The United States and Iran

THE UNITED STATES AND IRAN

POLICY CHALLENGES AND OPPORTUNITIES

ALETHIA H. COOK AND JALIL ROSHANDEL

palgrave
macmillan

First published in 2009 by
PALGRAVE MACMILLAN®
in the United States—a division of St. Martin's Press LLC,
175 Fifth Avenue, New York, NY 10010.

Where this book is distributed in the UK, Europe and the rest of the world,
this is by Palgrave Macmillan, a division of Macmillan Publishers Limited,
registered in England, company number 785998, of Houndmills,
Basingstoke, Hampshire RG21 6XS.

Palgrave Macmillan is the global academic imprint of the above companies
and has companies and representatives throughout the world.

Palgrave® and Macmillan® are registered trademarks in the United States,
the United Kingdom, Europe and other countries.

ISBN: 978–0–230–61811–4

Library of Congress Cataloging-in-Publication Data

Cook, Alethia H.
   The United States and Iran: policy challenges and opportunities / by
Alethia H. Cook and Jalil Roshandel.
      p. cm.
   Includes bibliographical references and index.
   ISBN: 978–0–230–61811–4 (alk. paper)
   1. United States—Foreign relations—Iran. 2. Iran—Foreign
relations—United States. I. Rawshandil, Jalil, 1944 or 5– II. Title.

JZ1480.A57I7 2009
327.73055—dc22   2008052689

A catalogue record of the book is available from the British Library.

Design by Newgen Imaging Systems (P) Ltd., Chennai, India.

First edition: August 2009

10 9 8 7 6 5 4 3 2 1

Printed in the United States of America.

Contents

Figures

Tables

Acronyms

bpd	Barrels per day (used in reference to oil supply)
CIA	US Central Intelligence Agency
CRS	US Congressional Research Service
EU	European Union
FEP	Fuel Enrichment Plant
GCC	Gulf Cooperation Council
GDP	Gross Domestic Product
GWOT	U.S. Global War on Terror
HEU	Highly Enriched Uranium
IAEA	International Atomic Energy Agency
IED	Improvised Explosive Device
IRGC	Iranian Revolutionary Guard Corps
MEK	Mujahedeen-e Khalq (aka MKO and NCRI)
MKO	Mujahedin-e Khalq Organization (aka MEK and NCRI)
MOIS	Iranian Ministry of Intelligence and National Security
NAM	Nonaligned Movement
NBA	U.S. National Basketball Association
NCRI	National Council of Resistance of Iran (aka MEK and MKO)
NGO	Nongovernmental Organization
NIE	U.S. National Intelligence Estimate
NNW	Non-Nuclear Weapons State
NPT	Nuclear Non-Proliferation Treaty
PA	Palestinian Authority
PFEP	Pilot Fuel Enrichment Plant
SAVAK	Sazeman-e Ettela'at va Amniyat-e Keshvar
SCFR	Iranian Strategic Council on Foreign Relations
SCIRI	Supreme Council of the Revolution in Iraq
SCO	Shanghai Cooperation Organization
SIS	British Secret Intelligence Service
TIPF	Temporary International Presence Facility
UAE	United Arab Emirates
UK	United Kingdom (adjectival use)

UN	United Nations
UNSCR	United Nations Security Council Resolution
U.S.	United States (adjectival use)
WMD	Weapons of Mass Destruction
WTO	World Trade Organization

Chapter 1

Introduction

In the midst of a chaotic international system, the U.S.-Iran relationship has become increasingly confrontational. The deterioration of relations is not a startling new phenomenon, but rather the culmination of decades of perceived betrayals, open challenges and mutual distrust. Many events and activities have influenced this decline. It is the purpose of this book to examine the major contributing factors in order to gain insights into the relationship and arrive at some potential approaches to ameliorate the conflict. Because the goal is to identify means to improve the situation, the authors strove to avoid bias and present both countries' perspectives.

Each chapter of the book is meant to shed light on the factors deemed to be of most significant importance to U.S.-Iranian relations and policies. These include the historical context of the relationship; the current political environment in Iran and the U.S. reaction to it; the allegations of Iran providing state support to terrorist groups; the pivotal role of Iran in Persian Gulf security; and the conflict over Iran's nuclear program. The process of examining each of these influential aspects of the relationship will bring the key conflicts to the forefront and allow for the identification of potential U.S. policy approaches to alleviating the tensions with Iran and forming a more constructive relationship in the region.

Iran's geostrategic relevance to the United States is based on three inter-related factors, its position as a significant regional power, its location in a vitally important but unstable region, and its significant oil reserves and other natural resources. Iran is second only to Saudi Arabia in the size of its oil reserves and also has the second largest natural gas resources in the world.[1] Iran's oil and natural gas reserves position it to be a major factor in world affairs long into the future. Beyond its natural resource wealth, however, Iran also has a position of importance in the region. Geographically, it is nestled among some of the most unstable countries in the world. Improved relations with Iran could allow the United States to have an ally in the region that is positioned to grow in power, industrialization, and wealth. However, the relations between the United States and Iran have been marked by a lack of effective diplomacy on both sides. In fact, during specific periods through time each side has seemed to exhibit little interest in improved relations.

Iran has been an important actor in the region for a long time. Its position in the region is arguably becoming more important (both to the region and to U.S. policies) because of U.S. actions in the Middle East. A potential power vacuum has been created in the region by the U.S. toppling of Saddam Hussein and the war in Afghanistan. Recent unrest in Pakistan may also contribute to the general instability in this region. Amidst this turmoil, Iran seems to have the potential to arise as a resource-rich, relatively politically stable country. It could serve as an arbiter of these disputes and assist the United States in dealing with this regional strife. However, lack of cooperation between the United States and Iran makes this somewhat unlikely at the present time.

Evidence of the importance the United States is placing on the relationship with Iran is found in a recent set of hearings being held by the House Committee on Oversight and Government Reform's National Security and Foreign Affairs Subcommittee. That Subcommittee held hearings on October 30, November 7, and November 14, 2007 during which scholars, diplomats, and representatives of the U.S. military discussed the risks and mutual distrust associated with U.S.-Iran relations. Each of the key issues covered in this book was brought up by more than one of the invited speakers. The book then takes each of the issues and explores them in greater detail, providing both the Iranian and U.S. perspectives. The testimony addressed the issues of terrorism, regional and global consequences of U.S. military action in Iran, Ahmadinejad's domestic political situation and public opinion, U.S. diplomacy and alternative policy options to solving the problems with Iran.[2]

The historical context of U.S.-Iran relations has set the stage for distrust between the countries and the dismal state of their diplomatic relations. In the aftermath of World War II, Iran turned to the U.S. to help it improve on its economic management and industrialization. With the possible exception of a short period of time during Mohammad Reza Shah's return to power, this was the last time that there has been trust in the relationship. The U.S. sponsorship of the 1953 Coup that overthrew democratically elected prime minister Dr. Mohammad Mossadeq undermined that trust for most Iranians. The 1979 Islamic Revolution and subsequent hostage crisis served to solidify U.S. distrust of Iran. From the Iranian perspective, the U.S. role in the 1980–1989 Iran-Iraq War exacerbated the problem. Overall, the diplomatic relations between the states since the 1990s have been marked by vacillating interest on each side in engaging the other in a more constructive manner. Unfortunately, it has seemed that when either the United States or Iran has made overtures for improved relations, the other side has not been receptive at that time. The positive aspect of this inopportune timing is that it could mean that there are opportunities for the situation to improve.

Recently, three major points of contention have been challenging the relations between the states. First, the United States has accused Iran of being a state sponsor of terrorism. Given the U.S. Global War on Terror (GWOT), this accusation is clearly problematic. In particular, the United States has accused Iran of providing support to Hezbollah, Hamas, and al Qaeda. Iran was first designated a state supporter of terrorism in 1984 and has remained on the list ever since.[3] The United States State Department has declared Iran the most active state supporter of terrorism for 2006.[4] Iran, however, argues that the groups it supports are not terrorists. Instead, these groups have been deemed by Iran to be fighting against foreign occupation of their homeland and therefore in the right.

Second, the United States is concerned about the role that Iran has been playing in Iraq since the fall of Saddam Hussein's regime. Most significantly, the United States believes that Iran has been supporting insurgency activities in Iraq to undermine the U.S. actions in that state. It has been accused of providing weapons (some of them advanced), Improvised Explosive Devices (IED), training, financing, bomb-making materials, and in some cases even fighters to facilitate the insurgency and influence the future of the Iraqi state.[5] In November of 2007, Vice President Dick Cheney went so far as to argue that a U.S. withdrawal from Iraq could allow "competing factions" (in which he specifically included Iran) to "unloose an all-out war, with violence unlikely to be contained within the borders of Iraq...[resulting in] carnage [that would] further destabilize the Middle East."[6] Iran denies that it has played this role.[7] The United States has also expressed concern that Iran is expanding its ties with Iraqi Shi'ite factions and is attempting to influence the new Shia controlled Iraqi Government.

Finally, and certainly most importantly, the two states are locked in a battle over Iran's nuclear program. Iran claims that it is seeking a heavy water reactor and enrichment technologies to help fulfill its energy requirements and increase its energy security. As is discussed in greater detail later, Iran currently must rely on other states to provide fuels for its nuclear power plants. It is troubled by repeated imposition of sanctions and the impact that they could have on its access to the required fuel in the future. The International Atomic Energy Agency (IAEA) has visited Iran's heavy water reactor at Arak, confirmed that materials were not being diverted, and declared that Iran has been relatively truthful about its nuclear-relevant activities.[8] The United States (and many others in the international community) argues that the technologies desired by Iran would give it the capability to manufacture weapons grade materials and that the Iranian intention is to build a weapons program. The United States and others argue that there are other technologies available that could provide for power generation without fostering a weapons program. Among the potential solutions proposed are the building of a light water reactor rather than a heavy water reactor and the continued provision of nuclear fuel to Iran by other states (perhaps Russia) so it can create energy without producing nuclear fuel.

Messages from Iran about its nuclear weapons aspirations have been mixed. On the one hand, there are pronouncements from Iran's religious community that "Islam bans shedding blood of nations; on the same ground, production of a nuclear bomb and even thinking on its production are forbidden from Islamic point of view."[9] Similar statements have been issued by Ayatollah Khamenei, the Supreme Leader of the Islamic Revolution.[10] However, in other instances, Khamenei has stated that Iran would never give up its enrichment at any price.[11] Furthermore, Iranian president Mahmoud Ahmadinejad has made inflammatory statements that it is the sovereign right of nations to acquire nuclear weapons as well as threatening Israel with annihilation.[12] These seemingly contradictory statements from key members of Iran's Government tend to foster distrust of their intentions.

One thing that is relatively certain is that it will be very difficult for Iran to abandon its nuclear ambitions.[13] The country initially expressed its interest in a nuclear capability in the early 1970s under the Shah when it acquired its first nuclear reactor. Consistently since then Iran has expressed an interest in a nuclear option and the notion seems popular with the Iranian public.[14] Currently Iran sees the United States as its main competitor in the international system. It is aware that it cannot compete in a conventional war with the United States. In contrast, at present the United States would likely overstretch its already strained military forces if it chose to invade Iran.[15] Iran is also aware of the political power conferred with the acquisition of a nuclear device. U.S. activities may be able to forestall the eventual arrival at this nuclear capacity, but they would be unlikely to convince Iran that it should eschew nuclear weapons entirely.[16] More importantly, the United States should realize that there is definite potential that military strikes against suspected Iranian nuclear facilities might slow down the rate of progress but would be unlikely to stop the program entirely. Instead, such attacks might serve to unite the otherwise fragmented Iranian elites behind accelerated development of nuclear weapons.[17]

However, there are so many potential negative outcomes from a nuclear-weapons capable Iran that have been identified in the literature that the United States cannot afford to back down on the issue. Among the possible impacts that would be counter to U.S. interests are as follows: Iran attacking Israel or another U.S. ally in the region with their new nuclear weapon; Iran attacking U.S. troops in the Middle East with its new weapon; Iran's acquisition of a nuclear capacity resulting in a Middle East nuclear arms race; an increasingly conventionally confrontational Iran backed with a nuclear threat; nuclear proliferation from Iran to other states; general destabilization of the Middle East; or Iran providing a nuclear weapon to a terrorist organization.[18]

The confusion over Iran's nuclear aspirations highlights another fundamental problem with the relations between the two states. For most Americans, one of the least understood aspects of the conflicts between the states is the role that Ahmadinejad (or any Iranian president) plays in the country's domestic and international politics. The way in which Islam and religious leaders are incorporated into the government of Iran (or any Islamic state, for that matter) is unclear to many Americans. The Iranian case is particularly confusing because its government includes both authoritarian and democratic elements. This potentially causes Americans to attach too much significance to the statements of Ahmadinejad while too little attention is paid to Khamenei and other religious leaders. In fact, Ahmadinejad is suffering from decreasing approval ratings in Iran as he has generally failed to deliver on promises of economic improvements on which he campaigned in 2005.[19] Rather than being the authoritarian government ruled single-handedly by Ahmadinejad as many Americans perceive, Iran is a country whose government is marked by a lack of consensus at the highest levels.[20]

Given the complexity of U.S.-Iran relations, determining what the future holds for the two countries is challenging. Under what conditions might cooperation be achieved? It is possible that traditional diplomatic approaches can contribute to more constructive relations. However, there is much distrust on both sides, which makes it difficult for either side to negotiate effectively. What is likely to be required is a suite of comprehensive policy approaches.

A major component of almost all U.S. policy options would be to try to reconstruct diplomatic ties. The challenge here would be to overcome the mutual distrust in the relationship. It is likely that diplomatic activities through some third party, whether it be the United Nations (UN) or some other international organization or through an intermediary state, would be required to facilitate the process. The position of the George W. Bush administration that it would not negotiate with Iran until it suspended its nuclear enrichment program would be a barrier to such negotiations. It is unlikely that the Bush administration could back down from this stance as it would undermine its authority in the region and elevate Iranian influence. This means that there is an opportunity to change policy with the change in administration in the United States. Although it is clear that the Obama administration cannot simply decide to not address the nuclear issue, they may be able to set a new tone and set of policies for dealing with disagreements with Iran.

Second, and related to the first policy proposal, is that the United States could utilize economic engagement of Iran as a first step toward normalizing relations. This option would rely on negotiations through the European Union (EU) to generate support for reducing barriers to trade and perhaps permitting Iran to join the World Trade Organization. The Neo-Kantian logic here is that increasing Iran's integration into the global economy would provide incentives for Iran to cooperate more fully with international organizations.[21] It could encourage Iran to embrace international norms about nuclear nonproliferation and not supporting terrorism. It would also increase U.S. leverage against Iran if the United States had more normal trade relations with the country.

A third policy would be to engage Iran through track-two diplomacy. This would involve increasing interaction and collaboration among elites in Iran and the United States. A track-two diplomacy policy could be carried out through nongovernmental organizations (NGOs) that would conduct workshops among epistemic communities in military, industry, and other businesses. Such a strategy would offer the potential for creating support for international norms within the country and potentially pressure the government of Iran in favor of U.S. preferences.

There are, however, significant hurdles to this approach. First, there is increasingly deep pessimism and suspicion of U.S. intentions among the Iranian leadership. This suspicion was highlighted in actions by both governments in 2008. Iran refused to allow an actress to go to Hollywood to discuss a movie roll. This was her punishment for failing to seek the government's permission before her previous performance in an American film. On the American side, the National Basketball Association (NBA) was sent a letter informing it that U.S. laws prohibited it from recruiting a talented Iranian basketball player (Hamed Ehadadi). The NBA had to gain a special license that eventually allowed them to work with Ehadadi.[22] Although these are relatively minor issues, they exemplify some of the challenges to increasing person-to-person relations between Americans and Iranians.

Second, some in Iran believe that there is a conspiracy against their participation in international conferences. The perception from Iran is that the prohibition of participation of Iranian scholars in international meetings with political content undermines their participation in other venues. Most recently, Ahmadinejad's government has ordered Iranian scholars traveling abroad for pilgrimage or participation in conferences to go through a thorough security check to assure that they are not politically motivated in their travel or that they are not participating in a conspiracy against Iran.[23] Furthermore, scholars must have all of their presentation materials (papers and briefings) pre-approved by the Iranian government before they are permitted to participate. These attitudes create an environment where track-two diplomacy will have great difficulty being established and bringing about change. This situation was complicated by contradictory messages from Ahmadinejad's government. Vice president and head of the Iran Cultural Heritage and Tourism Organization, Esfandiar Rahim-Moshaie on August 10, 2008, stated that "Iran would be friends with both the Israeli and American people, despite political problems with the two countries. The statement was unique because an Iranian Government official recognized Israel using its name, rather than the normal rhetorical denomination of 'the regime occupying the holy *Quds*.'"[24]

A fourth policy activity could be to engage in secret diplomatic activities with Iran. This type of backchannel diplomacy would permit both sides to vent their grievances and begin negotiations outside of the public eye. It would provide both governments the protection from the possible domestic backlash associated with rapprochement while allowing them a more free dialogue in the discussions. This might be a good place to start the discussions as well as a policy that could be utilized for more contentious issue areas such as support for terrorism, energy security, and Iran's nuclear program.

The fifth policy, which would likely signal the failure of the preceding options, would be imposition of more targeted, multilateral sanctions. Sanctions rarely achieve their goals and frequently impose hardships on the least fortunate in the targeted states. However, they are certainly a punitive option short of military engagement by the United States or its allies. The key here would be to find ways to target the sanctions carefully so that they hurt Iranian elites more so than the common man. Furthermore, the sanctions would be more effective if there were global participation rather than the United States imposing penalties unilaterally. To the extent possible, the United States needs to create an international coalition of states who are devoted to changing Iranian behavior. Only through such a concerted effort could sanctions hope to be effective.

A final option, that the authors sincerely hope can be avoided, would involve the use of military force to resolve the disputes between the two countries. The prevention of proliferation rests on the newly stated doctrine of preemption whereby the United States may take any action it deems necessary to protect national interests as it relates to the proliferation of nuclear, biological, and/or chemical weapons that may be used against U.S. interests at home and abroad. This doctrine has already been utilized in Iraq where the necessity for immediate action was prompted by the inference that an imminent attack by Iraq on U.S. interests was in the works. Unilateral action was taken after the UN Security Council did not back U.S. interests. If Iran is taken to the Security Council and a resolution is not ratified establishing sanctions based on noncompliance, another unilateral military incursion could be instigated. A military infiltration into Iran could pose a greater threat to U.S. interests than a diplomatic approach.

Costs, benefits, and opportunities for success vary across these U.S. policy options. The range of response options from Iran also varies based on the selected approach. While any of the options will take time and dedication from the United States, the importance of Iran to the region necessitates a new approach. Continued refusal to address the problems with Iran will be very unlikely to result in improved relations and could end in catastrophic failure. However, the United States has to recognize that it will take an equal amount of will and determination from Iran to improve the current situation. If Iran were to take a continued recalcitrant or increasingly bellicose position, potential U.S. policy responses will be constrained.

To some extent, both sides will have to have willingness to make concessions in order to resolve their current disputes. Before any diplomatic or other actions are taken by the United States, it will need to evaluate what types of concessions might be acceptable and those issues on which the United States cannot afford to budge. The United States must also consider under what conditions it will engage Iran militarily. If the United States is unwilling to do so to achieve specific policy goals, then threats of the use of force should not be made. If they cannot be made credibly, then the United States should avoid putting itself in a position where Iran could call its bluff. Similar calculations will have to take place in Iran. It is likely that there are few actual deal breakers on either side. However, some creative policy alternatives may have to be available for areas where neither side is willing to give.

This book will delve more deeply into each of the issues that have been introduced in this chapter. There are several core arguments that will be made. Obviously, the work here is built on a key assumption that there are diplomatic and policy-based solutions to the conflict between the United States and Iran. It is the belief of the authors that resolving the outstanding disputes between the states and building a more constructive relationship is possible. However, this can only happen if both states' interests and perceptions are taken into consideration. The book is based on the notion that there are significant and valid historical reasons for the distrust between Iran and the United States that both sides must overcome. These underlying factors have created a specific mindset among members of government and the general population in both countries. Identifying potential policy solutions to the problem relies on the ability to understand both perspectives on the relationship and accommodate them in policies. Absent this understanding, policies put forth by either side are likely to fail.

In addition to understanding the historical context, it is important that the analysts make every effort to remain unbiased. Much of the literature that is currently available on U.S.-Iran relations seems to be pursuing an agenda specific to the interests of one side or the other. In contrast to these works, the agenda being pursued by this book is the identification of viable policy solutions to the problems. For that reason, an objective approach is necessary and appropriate. Just as a lack of historical context will result in faulty policy, the failure to perform the analysis in an unbiased fashion will result in policy proposals that will be unacceptable.

Organization

The book consists of seven chapters, including this introduction. The chapters are organized around the themes that have been identified by the authors as being key factors in the U.S.-Iran relationship. Each chapter has some common elements. One of the main instruments the book employs to aid the reader's understanding are the comparative perspective tables. A major challenge with understanding the difficulties in U.S.-Iran relations is a failure to realize that both sides have unique perspectives on historical events and the current political climate—both domestically and internationally. In an effort to clarify these differing perspectives in a convenient and straightforward manner, the authors have provided the perspective tables that summarize these differences of view. In each chapter, the Iranian perception of events is discussed more thoroughly after the perspective table. This is then followed by a section on the "View from the United States."

Once the arguments relevant to each issue area have been established, the chapter transitions to U.S. policy options for addressing the challenges with that aspect of U.S.-Iran relations. Again, for the sake of convenience and clarity, the U.S. policy alternatives are provided on a table which includes the policy option, anticipated impact or probability of each policy, and the authors' recommendations. Each policy option is then explored in greater detail. This includes a summary of the policy alternative, benefits of the policy's adoption (strengths), and the anticipated detriments of that policy's selection (weaknesses). The policy alternatives and the associated strengths and weaknesses were sometimes found in the literature and agreed with by the authors, in which case, appropriate citations were provided. However, in some instances, the strengths, weaknesses or alternatives were ideas of the authors not found elsewhere in the literature and therefore were not cited. In some cases, the authors could not arrive at significant strengths or weaknesses for a policy alternative. In those instances, the discussion was necessarily brief. Each chapter then closes with the authors' identification of the preferred policy option for the United States to pursue in the relevant issue area if it hopes for improved relations with Iran.

The second chapter focuses on understanding the political history and relations between the two countries. The chapter will discuss key historical events in the relationship including the 1953 U.S.-sponsored coup, the 1979 Revolution, the Hostage crisis, the 1980–1989 Iran-Iraq War, the post-9/11 Axis of Evil speech, and decades of failed diplomacy. In this chapter, a comparative perspectives table is provided for each pivotal point in time to emphasize the continued divergence between Iranian and U.S. interpretations of their relations. This history will help readers to understand the policy options that are deemed to be available to the United States and Iran today and in the future. The U.S. policy options section of this chapter focuses on ways that the history of the relationship might be overcome in the hopes of improved relations with Iran.

Chapter 3 discusses the political structures and power distribution in post-Revolutionary Iran. The roles of key actors and their relative power to impact Iran's international relations are discussed in detail. The goal of this chapter is to provide the reader with greater understanding of the ideological and political dynamics within the Iranian government. The relationship between the Government (represented in the current media by Ahmadinejad) and the religious institutions and actors will be emphasized. The focus will be on the power distribution impacts decision making in Iran. Understanding how the relevant actors and their relative power, perspectives, and predispositions will aid in defining which policy options provide potential solutions and which will be likely to be rejected by the relevant actors. It will also help readers to understand the relative importance of actors in Iranian government. Chapter 3 provides the reader with some relevant Iranian economic issues and their impact on Iran's relations with the rest of the world. Finally, the chapter identifies some key groups in Iranian government that have influence over policy and its implementation. Specific individuals who have held political power in Iran, their actions, and their relations with the United States are examined. It then provides for the reader a variety of alternate futures that could emerge in Iran within the next several years. U.S. policy alternatives for dealing with Iran based on the postures of the Iranian government that could emerge are then identified and compared.

Chapter 4 addresses the pivotal roles of Iran and the United States in Middle East stability and security. Iran is positioned in what is arguably the most important geostrategic region of the world for U.S. interests. Continued inability or unwillingness of the United States and Iran to reach diplomatic solutions to their disagreements poses a threat to the stability of the region as a whole. Specifically, this chapter will discuss the security climate for Iran, threats posed to the region, oil and its influence on the relationship, and the regional implications of a U.S. invasion of Iran. There are several significant regional issues that are also addressed in this chapter. The relationship between Iran and Israel is addressed. Another major issue today in the region is Iran's emerging relationship with Iraq and its implications for regional security. This is taken up at length in the chapter. Within this section, the special case of the Mujahedin-e Khalq Organization (MKO) terrorist group is also presented. In addition, the chapter addresses the role extraregional players have had in Middle East stability, Iranian policies, and U.S. interactions with Iran and the region. These include discussions of relations between Iran and Russia, China, and the EU, and the subsequent impact of these interactions on the region. It also includes discussion of the proposed natural gas pipeline that would link Iran, Pakistan, and India in political and economic relations—a move that is highly contested by the United States. U.S. options for helping increase stability in the region through its dealings with Iran are then provided.

Iran's alleged support for terrorist groups is the central theme of chapter 5. The United States and other governments have accused Iran of providing support for terrorist groups and for sponsoring specific terrorist attacks in the past. The evidence underlying these allegations will be examined in this chapter. Understanding the motivations underlying both U.S. accusations and Iranian actions is important to resolving the conflict. The United States must understand Iranian motives for supporting these groups if it wishes to develop policies to deter them from doing so in the future. The chapter will explore Iran's relationships with a variety of international groups, particularly Hezbollah, Hamas, al Qaeda, and insurgents in Iraq.

It will also provide a description of U.S. reactions to the alleged support through time. U.S. sanctions and their impact will be evaluated, along with the responses to those sanctions from Iran's government and population. Finally, the chapter provides proposals for U.S. policy approaches to addressing Iran's support for groups the United States has identified as terrorists and a preferred policy is identified through comparison.

The critical question of Iran's nuclear aspirations will be the focus of the sixth chapter. The claims of both sides will be examined, as well as the perspectives of the IAEA, the EU, and other international observers of Iran's activities. In an effort to establish the importance of this issue for U.S.-Iran relations, the implications of a nuclear-armed Iran for the region and the world will also be discussed. In addition, the impact of U.S. sanctions, policies and other actions relevant to the nuclear aspirations of the country on Iran and the region will be explored in detail. The main goals of this chapter are to establish the level of threat posed by a nuclear Iran, to examine evidence of Iran's intentions, and to determine what impact the U.S. response is having. The chapter includes a discussion of the role of the EU in attempting to achieve a diplomatic settlement to the dispute. The Iranian response (or lack thereof) to the EU overtures is also examined. The implications of Iran's recent missile tests are provided in this section as they are believed to be potential nuclear weapons delivery systems. At a minimum, they were intended demonstrate the length of Iran's reach into the region. In the end, the chapter examines a variety of different U.S. policy approaches for dealing with the question of a nuclear Iran. A suite of policy solutions is provided by the authors in this instance, as a variety of different approaches are likely to be necessary to achieve a satisfactory outcome.

Finally, conclusions are provided in chapter 7. It begins with a summary of U.S.-Iran relations and key aspects of their mutual perceptions. General policy propositions are then provided to identify consistent themes observed in the policy observations and alternatives in the preceding chapters. This is then followed by specific policy proposals. The chapter synthesizes the policy alternatives and preferences identified in the preceding chapters to identify a path for the United States to follow if it wishes to improve relations with Iran. The intention is to provide a set of more comprehensive and rational policies that may help the United States to deal more effectively with Iran across the broad spectrum of issues to be faced in future. The authors argue for a more constructive, structured, and consistent U.S. approach that is focused more on engagement than on coercion or punishment. The policy solutions recognize that there are many hurdles to overcome and improving relations will be reliant on both sides possessing the will to do so. Furthermore, both sides will have to make concessions in the interest of achieving more constructive bilateral relations.

This book is intended to provide background and context to policy-makers and students regarding this important international relationship. The recent hearings in Congress indicate that there is an interest among policy-makers in learning more about Iran, its challenges, threats and aspirations. A neutral approach to the issues is intended to facilitate learning more about U.S.-Iran relations without pushing a specific political agenda on the reader.

Several key questions will be addressed throughout the book:

- What potential futures could emerge from the current situation?
- What is the potential for a diplomatic solution to the current crisis with Iran?
- What are the most important aspects of the existing relationship that have to be overcome to arrive at a solution?
- What are the larger implications of U.S. accusations of Iranian sponsorship or terrorist organizations and its nuclear enrichment aspirations?
- What actors will be the most influential in negotiating the future relationship?
- What impacts do and will other states have on the relationship?
- How will the relationship impact the stability of the Persian Gulf region into the future?

Chapter 2

Iran/U.S. Political History

It is not uncommon for books on U.S./Iran relations to begin by recounting key time periods in their history. It is critically important for establishing the context of the current climate of distrust and animosity in the relationship. Understanding each side's perceptions about events at key points in time provides insights into each country's perspective on their ongoing diplomatic and political engagement. It is not the goal of this chapter to provide a comprehensive recounting of the history of the relationship. Instead, the chapter will provide an abbreviated discussion that highlights key points of divergence of perspective and their impacts on past and future U.S. foreign policy–making. This admittedly limited coverage of the history of the relationship is appropriate given the focus of this book on developing future policy recommendations rather than a comprehensive historical account.

Iran has had a history of being exploited by foreign powers. Natural resources such as tobacco, oil and caviar were sold off to the British and Russians by various Shahs. During World War II (WWII), the Russians and British worried that the Shah was leaning toward Hitler, so they invaded the country and occupied parts of it until the war's conclusion. When WWII ended, the Russians attempted to maintain their claim on Northern Iranian territories. In January of 1946, Iran took its case for the removal of Russia to the new UN Security Council and the U.S. backed the Iranian claim against the Soviets.[1] This was the first significant skirmish of the Cold War. Both this and the desire of the Russians and British to control Iran during the Cold War are evidence of its emerging geostrategic importance at the time. It is a position the country holds to this day.

The American role in the 1953 Coup will forever be viewed by Iranians as concrete evidence of American imperialistic intentions toward the Middle East in general and Iran in particular. There is validity to that interpretation of the events. A more charitable interpretation of the U.S. support for the overthrow of Mossadeq's government is that there was concern that the country would fall under the influence of the Soviets and the United States was acting to protect the geostrategically important region. There is also some truth to that perspective. The differing perspectives are provided on table 2.1.

Table 2.1   1953 coup

Iranian Perspective	U.S. Perspective
Perspective 1 (largely discredited): Mosaddeq's declining popularity resulted in the people supporting the reinstatement of the Shah.	Perspective 1: Mossadeq was not really democratic, so the United States was not involved in helping to overthrow a democracy.
Perspective 2 (widely held): The coup was led and sponsored by the U.S. Central Intelligence Agency (CIA), demonstrating the U.S. willingness to overthrow democratically elected regimes if they are unfriendly to U.S. interests.	Perspective 2: U.S. action was necessary to stabilize a geostrategically important region and was for the global good.
Perspective 3: This was an action designed to give the Iranian people control of the domestic oil supply and assert the sovereignty of the Iranian State. The United States (CIA) and United Kingdom plotted together to maintain their access to the lucrative Iranian oilfields.	Perspective 3: The United States, alarmed at the strength of Iran's Communist Party, which supported Dr. Mossadeq, felt it had no other option.*
A betrayal of the Iranian relations with the United States for many.	Many U.S. citizens have little knowledge of the coup or the U.S. involvement in it—however, starting in about 2000 members of U.S. government including Secretary of State Madeleine Albright have publicly expressed regret for the U.S. role.

Note: *See, for example, Elaine Sciolino, "Mossadegh: Eccentric Nationalist Begets Strange History," *The New York Times*, April 16, 2000 downloaded from http://query.nytimes.com/gst/fullpage.html?res= 9807E1D61631F935A25757C0A9669C8B63&sec=&spon=&pagewanted=all on July 15, 2008.

Source: Perspectives summarized and expanded from Ali Ansari, *Confronting Iran: The Failure of American Foreign Policy and the Next Great Crisis in the Middle East* (New York: Basic Books, 2006), p. 36.

The Western world, most importantly the United States and United Kingdom, were frustrated at the time by the lack of cooperation they were receiving from the democratically elected Premier of Iran, Mohammed Mossadeq. At the heart of the issue was Iranian oil. The British controlled Iranian oil because they had bought the rights to it in 1901.[2] The Iranian population had become frustrated that they were receiving little in return for the increasingly valuable national resource. This frustration was being manifested in Mossadeq's resistance to the West and a move to nationalize Iranian oil.

> All the oil that was produced in Iran was the property of one British oil company. And that oil company paid Iran only a very small amount for the oil that it took. It was inevitable that sooner or later Iranians would rebel against this. And that's what they did. By propelling Mohammed Mossadeq into the Prime Minister's office [sic]. Mossadeq's principle project as Prime Minister was to nationalize the oil company. And that's what he did.[3]

As stated by the CIA official historian, Donald Wilber:

> By the end of 1952, it had become clear that the Mossadeq government in Iran was incapable of reaching an oil settlement with interested Western countries; was reaching a dangerous and advanced stage of illegal, deficit financing; was disregarding the Iranian constitution in prolonging Premier Mohammed Mossadeq's tenure of office; was motivated mainly by Mossadeq's desire for personal power; was governed by irresponsible policies based on emotion; had weakened the Shah and the Iranian Army to a dangerous degree; and had cooperated closely with the Tudeh (Communist) Party of Iran. In view of these factors, it was estimated that Iran was in real danger of falling behind the Iron Curtain; if that happened, it would mean a victory for the Soviets in the Cold War and a major setback for the West in the Middle East.[4]

This interpretation of the Iranian situation caused the United States to be receptive when the British asked for assistance in resolving the situation. However until November 1952 there was no consensus on the coup. Before that time, "almost all US officials working on Iran" had a different view on the Iranian Tudeh Party. Mark Gasiorowski believes they all "shared the view that a Tudeh takeover was not imminent but might occur if conditions did not improve," but there was a lack of consensus in the U.S. approach, including Secretary of State Dean Acheson who was opposed to the U.S. backing the coup.[5]

In the fall of 1952, after Mossadeq had expelled British personnel he believed to be plotting against him, the British turned to the United States and requested the assistance of the incoming Eisenhower administration in overthrowing Mossadeq.[6] The United States CIA and British Secret Intelligence Service (SIS) jointly initiated the TPAJAX project (also known as AJAX) in 1953. The goal of the project was to engineer the overthrow of the Mossadeq government and reinstallation of the authoritarian government of the Shah, which would be more sympathetic to Western interests.[7]

The Shah himself was complicit in the Western plan in that he issued *firmans moloukaneh* (royal decrees) dismissing Mossadeq, appointing his Western-supported replacement General Fazlollah Zahedi, and calling on the Iranian Army to remain loyal to the Shah.[8] The firmans moloukaneh were supplemented by a propaganda campaign and news releases designed to stir up public opinion against Mossadeq. While the initial actions taken to overthrow Mossadeq were discovered, allowing him to try and take action to protect himself, the Western propaganda campaign was able to spin his actions as having been aimed toward deposing the Shah. Furthermore, American agent Kermit Roosevelt orchestrated mobs to assist in destabilizing the regime.

> He would have them surge through the streets of Tehran, break windows, beat up people, shoot their guns into mosques and shout "we love Mossadeq." Up with Mossadeq and communism. And as if this wasn't enough he then hired another mob to attack this mob to show that Tehran was in such chaos that anarchy was threatening and that just to bring Iran back to a measure of stability, Mossadeq had to be overthrown.[9]

This successfully mobilized the Iranian public in favor of the Shah, resulting in the ouster of Mossadeq. This was then followed by a major economic support package from the United States to assist Zahedi in consolidating his power.[10]

It should be noted that this accounting of the events of 1953 was taken largely from the CIA's official history and not from an Iranian source. It was selected due to the fact that, in spite of coming from a U.S. source, it does not present the U.S. actions in a favorable light or sugar-coat the U.S. activities. The history is described as an after action report about the incidents and was closely guarded (classified, with consistent refusals to declassify the document) by the CIA until it was released in part to the *New York Times* on June 18, 2000.[11]

After his return to power in 1953, few leaders of the world were more loyal to the United States than Shah Mohammad Reza Pahlavi. During the 1973–1974 oil embargo imposed by the Arab states in an attempt to balance U.S. support for Israel, Iran was more cooperative and continued selling the U.S. oil, albeit at a higher cost. Iran also allowed for the Israelis to open the only Israeli embassy in the Middle East at this time. (Ironically, after the 1979 Islamic Revolution the same building was given by the new regime to the Palestinians to establish their first ever embassy in the Middle East.) The Shah also allowed the United States to set up electronic listening stations in Northern Iran along the border with the Soviet Union. Most of these stations were scattered in the Guilan and Azerbaijan provinces under the cover of vast forest areas where huge lumber factories were located and run by Canadian and American experts who were hired by the Shah's government.

The Shah's regular arms procurements from the United States helped to ease the American balance of payments problem. The U.S. government was so supportive of the Shah during this time that it praised his governance. In December 1977, President Carter visited Iran and applauded it as "an island of stability in one of the most troubled areas of the world." He declared that the Shah was a great leader who had won "the respect and the admiration and love" of his people.[12]

Though many still criticize President Carter for his remarks, the Shah was truly very popular with wealthy Iranians and his wife, Princess Farah, was also popular in rural and poor areas of the country. At this time in Iran, political consciousness was relatively low, especially in rural areas. However, among intellectuals and in some poverty-stricken areas, there was political resentment. There was not much political movement against the Shah, however, with the exception of two small, armed groups: Mujahedin Khalgh (radical Islamist group that was very much like the Iraqi Ba'ath Party) and Fadayeen Khalgh (a radical Marxist Leninist group which included a new version of the Tudeh Party). What both the Shah and President Carter had failed to understand was the underlying religious culture and how little time the Shah had to enact his policy agenda. Led by a fundamentalist Islamic clergy and emboldened by what were seen as empty promises of free water, electricity, telephone lines and public services paid for by oil money, the Iranian masses soon turned against the Shah and his Westernized policies. Their hope was that the "Revolution would give them freedoms and independence in the political platform of Islamic Rule"—which was chanted by the masses confronting the Shah's military curfews.

This U.S. involvement in the coup continues to serve as an important reminder to Iranians, and many in the Middle East, that the United States is more interested in protecting its own interests than promoting democracies. They will point to this coup as evidence that the United States cannot be trusted as an ally. This was something that shaped Iranian behavior during the Revolution in 1979 and the subsequent hostage crisis.[13] The

U.S. defense of its actions is largely restricted to pointing out that they had the support of the Shah, Zahedi, and others in Iran for their actions.[14] This is held up as evidence that the Western interpretation of the problems with Mossadeq was at least partly accurate.

Relations between the United States and Iran maintained a stance of guarded engagement throughout the 1970s. Increasing oil revenues during the energy crisis allowed Iran to progress economically, to invest heavily in military hardware, and to begin to push its own agenda in the international system. While the United States enjoyed good relations with the Shah, it was leery of his emerging interest in nuclear technology and his tendency toward anti-Western rhetoric.[15] However in its attempts to improve relations with Iran and in deference to the Shah, the United States had decreased its intelligence gathering capacity inside the country.[16] This led to the United States lacking sufficient knowledge of the domestic situation in Iran as it moved toward the Islamic Revolution. The differing perspectives are presented on table 2.2.

Meanwhile, the Iranian people were growing weary of the presence of many Westerners in their country, most of which failed to adapt to Iranian cultures and values. There were also an increasing number of dissidents within Iran who were looking for leadership. This was forthcoming in the personage of Ayatollah Ruhollah Khomeini, an exiled cleric with whom the Shah had struggled for some time.[17]

Table 2.2   1979 Islamic Revolution

Iranian Perspective	U.S. Perspective
The goal was the establishment of an Islamic state.	The United States claimed that getting involved in the revolution "would be contrary to US policy [to] interfere in Iran's internal affairs."*
A distinct break from the past characterized by U.S. influence.**	It was not the revolution but the incidents in its aftermath (such as the hostage crisis and the idea of exporting the revolution) that destabilized U.S. friends and allies in the region.
Most Iranians see the Revolution as being the factor that most degraded U.S./Iranian relations since 1979.	

Notes: *Ali Ansari, *Confronting Iran: The Failure of American Foreign Policy and the Next Great Crisis in the Middle East* (New York: Basic Books, 2006), p. 85.
**Ansari, p. 71.

While instability was building within Iran, the Shah seemed to be becoming more and more insular. His tolerance for criticism from abroad or within his own country declined sharply. His willingness to listen to counsel decreased as demonstrations within the country grew in size and spread more broadly through the population. By late 1978, the Shah seemed to be losing control of the country.[18] "The truth is that the author of the revolution was the Shah himself—not so much because of what he did but as a consequence of a fatal inaction and inability to lead at the critical juncture when leadership was most earnestly required."[19]

The Revolution happened in an environment of emotion, anger, and lack of political awareness. There was a general lack of political knowledge among the average Iranian regarding alternate forms of government. If a revolutionary Iranian were asked what kind of system would replace the monarchy, he would have no alternative other than to say it is going to be Islamic. However, few had any perception of what an Islamic regime would look like.

In early fall of 1978, the revolutionary movements in Iran gained force. The monarchy was paralyzed by uncertainties and indecisiveness. Its policies altered widely between suppression of the revolution and conciliatory measures to try and silence the streets of Tehran. Many big cities were packed by the masses, many of whom took to the streets because the Shah had imprisoned a member of their family or was killed...by accident or intent of the Sazeman-e Ettela'at va Amniyat-e Keshvar (SAVAK—the Shah's secret police).

All through the Revolution, U.S. perception of Iran was based on inexact and perhaps inaccurate evaluation of the situation in Iran. This is sometimes blamed on the U.S. withdrawal of many of its intelligence assets from Iran out of respect for the Shah. As mentioned previously, the misperceptions and lack of information factored into the Revolution and subsequent hostage crisis.

Almost 30 years later, President Carter did an interview on *CNN* with Wolf Blitzer's "The Situation Room." At that time (October 10, 2007) Carter said: "Well, we couldn't stick with him [the Shah], he was not overthrown by anything the United States did, he was overthrown by his own people. And as I said earlier, after they did overthrow the Shah, we took care of the Shah as best we could and we also continued our conversations with—our diplomatic relations with the new regime."[20] To supporters of the Shah, this is seen as another case where the U.S. abandoned an ally in the region.

The Iranian hostage crisis consolidated American public opinion against Iran. For 444 days, Iranian students (including today's President

Table 2.3   1979 hostage crisis

Iranian Perspective	U.S. Perspective
Publicly and at the Early Stage: The Iranian Government argued that there was little it could do about the crisis as it technically was taking place on the sovereign U.S. territory of the embassy.	Initially, this was not taken very seriously by the U.S. government, as such sieges were not terribly uncommon and were usually resolved by the host government in a matter of days.
Iran attempted to negotiate settlement to the situation with the student hostage-takers, to no avail.	As the crisis continued, the United States decried the lack of assistance from the Iranian government and planned a rescue that intentionally violated Iranian sovereignty.
Privately and Later: It has been shown that the Ayatollah supported the hostage-takers as anti-imperialist forces against the Great Satan.	Some see this as the symbolic start of the collapse of relations between the United States and Iran.*
	Americans see this as being the factor that most degraded U.S./Iranian relations in 1979.

Note: *Ali Ansari, *Confronting Iran: The Failure of American Foreign Policy and the Next Great Crisis in the Middle East* (New York: Basic Books, 2006), p. 72.

Mahmoud Ahmadinejad) held 52 American diplomats, agents, and Marines hostage. The plight of the hostages and the duration of their captivity were televised daily in the United States, intensifying the anti-Iranian sentiment. The U.S. government seemed powerless to gain their release. The Iranian government claimed that it would have to violate the sovereignty of the U.S. embassy in order to carry out a rescue mission, and therefore could not act on the behalf of the U.S. captives. Table 2.3 compares the countries' perspectives on the hostage crisis.

From Khomeini's perspective, the hostage situation proved to be beneficial. There is little evidence that he authorized the hostage-taking or even that the students were confident he would be pleased by their actions. However, the events consolidated an otherwise fractious Iranian public, reducing potential threats to his new regime.[21] "For hardline revolutionaries, the seizure of the embassy became a second revolution, the moment when the Islamic character of the revolution was consolidated. For the United States, emerging from the uncertainties of the 70s, it was a grave humiliation."[22] While the hostage crisis arguably weakened the Carter administration and hurt his chances at reelection, it strengthened

Khomeini's position. Shaul Bakhash, who teaches history at George Mason University, was there at the time of the seizure and he described the scene:

> Had I not been there I would never have imagined how electric the seizure of the embassy was for society as a whole. I mean within hours of the seizure of the street and the whole area outside the embassy was full of tens of thousands of people and those crowds remained around the embassy for days maybe even weeks afterwards. It really was a galvanizing moment in the history of revolution and helped to consolidate the revolution and push it in a more radical direction.[23]

These mobs were generally facilitated by the Iranian government and the Iranian Islamic Associations (bonyads). The protestors were provided with transportation, loudspeakers, slogans, and posters to carry. Frequently the chief of the association or a nearby Islamic Committee member would guide the crowd to the embassy and after a half hour or so of nervous demonstrations by the crowd, they were free to go home for the rest of the day. Employees, school children, and almost everyone came to support these events. In addition, in these early days of the Revolution, all employees were looking for ways to prove their allegiance to the new regime and clear their past history of being pro-Shah. Participation was an easy way to demonstrate their support for the new leadership.

Carter was intensely frustrated with the situation and nothing his administration attempted to do to gain the release of the hostages worked. In April 1980 he broke off diplomatic relations with Iran. He then authorized an ill-fated rescue mission (Operation Eagle Claw) that resulted in the death of eight American service members in the Iranian desert. The mission was intended to transport U.S. Special Forces operators into Iran. They would then infiltrate the embassy where the hostages were being held captive, secure their release, and fly them out of the country. Several factors complicated the rescue attempt, including most significantly an unanticipated sandstorm at the site where the aircraft supporting the mission were supposed to set down and refuel. Although the sandstorm directly impacted the potential for the success of the mission, it must be recognized that the plan for the rescue was amazingly complex and involved a small band of dedicated Americans infiltrating a foreign country, storming a facility with armed guards inside, gaining the release of a very large number of hostages whose health uncertain, escorting them to a rendezvous point, and securing their extrication. There is significant possibility that the mission would not have succeeded even without the sandstorm. In the end, instead of rescuing the hostages, the United States lost eight American servicemen in an explosion that alerted anyone in viewing distance (which given the size of the explosion was quite considerable) to their presence on Iranian soil. Iranian zealots then converged on the scene and were shown in images pointing happily at the charred remains of the U.S. servicemen.[24] Iran also captured the equipment and classified materials that were abandoned in the desert. This was a major embarrassment for the administration and the United States.

The hostage crisis was finally brought to a close on January 20, 1981, mere moments after Ronald Reagan took office. The Algiers Accords brought about their release, with the United States promising not to interfere in the internal affairs of Iran and freeing-up $10 billion in frozen Iranian assets.[25] It seems that neither Iranians nor Americans have been able to forget the psychological and emotional effects of the 1953 Coup and 1979 Hostage Crisis. The two events will continue to shape the mentality of the decision-makers until they can overcome the history, and get past them in the interest of better relations in the future.

In a related incident, on November 21, 1979, a mob attacked the U.S. embassy in Pakistan. After a five-hour siege from the outside of the gates of the embassy compound, the mob broke the wall. During rounds of gunfire, a U.S. Marine was shot and killed on the roof of the embassy building. The mob eventually burned the U.S. embassy to the ground. The attacks were believed (at least in the United States) to have been stimulated by Ayatollah Khomeini stating that the United States was occupying Islam's holiest site, the Great Mosque of Mecca, on the previous day. The U.S. State Department denied this and called Khomeini's statement "irresponsible, outright, knowing lies."[26] This aspect of U.S.-Iranian relations is frequently overshadowed by the Revolution and the Iranian hostage situation. While there was some lack of clarity in Khomeini's role in the taking of the U.S. embassy in Tehran, in this case there is more direct evidence that he was supportive of such actions—at least at the beginning of his reign.

Saddam Hussein seized the opportunity of Iran's preoccupation with the U.S. hostages and the instability he believed to be associated with the recent Revolution to mount an invasion in 1980. He feared that the new religious regime in Iran would destabilize the balance between Sunnis and Shi'as[27] in Iraq, was angered at continued border disputes between the countries, and wanted to consolidate his power and take over Iran's position the most powerful state in the Middle East.[28]

In fact, the time leading up to the Iraqi invasion was marked by increasing hostilities between the two countries. Attempted assassinations by members of Dawa, a secret Shi'ite group with ties to Iran, and the subsequent execution of the group's leader (Mohammad Baqir al Sadr, the father of Moqtada al-Sadr) and his sister by Saddam Hussein certainly contributed to the deterioration of the relations. Furthermore, increasing border skirmishes between the two states were a contributing factor.[29] The comparison of U.S. and Iranian perspectives on the Iran-Iraq War is provided on table 2.4.

Despite the many reasons for Hussein's invasion, for most Iranians the motivation for the attacks was easily identified. "Few Iranians believed that Saddam Hussein would invade Iran on his own initiative, such was their contempt for their Arab neighbor. Iranians felt that an invasion would occur only at the behest of the United States."[30]

While the two states had experienced significant crises in the past, especially regarding the river/border region (referred to as the Shatt al-Arab in Arabic and the Arvand Roud by the Iranians), those tended to be limited in the scope of their goals. There were quite literally lines in the sand which each country would consider as an acceptable settlement of the dispute. This conflict was unique in its intensity and aim. "In 1980, Saddam Hussein broke with this tradition of carefully managed crises, and for the first time in three centuries launched the two countries into all-out war."[31]

Table 2.4   1980–1989 Iran-Iraq War

Iranian Perspective	U.S. Perspective
President Reagan encouraged and supported Saddam Hussein in his war against Iran by removing Iraq's name from the list of state sponsors of terrorism to make Iraq eligible for U.S. government funding and support.*	Uncharitable Interpretation: It was not in the U.S. interest to have either Iran or Iraq win the war and come to dominate the region and its vast oil reserves. U.S. support therefore tended to switch in favor of the combatant that was losing at any given point.
The United States proved itself, once again, to be an unreliable ally in the international system.	Charitable Interpretation: The United States could not stand by and watch either country be devastated by the other.
The United States and UN failure to react to Iraqi chemical weapons use against Iranian civilians is seen as being a particularly objectionable betrayal.	

Note: *Alex Lefebvre and Joseph Kay, "The Diplomacy of Imperialism: Iraq and US Foreign Policy," *World Socialist Website*, March 19, 2004, downloaded from http://www.wsws.org/articles/2004/mar2004/iraq-m19.shtml on July 14, 2008.

Interestingly, Hussein's timing of the attacks could not have worked out better for the new Iranian Islamic Republic. Hussein counted on the recent revolution and continued instability to aid in winning the war. His belief that Iran would fall easily, however, was ill-founded. Instead of crumbling, Iranians coalesced while facing this external foe. Cries for reform and other dissent collapsed to bring about national unity against Hussein's forces.[32] In many ways the war consolidated the power of the new revolutionary government and facilitated their ruling of the previously unstable country.

The war was particularly bloody and drug on for almost a decade. Throughout the war, the Iranian forces were typically deemed to be inferior to those of the Iraqis, but what they lacked in expertise and equipment, they made up for in sheer numbers. Saddam Hussein was frequently frustrated in the lack of success of his forces, which he thought should have won an easy victory. Iran's war rhetoric emphasized the difference between Hussein and his people. Khomeini and other officials emphasized that their war was with Hussein's Sunni power base and Ba'athist Party rather than with the majority Shi'ite population.[33]

The Iraqis sought to augment their forces by employing chemical weapons between May of 1981 and March of 1984. Iran has claimed that at least 40 Iraqi chemical weapon attacks took place during this time.[34] By 1986, the UN secretary general Javier Perez de Cuellar formally accused Iraq of using chemical weapons. Iraq was also charged by the UN for using chemical weapons in the Kurdish town of Halabjah in Northern Iraq in March of 1988.[35] The use of the gas was one of many atrocities committed during the war, but one of the few in which the international system should have (morally and probably legally) and could have intervened but failed to do so. There are those who argue that both Iran and Iraq used chemical weapons in the war, but the substantiated claims are generally restricted to Iraqi use.[36] No real penalties were put into place to punish Iraq for these actions. This was (and still is) perceived by many Iranians as a major betrayal by the United States and the international community. As it was said by Nasser Hadian, a political scientist at Tehran University, "we all thought that using of the chemical weapons would be a red line which never would be crossed. We thought the international community never would let happen. But to our surprise and our sorrow, deep sorrow, we found out that's not the case."[37]

Meanwhile, the United States and other countries applied significant economic sanctions against both of the combatants in attempts to bring the conflict to an end. However, even these were applied unevenly. According to Ali Ansari, "some sanctions, like those of the Europeans, limited the flow of arms to Iran and Iraq (although in practice arms sale restrictions to Iraq were more flexible)."[38]

More direct superpower involvement in the Iran-Iraq War did not come until 1986. Iran was making some gains and had captured territory in Iraq. This threatened the Iraqi oil facilities. In addition, there was increasing intensity of both sides' targeting of tankers in the Gulf. The superpowers were suddenly very interested in bringing about an end to the conflict.[39]

Another event that occurred during the 1980s that had an impact on relations was the Iran Contra affair of the Reagan administration. Under the plan, the United States would arrange for the transshipment of weapons (including TOW antitank missiles and Hawk missiles) through Israel to moderate factions in Iran who were opposed to Khomeini's rule. Funds for the transfer would also be funneled through Israel, with some making their way eventually to Contra rebels in Nicaragua. In exchange for the shipments, the Iranian moderates would do all they could to help secure the release of U.S. hostages being held in Lebanon. Strangely enough, the operation began as an effort on the part of the United States to increase relations between the United States and Iran. The idea was to establish friendly relations with this faction in Iran in the hopes that they would seize power on Khomeini's death and be open to normalization of relations with the United States.[40] It ended with members of the U.S. government breaking a host of laws, including the Boland Amendment and its prohibitions against provision of U.S. support to the Contras.[41] This episode was further evidence to Iran that the United States was willing and able to circumvent even its own laws in order to try and undermine its government.

Finally, the discussion of the relationship between the United States and Iran in the 1980s must also mention the case of the USS *Vincennes*. Toward the end of the Iran-Iraq War on July 3, 1988 the USS *Vincennes* shot down Iranian commercial flight minutes after it started its trip from the Iranian city of Bandar Abbas to Dubai, UAE. The downing of Iran Air Flight 655 was one of the deadliest in history, killing 290 including 66 children. The U.S. government justified the incident as human error or declared that the commercial airliner was inappropriately emitting signals identifying it as a military aircraft.[42] The Iranian government still maintains that the *Vincennes* knowingly targeted the civilian airliner. Despite Iran's expectation of a formal apology, the United States never admitted responsibility. However, in 1996 an agreement was made between the United States and Iran at the International Court of Justice for a final settlement of all disputes and United States agreed to pay $61.8 million in compensation to the families of the Iranian passengers killed in the incident.[43] The crew members of the *Vincennes* were given combat-action ribbons by the U.S. government and the air-warfare coordinator, Commander Lustig, was awarded the U.S. Navy's Commendation Medal for "heroic achievement."[44] Iran has insisted that the United States knowingly and intentionally shot down its civilian airliner.

This period of time is significant in that it established the foundation of the persistent political, geographic, and military dilemmas for Iran and its neighbors. Iran's sense of encirclement, discussed in greater detail on the regional chapter, was certainly influenced by the Iran-Iraq War. This sense was intensified because of the fact that many Middle Eastern states backed Iraq in the war. They did so because they feared that if Iran were to depose Saddam Hussein successfully it would create a domino effect through the region, giving Iran more and more power and greater control of the region's oil resources.[45]

The perception that the international system would not come to the aid of Iran and it had to be prepared to defend itself at all costs can be traced to the lack of international response to the Iraqi use of chemical weapons. The war increased the Iranian desire to be self-sufficient militarily and otherwise. Furthermore, while the country had been researching nuclear technology for some time, the desire to develop a nuclear weapon as the ultimate deterrent may have been intensified by the war.

Throughout the 1990s, the U.S. foreign policy regarding Iran was rather unremarkable—although it was frequently included among the U.S. government's lists of "rogue states."[46] The Clinton-era policy was focused on the conflict between the Arab states and Israel. The U.S. policy toward Iran and Iraq during this time has been described as "dual containment," in which the United States identified both states as potential threats and sought to deter both from aggressive behaviors. A wide variety of pieces of legislation created by the United States during this period demonstrate the commitment to containing both countries. Acts issued to try and change Iran's behavior included the Iran-Iraq Arms Nonproliferation Act of 1992;[47] the Iran-Libya Sanctions Act of 1996, which was based at least in part on the Iranian energy program;[48] two executive orders issued in 1995 that imposed severe sanctions;[49] the International Emergency Economic Powers Act of 1996 which penalized anyone who invested more than $20 million in Iran over a 12 month period[50]; the Omnibus Consolidation and Emergency Supplement Appropriations Act of 1999, which restricted aid to Russia for its assistance to Iran[51]; and many other policies. Sanctions were put into place against Iraq after its 1991 invasion of Kuwait and remained in place until after the 2003 invasion.

In the post-9/11 environment, the United States seemingly passed up on a potential opportunity to improve relations with Iran. In the aftermath of the terrorist attacks, Iranians responded to the U.S. tragedy with empathy and condolences. There were marches in the streets, but these

Table 2.5   Post-9/11—Axis of Evil?

Iranian Perspective	U.S. Perspective
Iran was supportive of the United States in its efforts against terrorism in Afghanistan after 9/11.	Iran formed and continued to support Hezbollah and was believed to be developing its nuclear weapons program.
Many Iranians were thoroughly offended when George W. Bush listed them as part of the "Axis of Evil" in his 2002 State of the Union Address.	Bush's exact statement about Iran: "Iran aggressively pursues these weapons and exports terror, while an unelected few repress the Iranian people's hope for freedom."*
Iran perceives the U.S. occupation of Iraq beginning in 2003 as a crusader war against Islam and Muslim countries.	Iran is a major threat in the Middle East and has to be controlled carefully.

Note: *The President's State of the Union Address, January 29, 2002, downloaded from http://www.whitehouse.gov/news/releases/2002/01/20020129-11.html on July 14, 2008.

were to condemn terrorism and not to praise it. President Khatami expressed his sympathy and condemned the attacks. According to Ali Ansari, "even the ritual chants of 'death to America' were suspended at Friday Prayers for several weeks as a show of respect, although some argued that this conservative gesture was more out of fear than respect."[52] While Iran was still engaged in activities that the United States would find objectionable (i.e., support of Hezbollah and a nuclear program), it was also being largely supportive of the U.S. activities to root out terrorism and the Taliban in Afghanistan. Cooperation for Iran was also advantageous, however, in that Iran was helping the United States to rid it of one of its main competitors in the region. A comparison of the Iranian and U.S. views is presented on table 2.5. Both the state support of terrorism and the nuclear program are treated at greater length in later chapters of this book. A good summary of this appeared in an article in *International Affairs* by David Dunn in 2007:

> This represented a lost opportunity for the United States. Iran was no friend of the Taleban [sic] regime and offered American forces operating in Afghanistan assistance in such areas as search and rescue of downed pilots, and refueling facilities. Washington was also encouraged by internal developments within Iran, such as evidence of debate about its foreign policy direction and the pro-American outlook of large numbers of young Iranians. As a result of this *rapprochement* many observers, including the Iranians themselves, were surprised and alarmed to find Iran lumped together with Iraq and North Korea as the 'axis of evil' in Bush's 2002 State of the Union Address.[53] (Italics in original)

This admittedly expurgated history of U.S.-Iranian relations identifies key divergences of views and actions between the two states. The two countries distrust one-another and question each others' motives in almost all things. Currently, the governments are dealing with the problem primarily by not talking to each other, which is an interesting approach to diplomacy. There are very few direct diplomatic contacts between the two states. Most of the discussions between the two countries are taking place through European intermediaries or through media releases intended for the other government's consumption. Neither side accepts the actions or words of the other at face value. Instead, each seeks to discover the hidden meanings into the other's behaviors. Even this brief history helps one to understand why that might be the case.

Any future improvement in this relationship will require both sides to overcome years of perceived betrayal and mistreatment. It is quite probable that only generations of confidence building measures between the two states will provide an environment in which trust can be rebuilt. In the interim, it is possible that utilizing backchannel diplomacy could prove fruitful. Portions of the public on each side would be displeased to see open diplomatic engagement between the states. Both governments would likely face domestic backlash if it seemed they were opening to the other. However, diplomatic relations could be reopened behind the scenes. This would protect the governments from public opinion. It would also allow each state to communicate more openly and to entertain policy solutions that would be unpalatable to their domestic population.

Most importantly, however, both sides need to have the political will to improve their relations. This may not currently be the case. Ahmadinejad's administration (discussed more thoroughly later in the book) has been benefiting from his hard-line posture toward the West, and the United States in particular. He has been using his defiance of the West to rally a population that otherwise might be more vocal in its concerns about his failure to deliver on promises of economic improvement that won him the election. This was emphasized when, during the writing of this book, Iran conducted missile tests in July and again in August 2008. General Hossein Salami, commander of Revolutionary Guard forces, directed the following comments at the United States and Israel:

> We want to tell the world that those who conduct their foreign policy by using the language of threat against Iran have to know that our finger is always on the trigger and we have hundreds and even thousands of missiles ready to be fired against predetermined targets...we will chance the enemies on the ground and in the sky and we will react strongly to enemy's threats in shortest possible time.[54]

The implications of Iranian missile tests and U.S. responses to them are taken up later in the nuclear debate chapter.

Likewise, there are few signs from the U.S. government that there is interest in improving this relationship. This was certainly the case during the eight years of the George W. Bush administration. Time will tell whether the Obama administration is more committed to building constructive relations with Iran.

View from the United States

The United States obviously has struggled with its diplomatic relationship with Iran. America's desire to exert influence over the country has remained constant. The geostrategic importance of Iran cannot be overstated. The United States would certainly like to see its relations with Iran improve and to be able to rely on Iran for assistance in ensuring regional stability. However, the United States has frequently pursued this goal with little grace, foresight or understanding of Iran or the Middle East. It was once said that the United States was like a "stupid, aggressive puppy."[55] This analogy was meant to indicate that the United States makes its policies without realizing that, like the sharp teeth of an aggressive puppy, they can inflict harm without intent. This seems to have been the case with the U.S. dealings with Iran. In the pursuit of its goals of maintaining access to oil and stabilizing the region, the United States has unintentionally hurt the countries and its relations with them.

The United States has continually been surprised with events in Iran. In part, this may be because of its misunderstanding and poor characterization of power relationships within the elites of Iran. It also is related to the lack of capable intelligence gathering assets inside Iran since the aftermath of the 1953 Coup. The United States was taken by surprise by the Revolution, the taking of U.S. hostages and Iran's governmental inability to secure their release, and by the Iranian response to the "Axis of Evil" speech. (This last represents the sincere hopes of the authors, who would hate to think that this was said with the intent of driving in the wedge between the United States and Iran even further. Somehow the United States being ignorant that the statement would have this effect seems better than that the United States intended for it to happen. The authors recognize that they could be misrepresenting the Bush administration's intentions in this regard.)

Currently, the United States sees the Iranian government as a somewhat enigmatic threat to the region. Ahmadinejad's aggressive behavior and threatening posture is easy for the United States to understand, but threatening nonetheless. There is even less understanding of Khamenei's role and influence over politics in Iran. From the U.S. perspective, however, Khamenei may be more conducive to improved relations as his stance toward the United States has been much less strident at times.

At the present time, the United States has somewhat limited contact with Iran and its government. Some signs of improvement were shown in summer 2008 when the U.S. government sent a high-ranking diplomat (William J. Burns, U.S. Under-Secretary of State for Political Affairs) to discuss Iran's nuclear program and released information that it was considering establishing an American diplomatic presence in Iran.[56] Both of these actions were the first such movements from the United States since the 1979 Revolution. The fact that the negotiations still ended in deadlock should not detract from the importance of the fact that formal diplomatic relations happened between the two countries for the first time in almost 30 years.[57] Sanctions have been imposed unilaterally by the United States and through UN resolutions in an attempt to alter Iran's behavior. These coercive diplomatic tools combined with U.S. government officials condemning Iran's behavior on a number of issues have been the extent of its relations with Iran for some time now.

U.S. Policy Options

The United States needs to identify ways that it can overcome the historical enmity in its relations with Iran and arrive at a more constructive relationship. The history detailed above places significant challenges in the path of this relationship. Iran will not forget the U.S. role in the 1953 Coup. Nor will it forgive the U.S. and international lack of response to the Iraqi use of chemical weapons against civilian populations in the Iran-Iraq War. Similarly, the U.S. memory of the lack of Iranian government action to secure the release of hostages is a hurdle. It should be recognized that the above historical incidents cannot be erased. As long as either side remains focused on this history, it may not be possible for the two to negotiate a more constructive relationship. Both countries would benefit from better relations. In order to improve the situation, the United States and Iran will have to develop relations that accept the past and focus on negotiating a basis upon which to build future relations. The U.S. policy options for this relationship are presented and analyzed on table 2.6.

Table 2.6 U.S. policy options: Overcoming history's impact

Number	Policy Options	Impact / Probability	Authors' Views
1	Continue to refuse to address the problems in the relationship and conduct relations through third-parties.	This strategy seems to be giving Iran the freedom it needs to engage in the behaviors we find objectionable.	Avoid
2	Work through the UN and allies to try and bring about more positive direct relations between the United States and Iran.	There is too much opportunity for mistakes in this option. Relations between Iran and allies or the UN could improve with no subsequent improvement for the United States.	Poor policy. Recommended only if 3, 4, and 5 should fail.
3	Engage fully and directly one-on-one with Iran to resolve our differences.	This would be difficult as both sides' domestic constituencies may object to the warming of the relationship.	Recommended
4	Backchannel diplomacy.	Would provide protection for both sides from domestic backlash from rapprochement. This option would take time and patience on both sides.	Highly recommended
5	Use track-two diplomacy between the two states to improve perceptions of one-another and create an environment more conducive to cooperation.	This could help to develop an environment in which future security cooperation would be more possible.	Highly recommended

Continue Current Path

The current relations between the United States and Iran can best be described as unconstructive. Neither country is happy with the state of relations but they remain unwilling to compromise. This has been seen in the fiery rhetoric from both Ahmadinejad and Bush, and from the slow pace of negotiations associated with any discussions.

Strengths

Neither side can be accused of giving too much to the other, for neither is giving an inch.

Weaknesses

The United States has refused to have direct diplomatic ties to Iran for decades. If Iran is deemed one of the most significant threats to international and regional security, refusing to communicate with them offers no hope of improving the situation. According to the U.S. State Department itself,

> [Iran] is the only country with which we effectively have no communications. We haven't had an embassy in Iran. We haven't had any military officials in Iran since 1979, 1980…There are very few American citizens living or working in Iran. It is a country with which we have been out of touch for the past twenty-five years.[58]

Given this lack of communication and diplomacy, it is hard to imagine a country with which it would be more difficult for the United States to build a constructive dialogue.

In many ways, the United States has put itself in a diplomatic corner with Iran. The United States currently has so many sanctions against Iran that it can no longer use trade to leverage Iran. The United States has relied almost entirely on indirect measures (i.e., negotiating through the EU, UN or other third parties) in its attempts to change Iranian behavior. It would seem that a country with as much potential to destabilize an incredibly important geostrategic region to the United States would merit significant direct diplomacy.

Work through the UN and Allies

This is also a status quo policy option. The United States would continue to rely on others in the international system to relay our interests to Iran and negotiate on our behalf.

Strengths

Using intermediaries might offer the possibility of a negotiated settlement to some of the disputes between the United States and Iran. It would protect both sides from the political ramifications of giving in to the other. They would be giving in to the will of the international system or the UN rather than one-another. Both sides would benefit from being seen as more cooperative internationally and willing to settle their disputes. This may be a good first step toward addressing the differences between the two countries.

Weaknesses

This option would likely take a long time to evolve to a mutually acceptable new relationship. It would likely take more time than backchannel diplomacy due to the added delays associated with using intermediaries in the process. Given the tense nature of the relationship and both sides' fears of the other resorting to a military option, time is of the essence.

Using intermediates in the diplomatic process also increases the opportunity for mutual misperception. Furthermore, there is always the potential that an intermediary will pursue their best interest in the negotiations rather than that of the disputing parties. While it would be nice to believe that this could not possibly happen in a situation of this significance, it cannot be excluded as a possibility. This type of indirect approach may be beneficial, however, if backchannel diplomacy and direct one-to-one negotiations prove to be ineffective.

Backchannel Diplomacy

Backchannel diplomacy would involve the United States and Iran engaging in secret talks hosted by third-parties to begin a dialogue between the two countries. The goal of such talks would be to get to the point where small, marginal policy changes toward one-another were possible. Eventually, it could lead to more direct and open one-on-one diplomacy between the two states.

Strengths

There would be two major benefits to using backchannel diplomacy to try and improve relations. First, because the relationship would evolve in secret, both sides would be protected from the domestic backlash that will likely be the response to warming.[59] The populations of both states cling to past grievances. If the governments were seen to be trying to forgive and forget, it could create dissatisfaction among hardliners at home. However, there are significant populations in both states that would be supportive of a warming of the relationship. Secrecy would allow for the relationship to warm gradually. Both governments could begin a process of exposing the warming to their people and allow them to slowly acclimate to the idea rather than springing it on them once the compromises are made. The U.S. and Iranian governments would also be protected in the event of failure of the attempts.

The second benefit to backchannel diplomacy (which is clearly related to the first, but deserves special attention) would be that the governments would be more free to express themselves without having to posture for the media.[60] Much of the escalating rhetoric between the two countries has been influenced by the fact that the world, including domestic populations, is watching what each President says. By discussing contentious issues in secret, the countries could be frank in their negotiations and potentially arrive at a better and longer-lasting relationship agreement.

Weaknesses

This process will take a long time. It would be impossible for two countries with such a long and contentious history to foster a new and more positive relationship in short order. Each side can be expected to withdraw from negotiations periodically. It will take dedication on both sides of the negotiations to bring about a positive end result. Some regimes in the countries have not had this kind of dedication, but perhaps future ones will be more amenable.

Track-two Diplomacy

Track-two diplomacy is an unofficial policy discourse that is conducted outside of the public eye. While such discussions rarely create radical changes, they may pave the way for change to occur. In the past, track-two diplomacy has allowed for elites in conflicting states to change the views and attitudes about one-another and have created an environment in which cooperation can be possible. These generally involve moderate actors (military, other elites or even academics) that have the potential to exert some influence in their state after the dialogue has been completed. They come together to discuss security issues and the value of cooperation.[61]

There have been track-two efforts in the past. The results have not been terribly successful. It is likely this lack of success was due to misperception and distrust. In some cases, the academics attending such meetings were persecuted on their return to Iran and banned from traveling outside the country.[62] Ahmadinejad's current policy includes imposition of a ban on the travel of university professors even for the purpose of pilgrimage.

> During a May 2003 conference in Athens attended by several prominent Israeli analysts and ex-officials, Mohsen Rezai, a former commander of Iran's Revolutionary Guards, presented what [Trita] Parsi [adjunct professor at Johns Hopkins University and President of the National Iranian American Council] describes as a bold strategic shift to a group of Israelis. Rezai's proposal at the conference, which is organized annually by the Greek Foreign Ministry and the University of California, Los Angeles, entailed a more moderate Iranian stance on the Palestinian issue in exchange for Israel dropping its opposition to rapprochement between Washington and Tehran.[63]

Unfortunately for the United States and Israel, Rezai was not in attendance at the meeting in any official capacity, but rather as an academic. This means that his position was not sanctioned by Ahmadinejad or Khamenei and holds little promise for improved future relations.

Strengths

Track-two diplomacy would permit the initiation of a security dialogue between the two states that would be unofficial but would allow the countries' elites to speak more frequently and openly than they have. The states could share views on regional security issues and the potential for future areas of cooperation. This would initiate the process of re-socializing the elites to more constructive attitudes. It could begin to correct misperceptions and faulty assumptions between the two states.[64]

Weaknesses

There are limits to the amount of change that can be stimulated through track-two diplomacy. These might include: ideological opposition of the sides' participants to greater cooperation; skepticism or hostility to the proceedings; the potential to develop more negative views rather than more positive among the participants; limited influence of the participants when they return home; a lack of domestic receptiveness to cooperation; or a shift in the regional environment that undermines the process.[65] This is a long-term process rather than a quick fix. It would require significant commitment from both sides to be effective. Absent such dedication, it is unlikely to improve the situation.

One-on-One Relationship Building

The United States could begin to relate with Iran directly, holding talks, reopening a U.S. embassy in Tehran, and engaging in full diplomacy.

Strengths

It seems that an attempt at this was begun when Madeleine Albright was secretary of state, but the Bush administration failed to follow through on it. In 2000, Albright admitted to the U.S. role in the 1953 coup and argued that Iran and the United States should attempt to improve their relations. She remarked on Iran's strategic importance to the United States and argued in favor of engagement.[66] This was a missed opportunity in the relationship, given the Khatami regime's leanings toward improving the relationship. Other U.S. elites have also advocated for improved direct relations between the two countries. "Zbigniew Brzezinski, former US national security adviser, urge[d] the United States to engage in bilateral talks with Iran on mutually contentious security and economic issues."[67]

This open and direct approach would be transparent to the domestic populations of both countries and could therefore have the benefit of building domestic public support in pace with the governments' progress. It would also clearly demonstrate both countries' commitment to the process to the international system.

Weaknesses

This is a time consuming and risky option. It is unlikely that it would proceed smoothly and each glitch in the process would become international media fodder. Both sides would have to be more guarded in their negotiations to avoid being seen as giving too much or receiving too little. This would impede the free exchange of ideas and information between the countries.

It is likely that this would be a difficult process, as was well-summarized by the U.S. Institute of Peace:

> Both Iranian and American sides come to the negotiating table burdened with years of accumulated grievances and suspicions. Their recent history has led both sides to assume the worst about the other and to see it as infinitely devious, hostile, and duplicitous. Yet, while talking to Iran may sometimes be difficult and unpleasant, it is also worth doing and may help both sides to find common interests lurking behind walls of hostility and distrust.[68]

Preferred Policy

Some combination of backchannel diplomacy, track-two diplomacy, and direct one-to-one negotiations offers the greatest promise of warming the relations between the United States and Iran. There are many sensitive issues between the two countries that would best be settled out of the public eye through backchannel diplomacy. This may include official apologies for some past misdeeds, agreements about the Iranian nuclear program's progress, and other areas where both countries' general populations may object to giving concessions to the other. Iran's forgiveness of other regional powers that backed Saddam Hussein in the 1980–1988 war may indicate that it would be willing to forgive past deeds if there was a larger benefit to doing so.[69] The United States should explore what larger benefits could be achieved by Iran through cooperation and forgiveness, even if it is temporary.

Track-two diplomacy requires a long term commitment from both sides, but that commitment is ideological. It is actually a relatively low-cost (economically, politically, etc.) and low-risk activity that could be on-going while other measures are pursued. If nothing is achieved through the process, there is little lost. The worst case scenario would be the development of less favorable perceptions among the participants. Careful selection of the participants and management of the process could help to protect against this eventuality. It should also be recognized that the process can be risky for some participants, especially if their government is not supportive of their participation. Careful attention should be paid to assuring that participants who might be at such a risk are protected from media leaks and other incidents that might reveal their participation.

Direct negotiations would also be beneficial as the countries move toward normalizing relations. This should be a gradual process where the open negotiations are supported with backchannel activities for more sensitive issues. Once agreements had been arrived at in the backchannel, they could gradually be unveiled. A slow and controlled rapprochement would likely be more supported than one that was just sprung on the public. Furthermore, this would allow both sides to build domestic constituencies in favor of the policy proposals. These individuals could then help the governments to convince the public that these are policies that are beneficial to all.

Chapter 3

Modern Iranian Politics

It is important at this point to examine the governing structures, personalities, and trends in Iran since the Islamic Revolution. Two main characteristics should be emphasized. First, the relative power of the different members of the executive branch will, as in other dual-executive governments, vary with the personal power and popularity of the actors. In the Iranian case, this means that the role of the president will change based on his own power base and personality as well as that of the Supreme Leader during his administration. Second, and very much related to the first, the presidency in Iran was designed to favor power for the Supreme Leader, with less power vested in the presidency itself. Through time, then, the power-sharing relationship between the Supreme Leader and president can change, and indeed this has been the tendency.

The role of the Supreme Leader is unique to the Islamic Republic. He serves the role of the Velayat-e Faghih (Guardianship of the Islamic Jurists), which serves as the justification of the representation of the Islamic clergy in almost every aspect of the Iranian government and, in fact, in daily Iranian life. Faghih itself can be defined as jurisprudence. It is further defined as "a general normative value system on the basis of which all forms of social-humans relationships can be organized."[1] Velayat-e Faghih is an Iranian governing concept that intertwines Muslim clerics with elected government. It is personified and led by the Supreme Leader. It makes having an Islamic Republic style of government possible. Constitutionally, the Velayat-e Faghih could be an individual or a group. Since its initiation, it has been one person, the Supreme Leader. However, it could be a council three or five fully eligible clerics to form a Leadership Council. This form of plural members has never materialized. (The Constitutional power structures are depicted on figure 3.1.)

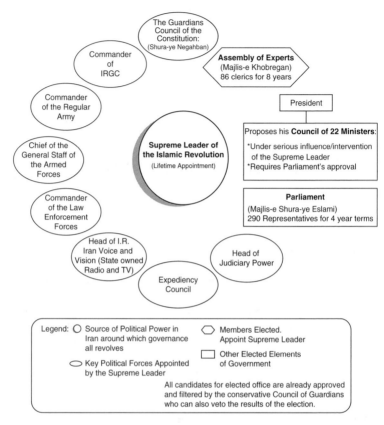

Figure 3.1   The constitutional power structure in Iran

This instrument of religious governance was initiated by Ayatollah Khomeini. Under the 1979 Constitution, he was given absolute power to rule Iran, including the powers to overturn actions from the elected elements of government and to declare war. Iran's Constitution established that the Supreme Leader was the theological protector of Iranian Muslims.[2] Khomeini believed he received his power to govern directly from God.[3] His chosen successor, Hossein Ali Montazeri, disagreed with Khomeini's interpretation and was therefore relieved of his designation as successor mere months before Khomeini's death. This was the reason that Khamenei was able to come to power. A council was formed to select the Supreme Leader and it was at the time claimed (undocumented) that Khomeini had positive views on Khamenei being the next Supreme Leader. This is part of why Khamenei found it difficult to take over power from Khomeini after his death. (It should be noted that the Revolutionary intent was to put in place a democratic form of government, not an authoritarian regime. Khomeini vested that power in himself after the Revolution.)

There was a long argument of whether the government should be an Islamic Republic or simply the Republic of Iran. Finally, agreement was reached that it should be the Islamic Republic. At that time, there was no clear definition as to what an Islamic Republic would be. Those involved in writing the Constitution would often describe what an Islamic Republic is not in order to give an impression of what it would be.

Khamenei did not share Khomeini's power or charisma. Many Shi'ite clerics questioned the concept of Velayat-e Faghih when the power was vested in Khamenei and it continues to be challenged to this day. However, it remains in place and is a major force in Iranian government.

Both Prime Minister Bazargan and President Khatami lost their grip on power because they could not come to agreement with the Velayat-e Faghih. The Velayat-e Faghih has the ultimate power in every aspect of Iranian Muslims' lives.

The Velayat-e Faghih has many duties and unlimited authority. It selects six religious jurists to serve on the Guardian Council, with the other six being constitutional experts appointed by the *Majlis* (Parliament). The Guardian Council vets laws passed by the Majlis, confirms the constitutionality of all legislation, appoints heads to the Judiciary and Armed Forces, and selects members of the Expediency Council, the Supreme Council and the Council of Defense. The Velayat-e Faghih endorses the appointment of the president, who is technically popularly elected.

Of the two power centers (president and Supreme Leader) in Iranian politics, the Supreme Leader at the head of the religious element of government generally exercises more functional power than the president. The first Supreme Leader was Ayatollah Khomeini. He ruled from the Revolution in 1979 to his death in 1989. Ayatollah Khamenei has played the role of Supreme Leader since 1989. In that position, he has power over the Iranian Revolutionary Guard Corps (IRGC), the intelligence and security services, other aspects of the military, the judiciary, and other Iranian government agencies. This is something that many Americans fail to grasp. The Iranian presidency is more visible than the Supreme Leadership, but in reality it is a frequently a ceremonial position that lacks real decision-making power. The current American misperception is likely influenced by the more vocal and visible role that has been played by President Ahmadinejad. This is likely part of Ahmadinejad's strategy to mobilize public opinion in favor of his policy preferences through his rhetoric and blatant challenging of the West. In this way, the Iranian president might wield power through public opinion to sway the Supreme Leader in favor of the president's policy preferences.

Beneath the Supreme Leader in this religious power structure are high-ranking bureaucrats in the Basij, IRGC, and other influential groups. Additional informal power is held by interest and pressure groups, people retired from positions of power, and the Bonyads (Islamic Foundations).

Immediately after the Revolution, Ayatollah Khomeini had so much personal power and popularity that neither the president nor the prime minister wielded much effective power. In foreign policy, Chapter 8 of the Iranian Constitution gave the Supreme Leader broad powers including: "determining the general policies of the system; the supreme command of the armed forces; the power to declare war or peace; and the appointment and dismissal of the chief of the Joint Staffs, the chief commander of the IRGC, the chief commanders of the armed forces, and the chiefs of the police forces."[4] This meant that Khamenei, who was president during Khomeini's leadership, was a figurehead. When Khomeini died, however, Khamenei was his successor. The problem at the time was that there was little faith in Khamenei and his power was relatively low. Because of this, he was a much weaker Supreme Leader initially than Khomeini had been. This, combined with the constitutional elimination of the position of the prime minister, allowed President Hashemi Rafsanjani to wield much more political power as president than Khamenei had.

Today, Velayat-e Faghih sets general policies in consultation with the Expediency Council. He also supervises administration of policies. Most importantly, the Velayat-e Faghih is the final arbiter for all legislative disputes and has the power to control or revoke all governmental appointments. Some even claim that his words and oral orders replace the written text of laws. There have been cases where the Supreme Leader's orders were immediately put into effect.

The Majlis has 290 members who are elected for four-year periods. The government is comprised of the president and about 23 ministers who form the Cabinet, typical of a parliamentary system. The president is to lead the executive branch of government. He nominates the Cabinet members and seeks their endorsement from the Majlis. All the laws passed by the Majlis have to be vetted by the Guardian Council. Where an agreement cannot be reached between the Majlis and the Guardian Council, the final decision is made by the Expediency Council. There are currently several pending issues at the Expediency Council because the Guardian Council objected to them and the Majlis was unwilling to alter the bills to meet the Guardian Council's requirements.[5]

Table 3.1 Modern Iranian leadership

Position	Individual	Dates	Characteristics and Outcomes	Relations with the United States
Supreme Leader	Ayatollah Khomeini	1979–1989	A steady hand on the tiller of the Islamic republic.*	Were strained and deteriorated with the Hostage Crisis.
President	Seyyed Ali Khamenei	1979–1989	Almost no role due to power vested in Prime Minister and Supreme Leader.	Were strained and deteriorated with the Hostage Crisis.
Supreme Leader	Seyyed Ali Khamenei	1989–Present	Relatively weak initially. However, he has gained power through time as he has consolidated supporters and been countered by less personally powerful presidents.	Khamenei has never missed an opportunity to blame the United States for all bad things that happen in Iran. He has often condemned U.S. policies toward the Middle East and Iran, yet there may be some opening for negotiations.
President	Hashemi Rafsanjani	1989–1993	Prime Minister position eliminated. A president determined to reconstruct Iran and expand Iranian wealth and influence. Seen by some Iranians as too focused on materialism rather than spirituality.	Rafsanjani argued that the United States should take more positive steps and relinquish its hostile attitude. He left the door open for resuming relations, but insisted the United States would have to deal with him rather than others in government.

Continued

Table 3.1 Continued

Position	Individual	Dates	Characteristics and Outcomes	Characteristics and Outcomes	Characteristics and Outcomes
President	Hashemi Rafsanjani	1993–1997	President under siege for his embracing of capitalism.**		He condemned both the United States and Iraq during the 1991 Gulf War, but later said that he would be willing to help Iraq. He argued under sanctions that he might be willing to compromise, but was constrained by the domestic situation. In about 2005 he started arguing for thawed relations with the United States during his campaign for a third term.
President	Mohammad Khatami	1997–2005	Initiated a failed movement toward democracy. Aimed to reform Iranian society and government. Genuinely popular among his people.		Warming until the United States alienated him and the Iranian public with the "Axis of Evil" speech.
President	Mahmoud Ahmadinejad	2005–Present	An outspoken champion of the return to the Revolution. Hardline conservative.		Strained and poor.

Notes: *Nathan Gonzalez, *Engaging Iran* (Westport, CT: Praeger Security International, 2007), pp. 86–87 and Glenn Kessler, "In 2003, US Spurned Iran's Offer of Dialogue: Some Officials Lament Lost Opportunity," *Washington Post*, June 18, 2006, p. A16.

**Ali Ansari, "Iran under Ahmadinejad," *Adelphi Papers*, Vol. 47, No. 393, p. 12.

The Iranian government is a very centralized administrative system. There are 31 Ostans, which are administrative provinces. These are divided into 195 governorships, 5,001 divisions, 496 cities, and 1,581 village-districts. Even at the local levels, there are Imam Jome'h and local clergy to whom the elected government members must be responsive.

As time has progressed, Khamenei has expanded his power and influence in Iran. That, combined with the significant lack of popularity of Mahmoud Ahmadinejad, has led to the situation in the mid-2000s of the decreasing power of the presidency that is described in greater detail below. The modern leaders of Iran, their positions, and the authors' assessments of their characteristics and relations with the United States are presented on table 3.1.

Modern Iranian Government and Economic Performance

Rafsanjani and President Mohammad Khatami worked to reform Iran. They wished to increase electoral freedoms and hold government accountable to the people. These ideas were objectionable to hardliners in Iran. Unfortunately, normal business practices in Iran, and no doubt the fresh memory of the nationalization of oil in 1953 and the 1979 Hostage crisis, made Iran an unfavorable option for most investors. Furthermore, Khatami's push for democracy was not embraced by many in society. "[The failure of reform] was not caused by the violent obstruction of conservatives, as reformists charged, but by the failure and inadequacy of the very idea of democracy, an idea, it was argued, which was ill-suited in Iran, at least in its present circumstances. The notion that all could participate in politics was [viewed as] nonsense."[6] Khatami's administration was eventually known for its relative powerlessness and his inability to implement his social and economic policies. This ultimately undermined his desire to improve relations with the United States, as his political opponents capitalized on his weakness to impede his efforts. The United States was not particularly interested in his rapprochement anyway. This was demonstrated after the U.S. invasion of Iraq when, fearing that Iran was next, Khatami sent a secret letter to the White House through a Swiss ambassador offering to engage in comprehensive talks. This included full cooperation on nuclear programs, acceptance of Israel, and termination of support for militant groups. Far from being receptive, the Bush administration actually chastised the ambassador for serving as the courier of the letter.[7]

Under Rafsanjani and Khatami's leadership, some in Iran felt that they had moved too far away from the original intent of the Islamic Revolution.[8] Ahmadinejad appealed to those people. They rejected the materialism and capitalism of the preceding eras and called for a return to a time reminiscent of the Revolution's intent. Ahmadinejad and his supporters have argued that integration of Iran within the world community and engagement in international collaboration are actually counter to the country's Revolutionary purity.[9]

However, Iranian discontent with the system of government, current economy, and isolation from Western markets is reportedly widespread.[10] Mahmoud Ahmadinejad was elected in 2005 after campaigning on the need to reform the economy and improve the standard of living for every Iranian. He was merely the mayor of Tehran, had unorthodox religious views, and was not deemed a serious competitor by the reformists. As put by Ali Ansari:

> He succeeded [in getting elected] in part precisely because his reputation for ineptitude and eccentricity meant that he was not taken particularly seriously, and many reformists believed that this ineptitude meant he would not be in post for long. Significantly, this was a view shared by many conservatives, even hardliners, who regarded Ahmadinejad's track record as largely unimpressive and his obsession with the Twelfth Imam unhealthy.[11]

In fact, there are some (including Rafsanjani, his opponent in the run-off elections) who claim that Ahmadinejad won the election through corruption rather than the democratic process. The IRGC is accused of having stuffed ballot boxes for Ahmadinejad based on orders from Khamenei, who had personally selected Ahmadinejad as the next president. Rafsanjani was quoted as saying that "all the available resources of the regime were used in an organized and illegal way to intervene in the election"[12] Soon after the election, people were already turning against Ahmadinejad, leading one author to comment that it was difficult to find people who would admit to voting for Ahmadinejad because so many were embarrassed to have done so.[13]

Ahmadinejad proposed to distribute the country's oil wealth more evenly. As of the time of this writing, he has failed to provide the benefits he promised (table 3.2 presents key statistical information about Iran). His domestic popularity has been decreasing as the economy has failed to flourish. Ahmadinejad and his faction have attempted to depict the economic difficulties as being the result of U.S. imperialistic sanctions placed on the country.[14] Outside of Iran, the country's poor economic performance

Table 3.2   Vital Statistics for the Islamic Republic of Iran[a]

Population Statistics[b]	
Population (million)	68.6
Per capita GDP	2,802
Poverty Rate	20.9%
Population Growth Rate	1.5%
Unemployment Rate	11.5%
Other Economic Information	
Inflation Rate (consumer prices)[c]	20.68%
Oil Sector Contribution to Government Revenues[d]	71%
Aggregate Output and Expenditure[e]	
Hydrocarbon GDP	10.9%
Agriculture	13.8%
Industry	24.6%
Services	50.1%
Key Exports[f]	
Oil	80%
Gas	
Chemical and Petrochemical Products	
Pistachios	
Military Force[g]	
Army	350,000
Islamic Revolutionary Guard Corps	125,000
Navy	18,000
Air	52,000
Paramilitary	40,000
Defense Budget[h]	
Budget Excluding Defense Industry Funding (Billion US Dollars)	7.16

Notes: [a]Where available, data were collected from the International Monetary Fund or the International Institute for Security Studies in spite of the fact that the data were sometimes older than data available from the U.S. Central Intelligence Agency.

[b]Juan Carlos Di Tata, Leo Bonato, Roman Zytek, Rakia Moalla-Fetini, and Nisreen Farhan, *International Monetary Fund: Islamic Republic of Iran: Statistical Appendix*, pp. 3+20.

[c]Up to date statistic from International Monetary Fund website on Iran: http://www.imf.org/external/country/IRN/index.htm on 6/30/08.

[d]Authors' calculations based on IMF data from Tata et al., p. 5.

[e]Tata et al., p. 4.

[f]Tata et al., p. 3 for list of exports; Central Intelligence Agency, "Iran," *World Fact Book,* 2008 downloaded from www.cia.gov/library/publications/the-world-factbook/print/ir.html on 6/30/2008 on June 30, 2008 for the percent of exports for oil.

[g]International Institute of Strategic Studies (IISS), *Military Balance, 2008* (Wales: Routledge), p. 242.

[h]IISS, p. 242.

is largely attributed to mismanagement of the economy, the perception that Iran is politically unstable and therefore a poor candidate for foreign direct investment, and the economic sanctions that have been applied against the country since the Revolution.[15] Internationally, Ahmadinejad's regime's inflammatory rhetoric has increased tensions with other states and served to marginalize the country.

Ahmadinejad's actions since taking office have surprised many among the elites of Iran. While in his election speeches he emphasized skill and merit as prerequisites for attaining higher office, in practice he appointed largely loyalists, regardless of their lack of experience. These appointments upset many. For instance, Ahmadinejad appointed Tehran's chief prosecutor, Saeed Mortazavi, to be Iran's Human Rights Envoy to the UN. This was a surprising (and for some offensive) appointment given Mortazavi's notoriety and his having been implicated in the murder of a Canadian-Iranian journalist.[16] Ahmadinejad has also insisted on being personally involved in areas (such as economic projects) for which he has little experience or expertise. This has reportedly caused many problems.[17]

Ahmadinejad's election took Iran in a very different direction than the preceding Khatami regime had been headed. Khatami had attempted to engage Iran more fully in the international system. His stance was much more open and inviting to the West, whereas Ahmadinejad's has been openly hostile. Ahmadinejad's aggressive rhetoric internationally is likely the one saving grace for his administration domestically. This is because "resisting the foreign oppressor is so central to Iranian nationalist mythology, and so broad in its appeal, that Ahmadinejad has been able to use it to project an inclusivity which his other approaches deny him."[18] In other words, Ahmadinejad has engaged in the age-old tactic of attempting to unify the domestic population through the invoking of external threats. He has thereby relatively increased his power at home by creating a crisis mentality. This is not to say that he has become popular. However, he has been able to increase authoritarianism and keep the nation's attention focused abroad, to some extent, to protect his administration from the backlash over the poor performance of the domestic economy. However, there is evidence of the continued lack of popularity for Ahmadinejad's regime in its poor performance in the December 2006 municipal and Assembly of Experts elections.

While the recent increase in the price of oil has improved the Iranian economy, it has not solved the problems of inflation and poverty for the country. One of the key problems, which will be mentioned again in the nuclear chapter, is that while Iran is the world's second-largest oil producing country, it does not have sufficient domestic oil refining capacity. What few refineries exist in the country are antiquated and in bad need of maintenance and upgrades. This means that, in spite of its wealth in oil, Iran must import its petroleum products. In fact, Iran is the world's second largest gasoline importer after the United States.[19] "Some analysts raise questions about the economy's long-term viability and contend that currently rising international oil prices mask vulnerabilities in the economy."[20] Furthermore, the oil wealth that has been pouring into the country in the past several years has been held in the hands of a small minority of Iranians.

Inflation in Iran is high and rising, from 11.7 percent in 2006 to a projected 20 percent for 2008. Many in Iran are struggling to meet the increasing costs of staple items and housing, which has depressed real wages throughout the country. Unemployment levels were at about 11.5 percent in 2005/2006. According to one estimate, Iran has to be creating at least 700,000 jobs per year to offset its rising population and keep unemployment rates around the twelve percent rate.[21] In order to do this, Iran has to grow its economy. For that to happen, it has to have access to international markets and to be able to expand its energy production capacity.[22]

To offset economic problems, the Iranian government offers subsidies to the general population for things like gasoline, food, and housing. These subsidies amount to about 25 percent of Iranian Gross Domestic Product (GDP). While this does provide the average citizen with more affordable commodities, it fails to correct the underlying problems of consumer inflation and falling standard of living. The government also uses oil revenues to subsidize the costs of labor for important industries and to quell political unrest in the country by increasing wages beyond what they could be absent the oil revenues.[23] These subsidies skew depictions of poverty and wealth in Iran. While the 2004 GDP per capita in Iran was $2,320, the purchasing power parity GDP was $7,530. It is estimated that absent the subsidies the purchasing power parity GDP would be much closer to the real GDP per capita.[24] The most recent five-year plan under Ahmadinejad was intended to help alleviate some of the economic problems the country and its citizens are suffering. Reports differ in their assessments of the success of the plan.

This mix of increasing national income and increasing inflation at the same time has created a small Iranian middle class. These individuals are forming a new consumer market hungry for Western goods. However, U.S. companies are forbidden from competing in these markets by U.S. sanctions on Iran. This benefits other countries as their firms have opportunities to meet the needs and desires of Iranians in a less competitive marketplace.[25] This, in turn, has created international tensions as the United States has attempted to convince other countries to impose sanctions on Iran comparable to those from the United States. Getting other

52 THE UNITED STATES AND IRAN

countries to participate in sanctions has been a particularly hard sell for the
United States, especially with those EU nations that are even more dependent on Middle Eastern oil and markets than the United States is. This
tension has gotten to the point that some have suggested that Iran is intentionally attempting to drive a wedge between the United States and the
EU, effectively isolating the United States, as the United States has tried to
isolate Iran.[26] The United States has been, until very recently, similarly
unsuccessful in convincing countries such as Russia and China to adopt
restrictive sanctions against the Iranian regime.

Within Ahmadinejad's administration, most of the elites have little
experience with foreign policy. Ahmadinejad's tendency toward alarming
statements in the international media led Khamenei to create a new governing structure. In 2006, Ayatollah Khamenei created a new body in
Iranian government called the Strategic Council for Foreign Relations
(SCFR). (Which was seen referred to variably as the SCFR, the Foreign
Policy Council, and the Supreme National Security Council). This entity
was specifically created in "an attempt to balance the brash and inexperienced foreign affairs apparatus of President Ahmadinejad with the more
measured input of elder statesmen."[27] The body is comprised of approxi-
mately 15 heads of various military and governmental bodies. Their
responsibilities are as follows: determine national defense and security policies in accordance with the general policies of the Supreme Leader; coordinate governmental and social activities with regard to defense and
security policy; and exploit the resources of the country for dealing with
internal and external threats.[28] "The creation of a Foreign Policy Council [...]
to carry out the Supreme Leader's foreign policy—rather than Ahmadinejad's
slogans—is another sign [that] the real decision-making circles in Iran are
located beyond the inexperienced president's office of the foreign
ministry."[29]

The creation of this new body has not, however, tempered Ahmadinejad's
rhetoric. In July of 2008 the Nonaligned Movement (NAM—a group that
brings together more than 100 members of the international community
who largely oppose the West and accuse them of keeping Third World
countries down) Iran took leadership of the organization and Ahmadinejad
gave a fiery speech containing several thinly veiled criticisms of the United
States. In his written statement, Ahmadinejad condemned: "unilaterally
imposed measures by certain states... the use and threat of the use of force
and pressure and coercive measures as a means to achieving their national
policy objectives;" the unilateral categorization of countries as good or evil
based on unjustified criteria; and the UN Security Council as a tool of the
haves against the have-nots. The document also called on the NAM to
object to sanctions against Iran for its nuclear program and declared that

"the big powers are going down."[30] Though Ahmadinejad may be among the least powerful members of the government, he still has managed to mobilize public opinion to demonstrate popular support for his policy preferences.

Inconsistencies in Iran's policy preferences can sometimes be traced back to the factional struggles within the country and the counterbalancing of the president and the Supreme Leader. For instance, after Ahmadinejad wrote an unprecedented (and rambling) letter about the nuclear program to Bush, the former lead nuclear negotiator Rowhani quickly countered with the release of his own compromise proposal to *Time* magazine.[31]

Other Important Political Actors in Iran

The *IRGC* is a significant part of Iran's military. It is Constitutionally tasked with upholding and protecting the Revolution and its achievements.[32] The IRGC has pursued an arms procurement and production capacity independent of the rest of the Iranian military. They have also expanded their influence by becoming more involved in the Iranian economy through post-Iran-Iraq War reconstruction and infrastructure building projects. They have since evolved to impact the Iranian economy in the areas of construction, oil and gas, and telecommunications. Not everyone in Iran is pleased with the increased role that the IRGC is playing in Iran. "Clearly, the IRGC is among the most autonomous power centers in Iran, and it has resisted subordination to any civilian authority, from the presidential executive to the clerical control apparatus embodied in the Supreme Leader's representatives."[33] Some have even accused the IRGC of becoming involved in the black market economy.[34] The U.S. claims that the IRGC is proliferating Weapons of Mass Destruction (WMD), resulting in the United States imposing sanctions specifically against dealing with the group.[35]

The *QODS FORCE* is an elite arm of the IRGC that has been tied to Iranian support for Hezbollah. The Qods Force is an intelligence and unconventional warfare component of about 5,000 men. The Force is divided regionally, with a force for Iraq; one for Israel/Palestine and Lebanon; one for Afghanistan, India, and Pakistan; one for Turkey and the Arabian Peninsula; one for the republics of the former Soviet Union; one for North Africa; and one for Europe and North America.[36] They have provided support to Hezbollah, Hamas, and other Palestinian groups. Its budget is established directly by Khamenei and is not reflected in the official Iranian budget. It also plays a role in training for radical groups and others in unconventional warfare and is accused of working to train sectarian forces in Iraq.[37] It has also been linked by the U.S. government with violent factions in Afghanistan by providing training and weapons. The Qods Force was officially designated as a supporter of terrorist organizations by the U.S. Department of State on October 25, 2007.[38]

The *BASIJ* is a militia of the masses. It is an all-volunteer organization which began as a supplemental force to the military in times of struggle. The Basij are commanded by the IRGC. Their official strength is about 90,000, but they claim to have the capacity to call up to one million into service in crises. Their membership consists mostly of youths, men who have completed their service to the country, and the elderly.[39] They were very active in the Iran-Iraq War. Through the years its power has expanded and it now serves to supplement government policing and emergency management forces more broadly. Today it also plays a role in enforcing Islamic law in the cities of Iran.[40] This is contentious as it brings in the possibility of the military using the Basij forces to suppress and harass the domestic population. Ahmadinejad's regime has reportedly used the Basij to reinforce his repressive leadership at the street level, but he has been losing some support among the Basij of late.

The *BONYADS* are a unique aspect of Iranian political life. These are charitable Islamic foundations that compete with relative freedom in Iranian markets. They are governed by the Supreme Leader, not the other aspects of Iranian government. The bonyads are similar to major corporations with affiliations that reach into many aspects of Iranian life. They enjoy tax, credit, and foreign exchange benefits that are not available to other types of Iranian businesses. This may give the bonyads a competitive advantage to "normal" companies.[41]

Iran's Alternate Futures

It is uncertain what the future holds for Iran's domestic politics, and therefore difficult to predict what U.S. foreign policy alternatives might be. Obviously, Iran's stance toward the United States and the international system in general will impact the available policy alternatives for the United States as well as the relative rank-ordering of policies. If nothing else, it will constrain the options available to the United States. The authors have identified several paths that Iran could potentially take, which are discussed with their implications for the United States in this section.

If Iran were to keep Ahmadinejad as its president, or someone comparable to Ahmadinejad were put into office in the next elections, it could signal that the current relationship of Cold War–like combative rhetoric would continue. News reports in August of 2008 seemed to indicate this would be the case. The IRNA news agency quoted Khamenei as having told Ahmadinejad to:

> Work as if [he] will stay in charge for five years. In other words, imagine that in addition to this year, another four years will be under your management and plan and act accordingly. Some bullying powers and their worthless followers have attempted to impose their will on the Iranian nation. The president and the government have stood up to their excessive demands and moved forward.[42]

This would likely mean continued waves of rhetoric from both sides interspersed with periods of ignoring one-another or icy silences. Although a continuation of the current trend would not be the best possible outcome for the United States, there are certainly more negative situations with which it could be faced.

The worst case scenario would be one of an increasingly bellicose Iran. At several points in time since 2005, it has seemed that Iran was headed in this direction. Ahmadinejad's rhetoric and Khamenei's apparent failure to rein him in have led some to fear the worst. Iran simply has too much impact (or potential for impact) on this very important region. It could easily disrupt trade in the Gulf or impact the international economy by intentionally decreasing the oil supply from the region. It is near to being a nuclear power and has some fairly powerful allies. If Iran were to decide that it were completely not in its interest to cooperate internationally, it could destabilize the region significantly and have a commensurate impact on international stability.

It is possible that Iranian elites that are pushing for greater engagement with the West, and with Western economic markets in particular, will win out in the domestic struggles. This could lead to increased compliance with Western demands and cooperation with the international system. This path is predicted by a Policy Memo from The Stanley Foundation which was released in August 2008. They argued that it should be expected that the Iranian domestic situation should be "viewed as trending strongly toward widespread acceptance of broad-scale engagement with the West."[43] However, the Memo cautioned that this would not lead to immediate solutions to long standing problems between Iran and the West.[44]

Iran also could continue on its current path with the United States while warming significantly with other countries in the world. The EU has been working to influence Iran's nuclear program for some time now and has had much more diplomatic interaction with Iran than has the United

States. It is possible that this increased exposure and engagement between the EU and Iran could lead to warming of those relations with no benefits spilling over into its relations with the United States. There are many other countries in the international system with which Iran continues to have relatively normal relations. If Iran were to become even more disillusioned with the United States than they currently are, they could attempt to solidify relations with other countries in the world. This would give Iran greater leverage in dealing with the United States through the UN. Convincing Russia, China or France to side with it against the United States would be a major political coup for Iran. It would not likely be a terribly difficult endeavor with these countries, all of whom could influence the UN Security Council's votes. Each of these countries has major economic ties to Iran that could be incentive for them to cooperate.

A final scenario would be that Iran could become more bellicose with most of the rest of the world, while forming a bloc of countries with other potentially or openly belligerent states such as China, Russia, Venezuela, North Korea, Cuba, and others. In 2007, President Hugo Chavez of Venezuela took an international tour and spent time in many of these countries trying to develop this sense of shared identity among the nations' governments.[45] If Russia and China were to provide support for a bloc of disaffected states in the Western-dominated international system, it might be an attractive alliance for Iran. This would protect it from U.S. sanctions and other coercive U.S. tools because Iran would be able to meet its domestic needs through the bloc. It would also add the threat of Russian or Chinese retaliation to guard against a U.S. military invasion. Again, the authors believe this is one of the less likely scenarios to evolve, but one that should not be ruled out entirely.

View from the United States

U.S. public opinion about Iran is largely negative. This was emphasized by a December 2007 Gallup Poll in which Americans were asked to name the country that was the greatest threat to global stability, 31 percent responded that it was Iran.[46] However, 73 percent of Americans in the same survey preferred for the United States to utilize economic and diplomatic means to alleviate the problem rather than military action.[47]

The continued tense relations between the two countries led Vali Nasr to comment that "for much of the past three decades, the United States and Iran have been locked in a hostile stalemate."[48] This simple statement accurately and insightfully sums up the relationship. The question is, how do the countries move beyond this?

It will be interesting to see how the election cycles in both states impact the relations between them. The United States election in 2008 will necessarily usher in a new American administration. Ahmadinejad is eligible to stand for election to his second term in 2009. However, popular discontent with the failure of his economic plans may translate into a new administration in Iran as well. Given the radical change in policies from Khatami to Ahmadinejad, there is precedent to believe that a new administration could engage with the international system completely differently than Ahmadinejad has, in spite of the continued influence of Khamenei.

At present, the United States does not trade with Iran in any significant way. In large part, this is due to unilateral economic sanctions that have been levied against the state. In some ways, this has reduced American leverage to try and change the country's behavior. As president Bush himself has remarked, "We are relying on others because we have sanctioned ourselves out of influence with Iran."[49]

In addition to being labeled a state sponsor of terrorism and WMD proliferant, the United States has accused Iran of the following:

- Discriminating against religious minorities in the country, who are constitutionally forbidden to hold elected office, engage in public religious expression, be officers in the armed forces, and must study Islam in public schools and obey Islamic law regardless of their personal faith[50];
- Being "a source, transit, and destination country for women and girls trafficked for the purposes of sexual exploitation and involuntary servitude"[51];
- Facilitating the international trade in illicit narcotics[52]; (The narcotics trade and trafficking in women and girls may be influenced by the IRGC, which has control of the country's borders and is believed to be involved in smuggling.)[53]
- Breaking international law by executing juvenile offenders[54];
- Violating the human rights of its citizens—including criminalizing dissent, imposing the death penalty for insults against the Supreme Leader, brutal punishment of prisoners, stoning of adulterers, and lack of freedom of the press and speech;[55] and
- Most recently, Iran and specifically Ahmadinejad's regime have been accused of stepping up their arrests and persecution of Iranian dissidents, in particular those that have expressed their dissatisfaction with Iranian government online.[56]

A good example of typical U.S. rhetoric about Iran is provided at figure 3.2.

THE IRANIAN REGIME:
A Challenge to the World

"The international community is (also) speaking with one voice to the radical regime in Tehran. Iran is a nation held hostage by a small clerical elite that is isolating and repressing its people, and denying them basic liberties and human rights. The Iranian regime sponsors terrorists and is actively working to expand its influence in the region. The Iranian regime has advocated the destruction of our ally, Israel. And the Iranian regime is defying the world with its ambitions for nuclear weapons. America will continue to rally the world to confront these threats, and Iran's aggressive behavior and pursuit of nuclear weapons is increasing its international isolation."
—President George W. Bush

ADMIRATION FOR THE IRANIAN PEOPLE

The United States admires and respects the Iranian people and supports their right to determine their own future. As the President has stated, the United States hopes one day soon to be the closest of friends with a free, sovereign and democratic Iran.

The United States:
- Stands with the Iranian people as they confront a corrupt, repressive regime.
- Supports their efforts to promote positive political change, economic prosperity, and freedom.
- Offered assistance in the aftermath of earthquakes in 2003, 2005, and 2006.
- Asked Congress to fund an ambitious program offering the Iranian people:
  - unbiased information
  - empowerment of local activists
  - development of civil society
  - civic education and advocacy training

HUMAN RIGHTS VIOLATIONS

Iran's human rights record is abysmal and its democracy deficit is growing.

The Iranian Government regularly commits:
- Summary executions
- Disappearances
- Torture
- Arrest and detention of activists, journalists and religious minorities

NUCLEAR NON-COMPLIANCE

The international community has been clear that we cannot tolerate a nuclear-armed Iran. Under the Nuclear Nonproliferation Treaty, states have a right to develop nuclear energy for peaceful purposes, but the international community does not accept Iran's right to manipulate its access to peaceful programs to develop nuclear weapons.

Iran has:
- Abused its Nonproliferation Treaty privileges for years in its pursuit of nuclear weapons.
- Pursued a clandestine nuclear program for 18 years.

On February 4, 2006, the International Atomic Energy Agency (IAEA) voted 27-3 to report Iran's program to the UN Security Council.

On March 29, 2006, the UN Security Council issued a Presidential Statement (PRST) calling on Tehran to fully suspend its enrichment-related activities, cooperate with the IAEA, and implement the Additional Protocol.

SUPPORT OF TERRORISM

Iran remained the most active state sponsor of terrorism in 2005.

Iran has:
- Refused to start judicial proceedings against, render to countries of origin, or identify publicly senior al-Qa'ida members.
- Played a high profile role in encouraging anti-Israeli terrorist activity, including public threats to wipe Israel off the map as well as provision of financial and military assistance to Hizbullah and Palestinian extremists, enabling them to launch terrorist attacks.
- Provided financial and lethal support, including explosives-related components, to Iraqi Shia militants who have attacked Coalition forces.

Figure 3.2 U.S. State Department Fact Sheet from 2006 with typical rhetoric about Iran

Source: Taken directly from the U.S. State Department's Web site at http://www.state.gov/documents/organization/65664.pdf on March 4, 2008.

U.S. Policy Options

America and Iran are potentially at a new crossroad in their relations, if both countries are willing and able to recognize it as such. The Obama administration in the United States and impending elections in 2009 offer an amazing opportunity to start a new era between the two states. Table 3.3 presents policy options available to the United States in this issue area.

During the 2008 U.S. presidential campaigns, both U.S. candidates took positions on Iran as they campaigned, with John McCain's being more definitive than those of Barak Obama. In February 2008, McCain said: "I intend to make unmistakably clear to Iran we will not permit a government that espouses the destruction of the State of Israel as its fondest wish and pledges undying enmity to the United States to possess the

Table 3.3   U.S. policy options: Dealing with Iran's government

Number	Policy Options	Impact / Probability	Authors' Views
1	Attempt to intimidate the next regime.	Khamenei is the key, and the United States has been unsuccessful in intimidating him.	Avoid.
2	Isolate the new Iranian regime.	This would intensify animosity rather than alleviating it.	Avoid...unless new regime is more inflammatory and confrontational than Ahmadinejad's.
3	Seek to influence the outcome of Iran's forthcoming elections.	This is unlikely given Khamenei's wariness of U.S. intentions.	Attempt limited influence through overtures from the new U.S. administration to Khamenei.
4	Prepare to court the next president of Iran.	Could start off relations between the two new administrations on the right foot. It would give at least four years to build trust and cordial relations.	Highly recommended.

weapons to advance their malevolent ambitions."[57] McCain also upheld the Bush policy that negotiations with Iran should be conditioned on Iran's acceptance of certain U.S. demands, such as ceasing its enrichment or support for terrorism.[58]

Barak Obama was less strident in his position. In a speech to the American-Israel Public Affairs Committee (a group that would likely appreciate a tough stance toward Iran), Obama identified Iran as a threat to U.S. interests and international security. He refused to take the military option off the table. However, he has also, in the same speech, argued in favor of "aggressive, principled diplomacy without self-defeating preconditions."[59] He also said that it "would be a profound mistake for us to initiate a war with Iran."[60] That these statements were made in front of a group that would have been supportive of a more aggressive stance toward Iran is important. This is probably indicative of a greater willingness to work toward a diplomatic solution for disagreements between the two countries from Obama.

Attempt to Intimidate the Incoming Regime

A new regime might be more vulnerable to intimidation than the Ahmadinejad administration has proven to be. The United States could use rhetoric and threats to try and compel a new Iranian president to agree to compromises that would not have been deemed acceptable by Ahmadinejad.

Strengths

A new regime may be more open to U.S. pressures than Ahmadinejad has proven to be. It may be that the United States could more easily impose its will if there were a new regime in place that had yet to consolidate power.

Weaknesses

This approach would fail to recognize that the real source of political power in Iran is that of the Supreme Leader. Even after the president of Iran has changed (assuming that it does) Khamenei will continue to hold the reins of power in that country. Intimidating or attempting to intimidate the new president would be portrayed in the Iranian media as further U.S. moves to subjugate Iran to its will. It would actually probably benefit the incoming regime if it were shown to stand firm in the face of U.S.

attempts to impose policies on it. This lack of success could easily be seen as another foreign policy failure by the U.S. population.

Isolate the New Regime

The United States could choose to continue its current policy of attempting to isolate Iran within its region and the world. The goal would be to push Iran into capitulation by hurting it economically and politically in the international system.

Strengths

The only circumstance in which further isolation of Iran would become a preferred option would be if the next president of Iran were more bellicose than Ahmadinejad. Someone equally hostile as Ahmadinejad has proven to be would be detrimental, but it would still be in the best interest of the United States to try and improve relations. If the new Iranian administration were worse, the United States would in all likelihood have only isolation as a policy option. A new regime that was more aggressive would be a clear threat to the region and U.S. interests there. It would be likely to increase support for terrorism and accelerate the nuclear program. This would require the United States to take a more strident position with the new regime. It would signal the support of the Supreme Leader and (to a lesser extent) domestic public opinion for Ahmadinejad's hard-line approach to the international system. Because it is unlikely that such an Iranian regime would be open to U.S. overtures, U.S. options would be restricted to further isolating Iran or taking military actions to replace the regime.

Weaknesses

This is the most negative possible scenario arising from the next Iranian elections.

Influence Iranian Elections

The United States could adopt a policy that involved working to influence the Iranian elections. This should not be read to mean that the United States would use covert operations to change the will of the masses. That would be an inappropriate strategy for the Iranian political system. Rather, this would entail signaling to Khamenei that the United States is committed to improving relations and would appreciate a regime that would be more interested in rapprochement than the existing one.

Khamenei's influence over candidate selection and electoral politics in Iran was well-documented in the last election. Ahmadinejad was really no one's preferred candidate aside from Khamenei. Because the Supreme Leader has so much influence, the only way to impact the election's outcome would be to appeal Khamenei himself.

Strengths

Clearly, identifying and being able to get elected an individual that would help serve the U.S. interests in Iran and the region would be beneficial. If the United States could choose among the Iranian elites someone who was focused on true economic integration of Iran into the international system, this would likely go a long way to achieving U.S. goals. To engage more fully in the international economy, Iran would have to denounce the use of terrorism and its nuclear enrichment aspirations. These two factors alone would improve U.S. relations with Iran and the stability of the region. Similarly, the Iran Policy Committee argued in 2005 that the United States could maintain all its military and diplomatic options while aiding the Iranian opposition in moving toward regime change.[61]

Weaknesses

While there are obvious benefits associated with the United States influencing the selection Iran's next leader, it is highly improbable. Khamenei's cooperation is unlikely given his wariness of U.S. influence. Furthermore, if it were to come to light that Khamenei placed a "puppet" or "crony" of the United States into power, the public response in Iran would be negative.

Another problem with this option is that it is unlikely that the United States has sufficient information about potential candidates to select well. The U.S. intelligence capabilities have become notoriously ineffective. Knowing exactly who among the Iranian elites would be the best choice for the United States (i.e., moderate, Western-leaning, pro-market economy, etc.) would be practically impossible. In addition, if U.S. influence were discovered, it would further damage the U.S. reputation in the Middle East and the international system. According to one scholar, "such activities aimed at regime change from within, however, paradoxically serve to bolster the authority of the present regime, allowing it to portray any and all opposition to it as agents of the American state."[62]

Some limited attempt at influence, however, might be worthwhile. These would consist of appeals to Khamenei. The United States would have to convince him of its sincere desire for improved and more stable relations with Iran. If this could be achieved, it might at least result in Khamenei's support going behind someone who is less adamantly anti–United States than the current regime. Any amount of improvement would open doors for the U.S. and pro–West Iranian elites to engage more fully.

Court the Next President of Iran

The Obama administration has an opportunity to write a new relationship for the United States and Iran, assuming that Ahmadinejad is not reelected in 2009. Two fresh perspectives on the relationship may give it a new start. However, if Khamenei was sincere in his August 2008 assurance to Ahmadinejad that he had another term to look forward to, the United States may be denied this option for another four years.

Strengths

If the next Iranian president were more moderate than Ahmadinejad has proven to be, there is great potential for improving relations. The new U.S. administration took office in January of 2009. Iran's elections will be in summer 2009. That means that the U.S. administration has months to craft new policies toward Iran and position itself so that it is ready to respond depending on the politics of Iran's regime. The United States could examine past incentive packages and negotiations for options that were received positively on both sides and repackage these into a new offer to the regime.

If there is a new Iranian president, the new administrations also offer an opportunity because it would not be the case that either Bush or Ahmadinejad had backed down from their rhetoric. This would be two new actors who would be free to craft a new relationship if they wished. Clearly domestic public opinion and the history of the relations would have to be considered. However, there are elites on both sides that see the benefits of improved relations and would like to go down in history as the ones who overcame the historic impasse between the two countries.

Weaknesses

This is highly dependent on the individual who is selected to be the next president of Iran. It is probable that President Obama will be more open to improving relations than the Bush administration has been. However, the continuation of the Ahmadinejad presidency, or the election of someone equally or more radical than he is, could create a situation where the U.S. options for improving relations are severely constrained.

Preferred Policy

Three policies may be pursued simultaneously here. First, the United States could attempt to get word to Khamenei that they genuinely have an interest in improving relations. The United States could signal its willingness to rescind some sanctions or engage in more normal trade with Iran. Khamenei may be swayed through inducements to put a new president in place that would be less adamantly anti-United States. It should be recognized that it is unlikely that someone that is "pro–United States" will be the next president of Iran. However, any improvement in this regard will benefit the United States as it attempts to improve relations gradually over time.

The second policy to pursue would be identification of an inducement package that would be attractive to a new president and Khamenei. While there has been little positive response to recent U.S. and international inducements to Iran, this may change if Ahmadinejad were no longer president of Iran. The U.S. investment in going back through negotiations and determining which aspects of past proposals have been most attractive to Iran would be minimal.

Furthermore, the United States should consider negotiations without conditions. To do otherwise is to insist that Iran give up what it wants before the negotiations even begin. This is true even if the U.S. preconditions are temporary. This seems to the Iranians to be counterintuitive and insulting. They have to agree to give up what the negotiations are supposed to be deciding if they have to give it up or not? That makes little sense when viewed in that light. It would go a long way to showing that the United States was dedicated to a negotiated settlement if we removed these preconditions. Furthermore, a U.S. approach that was committed to turning the Iranian nuclear program back to a zero capacity basis will likely fail.[63] While there are obvious disadvantages to accepting Iranian enrichment capacity at some level, there are greater problems associated with failing to bring Iran to negotiated settlements.

This three-policy approach is similar to one that was recommended by U.S. ambassador Dennis Ross. His position is that the United States should engage without conditions but with pressures. He argued that the United States should attempt to continue to put pressure on Iran while at the same time attempting to provide "face-savers" and inducements for the country. He stated that the United States could remove the preconditions and thereby increase pressure on the Iranians by demonstrating U.S. dedication to reaching an agreement.[64]

Chapter 4

Iran, the United States, and Middle East Stability

The Middle East has historically been a geostrategically important region. During the era of colonialism, it was an important overland trade route that was coveted by the major imperial powers. The oil deposits of the region and global movement toward industrialization guaranteed the continued importance of the region in the postcolonial period. States within the region were highly coveted pawns during the Cold War both for their geostrategic location and oil supply. The continued global reliance on petrochemicals likely will make the region important for the foreseeable future.

There are many potential conflicts that could resurface in the region and directly impact Iran's security. The past conflicts with the United Arab Emirates (UAE) and others over the Persian Gulf islands (as exemplified by the Gulf's varying names: Persian Gulf, Arab Gulf, or simply the Gulf) is not currently an issue between Iran and its Arab neighbors. Similarly, the border conflict with Iraq and the conflict with Afghanistan over the border river are not hot topics of discussion in Iran today. These conflicts are not currently of concern for Iran, but they could resurface and destabilize the security environment for the region.

On the other hand, a conflict that does not directly impact Iran has been taken up by the country as a security interest. This is the Palestinian/Israeli situation. Looking rationally at this over 65-year-old conflict, there is no reason that Iran should be involved, but the Islamic regime leaders have assumed it is a religious responsibility to intervene in this conflict and take it on as one of their concerns. There are several reasons why Iran may be taking on this peripheral issue: it could be attempting to demonstrate its credentials as the defender of Islam in the region; the goal may be to make

Iran part of a global problem in order to solve their problems in the international system; or it could be that the country is trying to move attention away from domestic problems by refocusing attention on an international issue.

Seen from Iran, a different picture emerges. Iran's perspective could be best described as feeling encircled in the region (figure 4.1). There are several ongoing issues that could contribute to insecurity in the region:

- Disagreements about the Persian Gulf islands;
- Arab-Persian hostilities;
- Sunni-Shi'ite conflicts;
- Major U.S. troop deployments and bases throughout the region;
- The irredentist tendencies of the Kurdish population that is spread among states in the region; and
- An increasing wariness of Iran's neighbors that it is intent on exporting Islamic fundamentalism.

Iran is unique in its region. As it was put by the *New York Times* reporter Stephen Kinzer when you are in Iran, "you're in the middle of the Arab world but you're not an Arab country. You're in the middle of the Sunni Islam world but you're not in a Sunni country."[1]

Iran sits at the intersection of the Middle East and Asia. It has 5,440 kilometers of land boundaries with seven states, none of which is noted for its political or social stability. Its maritime boundaries include the Persian Gulf, the Gulf of Oman, and the Caspian Sea.[2] This gives it a strategic presence on the northern Gulf as well as along shipping lanes in and out of the Strait of Hormuz. This location has brought Iran both promise and problems...including foreign occupation, refugees from neighboring states, and openly hostile neighbors.

Stability within the region has been a long-sought-after goal of the international community. Persistent conflicts, however, have made this goal unattainable. These include:

- The fight between the Israelis and the other countries in the region over the territory given to the world's Jewish population in the aftermath of World War II;
- Conflicts among the Persian populations and the Arabs;
- Religious strife among the various sects of Islam within the region;
- Struggles among states to become the leading power in the region;
- The challenges that state failures pose to the region and commensurate strife;

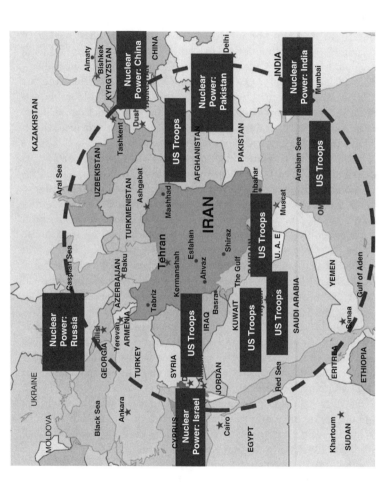

Figure 4.1 Feeling encircled

- Territorial disputes among the states in the region, including the Persian Gulf islands and various border disputes; and
- Concerns in the region that Iran is attempting to export the Islamic Revolution to its neighbors, as evidenced by Shi'a uprisings in Bahrain and elsewhere that have been traced back to Iran.[3]

The 1990s were marked with regional conflict over the Greater Tunbs, the Lesser Tunbs, and Abu Musa, three islands in the Gulf. These have been in dispute between Iran and the UAE since the British withdrawal from the region. Most of the Gulf Cooperation Council (GCC—whose membership includes Bahrain, Qatar, Kuwait, Oman, Saudi Arabia, and the UAE) have supported the UAE's claim to the islands.[4] This conflict was exemplified in February 2009, when a top Iranian official repeated the Iranian stance that Bahrain was the Fourteenth Iranian province, which was followed by Ali Larijani countering the claim.[5]

One of the major international concerns for the region is about its nuclearization. The entrance of Pakistan and India into the class of nuclear-weapons holding states on the periphery of the region was upsetting to many. The fear now is that the Pakistani nuclear arsenal (and the proliferation of A. Q. Khan, the father of the Pakistani nuclear weapon and head of a major proliferation network who was recently released from house arrest by the Pakistani government) increases the motivation for states in the Middle East to develop indigenous nuclear weapons programs. If one Middle Eastern state acquires the bomb, the argument is, the impetus will increase for others to do so. This could particularly be the case if Iran had nuclear weapons, which could be seen as a Shi'a state having the capacity to use against states dominated by other sects of Islam. This Western fear is not shared by all countries in the Middle East, however. Some believe that it would be a valuable regional counter-balance to Israeli military superiority and nuclear capacity, while others simply do not view an Iranian nuclear weapon as a threat.[6]

None of this should suggest that Iran has no friendly relations with its neighbors or the international community. Regionally, Iranian relations with Syria have been particularly close. During the Iran-Iraq War of the 1980s, Syria allied itself with Iran rather than siding with the West and the rest of the Arab League nations. Syria even shut down its end of the Iraqi/Syrian oil pipeline during the war, though it did receive subsidized oil from Iran in return. The two countries continue to enjoy relatively warm relations. In fact, they signed a mutual self-defense pact in 2005.[7] Although the move was largely political, it is symbolic of the long-term friendship and their joint commitment to withstanding outside pressures. Syria could be expected to support Iran if the United States were to launch hostilities against the Iranian nuclear infrastructure. Iran's relations with other Arab states remain cordial.[8]

Internationally, Iran has established close trade relations with Russia and China, who have been reluctant in their support of UN and U.S. sanctions against Iran. (Relations with Russia and China are discussed in more detail later in this chapter.) It has been developing a relationship with India, which needs Iranian oil as well as developing relations with Turkey based on the cultural and linguistic similarities among their populations. Alliances have also developed with Syria and Lebanon's Shi'a population and Hezbollah, generally based on their shared desire to deter and/or defeat the Israelis.

For the West, another fear about the region is its relative contribution to international terrorism. While regional terrorism is not new, the West's preoccupation with Islamist terrorist organizations and the states that may be facilitating their activities is a post-9/11 phenomenon. This offers both promise and peril for the region and for Iran in particular. The U.S. presence in both Afghanistan and Iraq has already had an impact on Iran (as is discussed later). Western charges that Iran is a state sponsor of terrorism (also discussed later) is a regional concern. Weak states in the region pose a particular threat, as they often make convenient operational hubs for terrorist organizations.

Table 4.1 presents the U.S. and Iranian perspectives on Middle East regional security. Iran hopes to be the leading state in the Middle East. According to Nathan Gonzalez, "when analyzing how Iran projects power abroad, we find the Islamic Republic pursuing a grand strategy of regional

Table 4.1   Middle East stability

Iranian Perspective	U.S. Perspective
Iran believes that the U.S. interference in the Middle East is the primary source of instability in the region.	The United States argues that Iran poses a significant threat to stability in the region due to its continued pursuit of nuclear weapons and state sponsorship of terrorism.
Iran sees itself as a major power in the region and wants to be seen as helping resolve regional disputes.*	The United States also feels Iran's hostile behavior can potentially jeopardize Israel's security, thereby generating further regional security dilemmas.

Note: *Mehran Kamrava, "The United States and Iran: A Dangerous but Contained Rivalry," *The Middle East Institute Policy Brief*, No. 9, 2008, p. 13.

dominance, or hegemony, and not a blind, religious mission to destroy Israel or simply cause massive death."[9] Given the instability in the region, the emergence of a strong regional leader may be beneficial...but it is unclear that Iran could or should be that state. From the regional perspective, "as a non-Arab Shi'ite state, Iran lacks a natural constituency."[10] From the American perspective, Iran's open hostility, sponsorship of terrorism and pursuit of a nuclear capacity make Iran an unpalatable candidate for regional leadership.

The U.S. invasions of Iraq and Afghanistan have actually brought Iran closer to its idealized position within the region by removing two of its most threatening rivals. Iran has a history of tension with both countries. This includes the Iran-Iraq War of the late 1980s, continued tensions with Iraq, and near-war with Afghanistan in 1998 after the Taliban killed 8 Iranian diplomats and a journalist. By removing Saddam Hussein's government in Iraq and the Taliban, the United States has also removed Iran's peer competitors and closest threats in the region. In many ways, the U.S. invasion of Iraq actually brought about the regime change there that Iran fought for in the 1980s. Iran never signed a peace treaty at the end of the Iran-Iraq War (they signed a cease fire) and it had maintained its policy preference of regime change for Iraq. U.S. actions have pushed Iran into a regionally dominant position.[11] According to Vali Nasr:

> By toppling Saddam and uprooting Ba'athism, the United States pacified Iran's premier regional rival. Iran benefited from the dissolution of the Iraqi military—the main barrier to Iran's expansionist aims since the 1970s. Today, there is no other military force in the Persian Gulf that is capable of containing Iran. In the political vacuum that followed Saddam's fall from power, Iranian hegemony quickly spread into southern Iraq—owing to the growing volume of trade (topping $2 billion in 2007) and impressive flow of pilgrims into Shi'a shrine cities (over 1.2 million in 2005–06).[12]

The fact that U.S. imposition of democracy in Iraq has led to it becoming the only Shi'ite, Arab country could be a factor in regional stability into the future. However, this windfall has been accompanied by increased Iranian fear that they are next on the U.S. list for aggression and democratization.

A related regional problem discussed in the literature is the potential impact of a hasty U.S. withdrawal from Iraq. Saudi Arabia has informed the United States that they could feel forced to intervene in Iraq if the United States withdrew, especially if they felt that Iraq's Sunni minority was at risk. A major conflict between Saudi Arabia and Iran over the disposition of Iraq would be a problem for the region and the world. This would be particularly true if the countries targeted each others' oil infrastructure as part of the hostilities, an option that has been deemed likely.[13] This would be a terribly destructive turn of events.

Part of the problem with the George W. Bush administration's relations with Iran early in its first term was that it did not seem to have decided on an approach between changing Iranian behavior or pushing for regime change. On the one hand, it was engaging Iran to help with the war in Afghanistan, while on the other it was labeling Iran part of the Axis of Evil. While some in the U.S. administration were pushing for increasing relations with Iran, others were resisting any concessions in the U.S. position.[14]

> For both the Clinton and Bush administrations, Iran has been perceived as a major threat to America's regional interests and policy objectives in the Middle East and elsewhere. In fact, the Bush White House has identified Iran as "a major threat" to the United States and its allies, aggressively seeking to isolate it and to bring about "soft" regime change [defined by Kamrava as overthrow of the government from fostered domestic uprising].[15]

As part of its attempts to isolate Iran in the Middle East, in July of 2007 the White House announced the unprecedented sale of over $50 billion in arms to the region. This sale included $20 billion in arms to Saudi Arabia, the United Arab Emirates, Kuwait, Qatar, Bahrain, and Oman over a 10-year period. It also included $30 billion in arms sales to Israel.[16] Table 4.2 compares each side's goals for the region.

Table 4.2   Policy goals for the region

Iranian Perspective	U.S. Perspective*
Expansion of the Iranian Revolution beyond its borders to unite the region in one *Ummah*.	Safety and security of the State of Israel.
Rejection of Western influence over the region's politics and economics.	Continued flow of oil from the region to Western markets.
Creation of an Iran-centered regional order to counterbalance the New World Order (whatever that means).	Containment of threats to U.S. interests, especially terrorism in the post-9/11 world.
Stability in Iraq under a democratic Shi'ite regime would best serve Iranian interests.	Iran's actions in Iraq are evidence of its desire to establish an Iranian style Islamic Republic in Iraq.

Note: *Mehran Kamrava, "The United States and Iran: A Dangerous but Contained Rivalry," *The Middle East Institute Policy Brief*, No. 9, 2008, p. 7, citing Robin Wright, "U.S. Plans New Arms Sales to Gulf Allies," *The Washington Post*, July 28, 2007, p. A1.

Another major regional point of contention is, of course, Israel. Iran under Ahmadinejad has increased tensions over this issue dramatically. Ahmadinejad has blatantly stated his desire to wipe Israel off the map and has denied the validity of the Holocaust—stating that it was made up by the West to give them an excuse to give Palestine to the Jews. While it is the case that Ahmadinejad is the less powerful executive in Iranian government, his pronouncements increase fears internationally that Iran is moving in a more hostile direction. Iran has, furthermore, strengthened its ties with Palestinian groups and increased its support to Hamas and Lebanese Hezbollah.[17] Iran has stopped short of open hostilities with Israel, but it has engaged Hezbollah in proxy conflicts with Israel. In particular, this was the case in the 2006 war in Lebanon.

The situation has gotten to the point where some are arguing that Israel is actually at war with Iran, but neither side is saying so directly.[18] According to one author, "The Palestinian struggle is no longer about creating an independent state. It is about being a front-line participant in the Iranian-led jihad to destroy Israel, evolving from a nationalist to a religious war...A real solution to the Arab-Israeli conflict can only be reached by dealing with its primary instigator: Iran."[19] Although this is an admittedly biased perspective, it is one that is held by some in the region and illustrates the extent of the potential problem and the perspectives of some in the region. Its interpretation is that Iran is using proxies to fight its war against Israel. Neither Israel nor Iran wants a direct war with the other. However, the proxy conflict continues through Hamas, Fatah, and Hezbollah and against the Palestinians, Israel, and Lebanon. Direct conflict with Iran would be devastating for Israel, but it may become more and more likely as Iran continues development of its nuclear program.[20]

This situation with Israel will have to be alleviated in some way to facilitate improved relations between the United States and Iran. So long as Iran continues its bellicose posture toward Israel, a major U.S. ally in the region, the United States will have difficulty normalizing relations. However, neither the authors nor the international community have arrived at a tenable solution for this complex and critical problem.

Clearly, the nuclear intentions of Iran also pose a potential threat to the stability of the region. The nuclear debate is taken up thoroughly in another chapter. However, it is appropriate to discuss the ramifications for Iran's nuclear aspirations for Middle Eastern political and military stability at this point. There are many countries in the region that are concerned about the implications of an Iranian nuclear weapon. One manifestation of this is the increasingly vocal arms acquisitions that have been undertaken by several states. This likely represents attempts to create stronger deterrent conventional capabilities. Saudi Arabia has been concerned about the increased Iranian influence in Iraq and Pakistan and has stepped up its regional role in response. There have also been talks about the development of a regional coalition of moderate states to confront the radical states that are being led by Iran.[21]

Of more concern have been the recent pronouncements by several regional powers that they wish to develop civilian nuclear programs. These states include Egypt, Jordan, and the GCC states as a group.[22] They approached the IAEA in 2006 to discuss their plans to develop their civil nuclear capabilities jointly.[23] Although many states have argued that they would prefer to have a nuclear free Middle East, few have foregone attempting to develop the technologies. Most have given in to the regional pressures and fears. What has resulted is competing programs where each state has attempted to grow their programs in pace with the others'. The fact that Israel has had the bomb for a long time and Pakistan (a neighbor to Middle Eastern countries and proliferator to them) has the bomb has increased this pressure.[24]

Furthermore, Henry Kissinger had an interesting perspective on the problem with an Iranian nuclear weapons capability. In an interview in 2005, he argued that Iran getting a nuclear weapon would move the world "beyond the point where nonproliferation can be a meaningful policy, and then we live in a world of multiple nuclear centers."[25] This notion that Iran may be a tipping point in nonproliferation is an interesting one and may be an exaggeration. However, it could be accurate if the Iranian acquisition of a weapon created a cascade of other states pursuing the capability.

Pakistan and its A. Q. Khan network have aided the nuclear programs in many states in the region. Pakistan's contributions to Iranian developments date back to the 1980s.[26] When Pakistan detonated their nuclear bomb in 1998, Iranian foreign minister Kamal Kharrazi traveled to Islamabad to congratulate the Pakistanis for their "Islamic bomb."[27] There is also evidence that the Saudis provided Pakistan significant financial support for its nuclear weapons program. Since the Pakistani detonation, the Saudis have received information and technology from the Khan network. The Saudis have also been working with the Russians on development of nuclear military and energy cooperation.[28]

It is not in the U.S. or global interest to have either a conventional or a nuclear arms race going on in the region. The instability associated with states in the region escalating their conventional and nuclear technology capabilities would certainly be difficult to manage. Although most Middle Eastern countries would prefer not to see Iran acquire nuclear weapons, a U.S. attack against the Iranian nuclear infrastructure could lead to increased anti-U.S. sentiments there.[29] Some countries might welcome the Western interference with the Iranian plan. However, none would be likely to support a U.S. attack openly for fear of retaliation from Iran.

A U.S. invasion of Iran would be inherently destabilizing not only for the region but also for U.S. relations with every country in it. Support for the United States among the governments and societies in the Middle East has been steadily eroding since the initiation of hostilities in Iraq. Furthermore, U.S. intervention in the region would likely also result in backlash within other regions and countries with large Muslim populations. Still other states may wish to distance themselves from the United States due to its bellicosity in the region.[30]

The Bush administration utilized "Nonlethal Presidential Findings" to authorize covert operations into Iran with the goal of destabilizing its government. These activities were reported in May 2007 through *ABC News* and later emphasized in *The New Yorker*.[31] These Findings have provided as much as four hundred million dollars for activities to support minority groups and dissident organizations, and to gather intelligence about Iran's nuclear program.[32]

A more radical stance toward Iran will likely now emerge with the election of Benjamin Netanyahu as Prime Minister of Israel. Among the major issues that will be instrumental in determining the next prime minister of Israel will be the candidates' Iran policy proposals. A significant problem within the region is that Israel sees an Iranian nuclear weapon, coupled with its attempted rhetorical and political intimidation, as a threat to its very existence. (The Iranian nuclear energy or weapons program is taken up in a later chapter.) However, it is important to note that the potential for an Iranian nuclear weapon has major implications for regional stability. While Iran has threatened to wipe Israel off the map, Israel has stated that a nuclear-armed Iran would be deemed to be an intolerable threat.

The Challenge of Iran's Iraq Policy

Iraq is of great importance to Iran's security within the region. The two have certainly had well-documented persistent hostilities in the past. They share a contentious border and have vied for power in the region. As mentioned previously, Iran has benefited significantly from the U.S. invasion of Iraq (as well as Afghanistan). However, Iran has not satisfied itself by sitting idly by and enjoying the improved regional atmosphere. Instead, Iran has been working hard to try and ensure that the new Iraq is one that will not challenge or threaten Iran in the region. In a later chapter, the issue of Iran's support for Iraqi insurgents is discussed. The purpose of this section is to provide information about Iran's attempts to influence Iraq politically, economically, and culturally.

When the governments of Iran and Iraq were both conservative monarchies, they tended to be better able to limit their competition. Then both regimes experienced revolutions that brought about the Ba'thist regime in Iraq and the Islamic Republic in Iran.[33] At this point, the countries turned against one-another. This state of affairs lasted for over 35 years; only actually becoming resolved with the U.S. invasion of Iraq and overthrow of the Ba'thist regime. One of the major problems that Iran had with the Iraqi system was that it was dominated by Iraq's minority Sunni population, which tended to treat Shi'ites like second class citizens, if not worse.

> During its seven-decade monopoly of power, the Sunni minority dismissed and relegated the Shi'ites to the margins of society. The Ba'thist regime would go on to extract a cruel revenge for any signs of Shi'ite political agitation and demands for representation commensurate with its demographic plurality...The Ba'thist retaliation took the form of summary executions, the razing of cities and massive deportations, which became the order of the day.[34]

Given Iran's Shi'ite majority, this situation was objectionable. This divide between the Sunnis and Shi'ites within Iraq continues to influence perspectives and goals within the country. Even their perspectives of the Iran-Iraq War differ. Sunnis reportedly see the war as a fight between Arabs and Persians and as a rallying point for Iraqi nationalism. Shi'ites apologize for the war and see Hussein's actions against Iran as comparable to his persecution of them.[35]

Since the U.S. ouster of Hussein and his regime, Iran has been working hard to exert its influence over Iraq's new government and society. Its activities have included a peculiar blend of diplomacy, working to assist Shi'ite allies, sending arms to Iraqi militias that are friendly, and supporting insurgents that are fighting against the U.S. presence.[36] This diverse policy approach to Iraq is seen by some as an attempt by Iran to "cover all its bases" or "hedge its bets."[37] Because of uncertainty over the eventual outcome of the state building process in Iraq, Iran has chosen to try and ally itself with as many Iraqi factions as possible. Iran's interests would be best served by an Iraqi government that was stable, governed by empowered Shi'ites, not dominated by the United States and not Western-oriented. However, "the overarching priority for Tehran is to prevent Iraq from once more emerging as a military and ideological threat."[38]

Having such a large U.S. presence in Iraq has been threatening to Iran. The United States has expressed its concerns that Iran is trying to export its revolution to Iraq. This does not seem to be the case. As it was put by Iranian foreign minister Kamal Kharrazi, "no Iranian official has suggested the formation of Iranian style government in Iraq."[39] Another Iranian politician, Muhammad Javad Larijani took this notion a bit further when he stated that, "Iran's experience is not possible to be duplicated in Iraq."[40] These do not sound like the comments of members of government bent on exporting the Islamic Revolution to Iraq.

Actually, the U.S. and Iranian interests are strangely aligned on the issue of Iraq. Both want to see a stable and democratic regime take hold in the country. Democracy in Iraq should translate into Shi'ite control of government, given that it is the majority religion there. Iran is hopeful that this would lead to improved security for its own interests.[41] Iran wants the stabilization of Iraq to occur as quickly as possible. The Iranian government knows that only through such stability will it gain the withdrawal of U.S. troops from Iraq. Conflict between Iran and Iraq or even within Iraq itself (especially if it turned in to a civil war) poses a significant threat to Iran's achieving its goals.[42] "Tehran wants to establish good relations with its one-time enemy, keep the government in Baghdad weak, and prevent a Saddam-like strongman from seizing power."[43]

However, at the same time, Iran is pursuing other goals in its relations with Iraq. Iraq's Shi'ite population has many similar interests to those of Iran. Where Iraqi Sunnis sought to identify with pan-Arab notions, both Shi'ite Iraqi elites and Iranian Shi'ites have a shared interest in downplaying Arabist arguments. Instead, Iraqi Shi'ites have consistently called for improved relations with Iran and Turkey.

Iran has reached out to new Iraqi government officials in the Dawa party,[44] the Supreme Council of the Revolution in Iraq (SCIRI)[45] party, and their respective militias. This includes the U.S.-supported Iraqi prime minister, Nouri al-Maliki.[46] Ironically, these are entities that have close ties with the U.S.-sponsored Iraqi government.[47] Furthermore, Iraq's Grand Ayatollah Ali al-Sistani, the leading religious authority, is a native of Iran.[48] Sistani's good will toward Iran was exemplified by his willingness to meet with an Iranian delegation while refusing to meet with leaders from the United States.[49]

Part of the reason that this process has been easy for Iran, aside from shared religion, is that many of the Shi'ite members of Iraq's new government lived in Iran after being exiled from Hussein's Iraq. In fact, during Hussein's reign, some Iraqi Shi'ite political parties made Iran their home base for operations, provided support for Iran's government, and planned for an Islamic government patterned after Iran's.[50] However, since gaining power, the Dawa and SCIRI parties have sought to create a government with a prominent role for religion, but have stopped short of striving for Iranian-style Islamic governance.[51] Both the Dawa and SCIRI parties would face significant challenges if the United States and Iran came to the point of direct conflict as they would be compelled to decide between maintaining U.S. support or joining the Iranian side. Dawa tends to be less dependent on Iran. When he was a member of parliament, Nouri al-Maliki once said "Dawa don't like Iranians, and I personally hate them."[52] His hatred seems to have tempered over time, but the sentiment that the Dawa are not terribly supportive of Iran is valid. SCIRI has a higher level of interaction and inter-dependence with Iran, and would therefore be more likely to be supportive of its position. If the two chose different responses to U.S./Iranian conflict, it could result in conflict between the parties as well as within them.

Iran has also developed close relations with the Iraqi Kurdish popula-tion. Again, these ties began during Hussein's time because of Iraq's perse-cution of the Iraqi Kurds.[53] However, there is also self-serving aspect of Iran's approach to Iraqi Kurds. Iran has a Kurdish population of its own. As with Kurds in most countries, the Iranian Kurds have irredentist aspira-tions. Iran is hopeful that good relations with Iraqi Kurds will create sta-bility for them and keep them from agitating Iranian Kurds.

Additional relations have been developed and maintained more quietly with radical Islamic cleric Muqtada al-Sadr. Iran has reportedly even sup-plied his Mahdi Army with some weaponry.[54] Al-Sadr's reputation and American concerns about him have been the cause for Iran's working behind the scenes to provide him support. Iran has not been terribly inter-ested in relations with al-Sadr, but has pursued some contact in the interest of spreading its influence broadly.[55]

As part of its efforts to expand ties with Iraq, Iran has also sent over two thousand religious students and scholars to study in Iraq. The U.S. govern-ment, however, believes that many of these students are actually Iranian intelligence agents that are spying on Iraq.[56]

Iran has been pragmatic about its relations with Iraq. While it is work-ing to develop increasing ties with Iraqi Shi'ites and political parties, it is aware that this will not result in Iraqi subordination of its interests to serve Iranian needs.[57] Instead, the Iranian expectation is that they will have a neighboring regime that will be less confrontational . . . and perhaps even friendly. Given the current environment, this is not an unrealistic expecta-tion. On July 7, 2004, for instance, Iraq's then defense minister, Saadun al-Dulaimi arrived in Iran and stated: "I have come to Iran to ask forgive-ness for what Saddam Hussein has done."[58]

An additional sign of Iranian pragmatism is the expansion of trade between Iran and Iraq. Trade between the two countries has risen steadily, from $800 million in 2004 to $1.8 billion in 2006, to $2.8 billion in 2007.[59] Iran is also providing Iraq with funding for infrastructure projects in southern Iraq.[60]

The Case of the MKO

The MKO is another factor in the Iran/Iraq relationship.[61] The MKO has been designated a terrorist organization by the U.S. State Department and many other states. (However, in 2006 the European Court of Justice attempted to overturn this designation but was not supported by the Council of the EU.)[62] It is a group that was formed in Iran in the 1960s and was expelled and ended up in Iraq during the 1979 Revolution. The group is based on a mix of Marxism and Islam and has both anti-West and anti-Iran ideologies. One of its main goals is to bring about the fall of the Iranian Islamic regime and replace it. The group uses a mix of propaganda and terror in its pursuit of this goal. Its National Liberation Army of Iran wing is responsible for its militant activities.[63] MKO has been responsible for many bombings against U.S. and Iranian targets. It also supported the 1979 U.S. embassy takeover and hostage taking.[64]

The group is led by Maryam Rajavi, who has established a personality cult around herself and claims to emulate the Prophet Muhammad. Members of the MKO view her has the president of Iran, in exile.[65] She was arrested by French authorities in 2003, which led to widespread riots among MKO members living in Paris. She was later released and is in hiding.[66] It has a global network of lobby organizations, such as the National Council of Resistance of Iran (NCRI) that has offices in Western capitals, including Washington, DC.[67]

The MKO has been a contentious point between Iran and Iraq. During the Iran-Iraq War, Saddam Hussein provided financing and equipment to the MKO in support of its work against Iran. Furthermore, it was revealed after the fall of Hussein that he had provided millions of dollars from the Oil-for-Food program (1999–2003) to the MKO. Evidence of Hussein's support to the MKO reportedly includes video of his handing suitcases of money over to known MKO leaders. MKO operatives were also shown as they were being trained by the Iraqi military.[68] Furthermore, the MKO has helped the Iraqi government in its suppression of Iraqi Shi'ites and Kurds.[69]

Iran made bombing runs against MKO bases in Iraq throughout the 1990s and into the 2000s. While the numbers and types of missiles used have been questioned, there is no doubt that Iran has been responsible for at least eleven attacks across the border in Iraq.[70] For 2001 alone, it is estimated that sixty-six Iranian missiles struck Iraqi MKO bases, which is a clear violation of Iraqi sovereignty.[71]

While the MKO's main headquarters is in Paris, it has a large number of members who are currently being held at Camp Ashraf in Iraq. The group was targeted by U.S. Coalition aircraft as part of Operation Iraqi Freedom. This resulted in its forces in Iraq surrendering in May of 2003 and their settlement into Camp Ashraf.

The future of the group is currently in question. In 2006, a plan was put into place for Bulgaria to work to secure the camp and begin dismantling the group. This was after there were complaints that the United States had been providing the group with its protection so that it could use the MKO as leverage against Iran. Others have argued that the United States is instead working to dissolve an incredibly coherent group slowly over time in order to avoid violent clashes with the MKO.[72] In 2004, the United States designated the MKO members protected persons rather than prisoners of war. The MKO reportedly thought this was a major favor from the United States. However, others have interpreted it as a U.S. move to gain the group's trust so that its leaders can be undermined more easily. Meanwhile, the United States has allowed the conditions at Camp Ashraf to gradually deteriorate. At the same time, the United States has been creating improved conditions at the Temporary International Presence Facility (TIPF), a facility at which MKO defectors are housed.[73]

Iraq's government claimed in 2007 that the United States has impeded their attempts to expel the MKO members from their country. The Head of the United Iraq Coalition, Abdelaziz Hakim has said that the Iraqi people want the MKO out of their territory so that they can avoid future Iranian strikes against the group.[74] He has also stated that, "Iran's support for the Iraqi nation and government in different junctures has guaranteed stability in the region and the stability is also useful for Iran itself."[75]

However, still in 2008 the MKO had not yet been expelled. In June of 2008 Iraq's cabinet approved bans on any Iraqi citizen or organization engaging with the MKO inside of the country.[76] Iraq formed a special unit to deal with the MKO as of August 8 and followed this up with giving the group six months to leave the country on the August 21, 2008.[77]

Extraregional Influences

Given the region's oil and other resources, most major countries in the world seek to influence it. This section is focused on the three entities whose attempts at influence have the most significant impacts on American foreign policy: Russia, China, and the EU.

Russia

Like the United States, Russia sees Iran as a key to stability in the Middle East. Russia and Iran have had good relations since Iran's Revolution, when Iran broke with the United States. Iran has increased its trade relations (almost tripling the trade volume) with Russia since 2000. Iran has received support for its energy sector, in particular assistance for the Bushehr nuclear power station, as well as weapons and military equipment. In exchange, Iran has exported fruit and cars to Russia.[78] As one Russian newspaper noted in 1995:

> Cooperation with Iran is more than just a question of money and orders for the Russian atomic industry. Today a hostile Tehran could cause a great deal of unpleasantness for Russia in the North Caucasus and in Tajikistan if it were to really set its mind to supporting the Muslim insurgents with weapons, money and volunteers. On the other hand, a friendly Iran could become an important strategic ally in the future.[79]

Russia also seeks to exert its influence over Iran to secure access to Iranian oil. A key difference from the U.S. motivation, however, is that Russia also sees Iran (as well as Turkey) as important to maintaining stability among the former Soviet satellites of Central Asia and Transcaucasia.[80] Furthermore, the U.S. Gulf War in the early 1990s isolated Iran in the region and increased its sense of threat. This pushed the Iranians closer to the Russians and increased Russian influence.

Russia has probably been the most significant international contributor to Iran's nuclear program since the mid-1990s. In 2002, it signed a ten year cooperation agreement with Iran to help with the construction of six reactors and the training of Iranian nuclear researchers and engineers. Russia has also helped Iran to learn more about uranium enrichment technologies and has an agreement in place to deliver uranium fuel to Iran six months prior to the starting of the Bushehr reactor site.[81] On February 25, 2009, Iran tested its first nuclear power plant with the support from the Russians and with a key Russian nuclear scientists on site to observe. It was anticipated at that time that a contract would soon be signed for Russia to provide nuclear fuel for at least ten years.[82]

However, there are still some signs of dissatisfaction in the Russian/ Iranian relationship. Iran has complained that trade between it and Russia

(1:20) is too imbalanced. On its side, Russia is worried about Iranian great power aspirations and its potential to cause instability in the region.[83]

U.S. unilateral sanctions against Iran have also given it added incentive to purchase its military equipment from Russia. Russia has been instrumental in helping Iran develop its arsenal of military equipment, and nuclear reactors and enrichment capacities. As a result of Russian assistance with the Iranian missile program, the United States placed sanctions on two Russian research institutions and eight additional Russian organizations.[84] Cooperation with Russia has also included the training of Iranian scientists at Russian facilities and the export of technologies. When the United States has pushed for increased and multilateral sanctions against Iran, it threatened these relationships. During the 1990s in particular, Russia was in need of the hard currency that Iran could provide for arms sales and argued against U.S. attempts to sanction Iran.[85] From the U.S. perspective, Russian development of close ties with Iran serves to undermine U.S. attempts to isolate Iran internationally.

Russia can be seen to be walking a careful line between its interests in its relations with Iran. There are numerous benefits to its positive relations with Iran: a market for its arms and energy technology; assistance in stabilizing the former Soviet states nearby; access to Iranian oil and other natural resources; and an ally to play against the United States. However, its willingness to exploit this relationship seems to be constrained by its desire to maintain good relations with the EU and the United States. While it (as is discussed in more detail later) has been reluctant to impose sanctions on Iran, in the end it did so.

Another thing to consider here is what the Russian reaction to U.S. military intervention in Iran might be. Russia's response will likely have a significant impact on regional stability and the U.S. chances for success. One of the potential ramifications of a U.S. attack on Iranian nuclear facilities might be a negative backlash from the Russian government and general population. The United States is currently not terribly popular amongst Russians.[86] Aggression against the Iranian program could easily be interpreted in Russia as more evidence of U.S. expansionist tendencies and desire to dominate the region. This could lead to Russia expanding its military forces or attempting to increase its military presence in the Middle East. It could also result in reduced Russian support for U.S. calls for sanctions against Iran. It is unlikely that the situation would go beyond making Russia more vocal in its condemnation of U.S. actions and increased reluctance for the imposition of sanctions. The situation, could, however, push Iran into a closer relationship with Russia—albeit one in which Russia might be less willing to sell weapons to Iran or provide support for its nuclear program.[87]

China

China's relationship with Iran is one that troubles the United States. In many ways, Chinese activity in the Middle East can be portrayed as it struggling to counter U.S. interests in the region. However, there are other reasons why the United States would like to disrupt Chinese and Iranian relations. These include:

- Iran's potential to impact regional stability;
- Iran's state-sponsorship of terrorism;
- Iran's desire to acquire WMD;
- Ahmadinejad's rhetoric and dedication to pushing the Iranian agenda in the region; and
- China is Iran's major conventional weapons supplier.[88]

The Chinese have been well-known violators of international prohibitions against the trade in technologies relevant to WMD. In the case of Iran, the United States is particularly worried about the potential for China to transfer nuclear weapons and delivery system technologies. The Chinese motives in these deals are rarely merely financial gain. China is focused on developing relationships with countries that are natural-resource rich so that it can feed the growth of its own economy. Iranian oil reserves are particularly attractive. "Iran's oil exports to China increased from 20,000 barrels per day (bpd) in 1995 to 200,000 bpd in 2000."[89] China's consumption levels of Middle Eastern oil are already high. However, they are anticipated to grow to be one of the world's major oil importers in the near future.

Similarly, direct Chinese access to Middle East oil would provide it greater protection from U.S. interruptions of their supply. Because of the U.S. tendency to support the use of sanctions to change nations' behavior, as well as the U.S. military capability to blockade oil traffic out of the Persian Gulf, China's interest in a sustainable direct supply of oil is high. This desire has caused China to coordinate diplomacy for the Middle East with other countries (particularly France, Germany, and Russia—who also value energy security from Middle Eastern oil), with the goal of developing a counterbalance to U.S. influence.[90] One of the major factors in this is China's willingness to be the supplier of military technology and equipment upon which the United States has placed restrictions to the Middle East. This has allowed it to develop closer military connections with many countries.[91]

Iran has purchased large quantities of military equipment from China. It has also acquired WMD technology assistance from China. This includes assistance with the Iranian ballistic and cruise missile programs. China has also provided expertise to assist Iran with its nuclear and chemical weapons program.[92] According to Barry Rubin, it is "Iran's pariah status that makes it an attractive market...or even a market at all...for China, as a supplier of last resort for certain conventional items and weapons of mass destruction."[93]

The Chinese influence is also present elsewhere in the region. It is known to have cooperated with the Pakistani A. Q. Khan network for proliferating nuclear technology, as well as providing some weapons schematics to the Pakistanis. They have also been linked closely with Saudi Arabia since the 1980s. It is known that the Chinese provided the Saudis with ballistic missiles, however little else is known about the relationship as it is typically conducted in secret.[94]

One activity that has been controversial is Iran's stated desire to join the Shanghai Cooperation Organization (SCO). The SCO is a regional cooperative forum between Russia, China, Kazakhstan, Tajikistan, Kyrgyzstan, and Uzbekistan. The group is seen by some as a post–Cold War regional counterbalance to Western influence.[95] The United States is concerned that this will form a power block in the region. Furthermore, if Iran were granted membership, it might lessen the impact of U.S. and UN sanctions on the country.[96] However, the SCO itself placed a moratorium on admitting new members two years ago. It allows Iran and others to be observers and has created a status of "SCO dialogue partner," but has been cautious about new membership. In particular, the group has been reluctant to grant Iran membership because of the tensions between Iran and the West.

EU

Relations between the EU, both as individual countries and as a group, and Iran have also varied based on the interests of the states and the issues of the day. The contact between Europe and Iran has been more consistent than that between the United States and Iran. This has allowed for better understanding of the many states' cultures, societies and governments to be shared between Europe and Iran. At various points in time, Iran has viewed Europeans as either protectors of their interests or threats to their security. Europeans, in general, have seen Iran as a trading partner in possession of a vital natural resource as well as a potential source for instability in the region. The threat of instability is an important one, as it would threaten the supply of oil, which is so badly needed by European states. On the other side of the relationship, Iran sells about one third of its oil supply to European states. Iranian trade links with the EU are fairly extensive and have been growing. In 2005, about 44 percent of Iranian imports were from European countries.[97] The importance of these trade relations makes it important to both the EU states and Iran to maintain positive diplomatic interaction.

In general, the EU has tended to take a more constructive path with Iran than has the United States. While the United States is imposing sanctions, pushing for more multilateral sanctions and discussing potential military action, the EU has been dedicated to trying to arrive at a diplomatic solution for areas of disagreement. More so than the United States, the EU has tended to treat Iran as a powerful state in its own right. This has resulted in the desire for more negotiated settlements rather than dictated ones.[98]

Because of the 1979 hostage crisis and following war between Iran and Iraq, throughout the 1980s many European countries backed the U.S. arms embargo against Iran. They also claimed neutrality about the Iran-Iraq War. However, in practice, only Germany actually maintained its neutrality and continued to trade with both Iran and Iraq. The primary reason European states supported the United States in these actions was that there was great concern that Iranian domination of the region would threaten the oil supply.[99]

There were actually, however, a minimum of four different approaches to relations with Iran: EU, France, United Kingdom, and Germany. While there were frequent arguments that the EU should take a cooperative approach to Iran, in reality each state's preferences and interests determined their bilateral relations with Iran. Things began to change in the early 1990s, when the EU adopted a more multilateral approach to Iran. There was European emphasis placed on what was known as the "critical dialogue," which was the official EU policy toward Iran. The focus of the critical dialogue was on engagement of Iran. The belief in the EU was that Iran was turning toward a more moderate approach. Social and humanitarian issues such as immigration, human rights, drug trafficking, organized crime, and terrorism were key aspects of the critical dialogue and the subjects of meetings between the states. The EU hope was that engagement would foster Iranian moderation. As the critical dialogue was playing out, trade negotiations were also underway and Europe became one of the major trading partners for Iran. France, Britain, and Germany increased trade with Iran radically.[100]

A significant change in the relationship occurred in the late 1990s. In 1997, the German Courts handed down the Mykonos Case verdict, which implicated high-level Iranian officials in a political assassination. This resulted in fifteen EU member states withdrawing their diplomats from Tehran and the suspension of the critical dialogue policy.[101]

However, by 2001, relations seemed to have recovered. At that point, high level diplomatic visits began with Iranian foreign minister Kamal

Kharrazi's visit to Brussels. This was followed by top EU leaders paying diplomatic visits to Tehran. In July 2002, a European Parliamentary delegation visited the Islamic Republic for the first time; with a return visit of the Iranian Majlis in June 2003.[102] These visits are significant indicators of the importance the EU and Iran place on improving relations.

However, points of tension still exist in the relationship. The EU has consistently pointed out four points that are of concern for it relevant to Iran: human rights, terrorism, nonproliferation, and the Middle East Peace Process.[103] While economic relations are important to the EU, it has stressed that Iranian behaviors have to change. However, the EU's approach to trying to change Iranian actions has differed from that of the United States. Where the United States has tried to use the stick...economic sanctions and threats of military action...the EU has leaned toward the carrots of improved trade and more integration into international markets. According to an EU report, the EU is Iran's main trading partner for both imports and exports.[104] This gives the EU more leverage in its dealings with Iran as well as making EU threats of sanctions against Iran more significant and potentially persuasive. However, the EU has recently agreed to participate in sanctions on Iran through the UN based on Iran's persistent refusal to negotiate about terminating its nuclear enrichment activities.

From a U.S. foreign policy perspective, the EU relationship with Iran is a challenging one. The U.S. benefits from and uses the continuing negotiations that the EU has with Iran. The EU has proven to be a fairly reliable and dedicated intermediary. However, EU relations with Iran could undermine the U.S. position in a number of different ways. First, if the EU or its member states continue to trade with Iran, it mutes the potential impact of U.S. sanctions. Second, diplomatic and trade relations between the EU and its member states and Iran are contrary to the U.S. will that Iran be isolated in its region. Finally, a close relationship between Europe and Iran could develop, potentially excluding the United States from future trade opportunities with Iran.

A Peace Pipeline?

Major natural gas reserves were found in the south of Iran in 1988. Since that time Iran has been negotiating with Pakistan and India for the building of a regional natural gas pipeline.

It would extend from about 690 miles inside Iran, span 440 miles across Pakistan, and go 530 miles inside of India. The project is currently estimated to require an investment of at least $7 billion.[105]

There are benefits for all concerned in such a deal. Iran, obviously, would benefit as it would have a guaranteed market for the sale of this resource. It would also benefit from the infrastructural investment that would have to be made to bring this project to fruition. India is in great need of energy resources to meet the needs of its masses. Its economic growth could also be stimulated by increased access to the natural gas from the pipeline. Furthermore, natural gas would provide India with a more environmentally friendly alternative to its current reliance on coal.

Pakistan, while possibly reluctant to provide a benefit to its major rival to the east, would reap the financial benefits of transit fees and other investments from both India and Iran while building and maintaining the pipeline. The project would guarantee Pakistan an additional future source of income. It would also provide Pakistan with the opportunity to increase its economic interactions with all of the countries involved in the project, which might include Russia, China, and some EU states. The pipeline would also provide natural gas that would improve its energy production capacity, which could have a ripple effect on the Pakistani economy.

The United States has significant concerns about the possible impact of such an arrangement on regional and international stability. The development of a strong alliance among the three countries would carry political and strategic benefits for them along with the economic impact. This is the main concern for Washington as it would hurt U.S. attempts to isolate Iran. The U.S. position was made clear by U.S. State Department official Steven Mann in 2006. "The US government supports multiple pipe-lines from the Caspian region, but remains absolutely opposed to pipelines involving Iran."[106] Warming relations between India and Iran have been underway since the 1990s.[107]

Among the U.S. concerns is that Iran will enter into this agreement with two nuclear weapons powers. Although it is possible that India and Pakistan could provide assistance to Iran in the development of improved power generation, the fact that they also have developed nuclear weapons makes the U.S. nervous about their sharing of technology with Iran.

A further complicating factor for the United States is the planned Russian participation in the project. The United States already worries about the potential for expanding Russian influence in the region. Russian cooperation with Iran has been (as discussed further in a later chapter) a point of contention due to Russian provision of enrichment technologies and assistance in building nuclear reactors in Iran.

Musharraf's resignation as president and replacement with Asif Zardari in September 2008 after the assassination of his wife, Benazir Bhutto, is evidence of this instability.[108] Pakistan's ability to maintain the security of the pipeline is uncertain. Another major factor in this regard is continued tensions between India and Pakistan, which have made negotiating the pipeline deal more challenging. Continued strife along the border between

Pakistan and India, across which the pipeline must obviously cross, could be a threat to the pipeline. The militant groups in this region frequently attack infrastructure and the pipeline would be a high-value target. Furthermore, India and Pakistan rejected a final deal from Iran in 2007 which called for a three-year review of the price of the gas.[109] Finally, India's votes against Iran at the IAEA over its nuclear enrichment program may signal trouble in that relationship.[110] In general, the sanctions that are in place against Iran would restrict the trade between it and both India and Pakistan. Until these are lifted, the pipeline will be hindered.

View from the United States

The Middle East is a region that is crucial to U.S. interests and those of the West more generally. The resources that are present in this region are critical to the economic well-being of every industrial state. Unfortunately, the region has proven to be highly unstable in the past and continues to be in today's international environment. Competition among the major international powers to exert influence over the governments of the region and thereby control access to its resources has been extensive. This competition obviously contributes to the regional tendency toward instability. During the Cold War, there were continued attempts by the United States and Russia to manipulate the balance of power in the region; either to maintain the status quo or to arrive at a balance that was more favorable to their position. In the post–Cold War world, the number of countries seeking to win favor among Middle Eastern nations has only increased and the competition seems to have intensified.

Among the major concerns of the United States is the security of Israel within the region. Iran's recent verbal belligerence toward Israel has been upsetting to the United States. Through time, the United States has sought to balance the power between Israel and its Arab neighbors in its attempts to maintain regional security. On the other side, U.S. support for, and special friendship with, Israel has been a persistent source of irritation for many countries in the Middle East.

Iran's stated desire to lead its region is, in many ways, a direct challenge to U.S. priorities there. This is particularly true so long as Iran is taking a hostile tone with the United States and the international community. Furthermore, the Iranian desire to export its Revolution to other countries in the area is not a preferred U.S. policy outcome for the region, to say the least.

Overall, it would seem that the United States currently does not know what to make of Iran or how best to handle relations with the country for the betterment of the region. The stark contrast between Khatami's seem-ing interest in normalizing relations and Ahmadinejad's apparent desire to sabotage them was certainly unsettling. Ahmadinejad has sought not only to disrupt his own country's relations with the United States, but has also attempted to derail U.S. interactions with other countries in the region.

Looking into the future two things seem to be clear. First, the United States will continue to have stability in the Middle East as one of its major foreign policy goals. Its geographic position and natural resource base must be protected in the furtherance of U.S. interests. Second, Iran's geostrate-gic position makes it incredibly important to the U.S. ability to achieve the first goal. U.S. frustration in its dealings with Iran likely comes from the knowledge that it is a major factor (obstacle) in the U.S. ability to achieve what it wishes to in the region.

U.S. Policy Options

There has been incredible frustration exhibited by the governments and peo-ples of the Middle East at the U.S. lack of consistency in its policies toward the region. The United States is seen as an unreliable ally, which causes the countries in the region to seek closer relations with any country other than the United States that can meet their needs. U.S. sanctions interfere with agreed-upon business and arms sales agreements. With the exception of Israel, U.S. allegiances are seen to shift with an unpredictability that cannot be under-stood. This does not serve the U.S. interests. No one feels they should listen to U.S. preferences due to the fact that they change so easily.

Further complicating matters is the regional objection to the U.S. posi-tion on Israel. The states in the region see the United States as applying a double-standard to Israel in relation to other countries in the region. Israel transships U.S. industrial technology and gets a slap on the wrist. It bombs U.S. ships to keep them out of regional conflicts, the United States accepts their apologies. Middle Eastern countries generally see this as a bias toward countries with Western cultures, as predicted by Huntington's "Kin Country Syndrome."[111] Table 4.3 provides policy alternatives that the United States could choose to pursue.

Take Sides in Religious Conflict

The religious divide between Sunnis and Shi'ites provides the basis for this policy proposal. The United States would have to determine which sect's

Table 4.3 U.S. policy options: Middle East stability

Number	Policy Options	Impact/Probability	Authors' Views
1	Take sides in the Sunni/Shi'a struggle to dominate the region.	It is unlikely that a religiously motivated set of regimes, regardless of the sect, would prove to be pro-U.S. in its orientation.	Avoid.
2	Militarily conquer any state in the region that seems to be acting contrary to U.S. interests.	This would be very difficult for the U.S. to do. It is already overstretched in its commitments to the region with Afghanistan and Iraq.	Avoid.
3	Continue to throw U.S. support behind any country in the region that seems to be losing power to others in an attempt to maintain a regional status quo.	This seems to work in the short term, but fails to bring about long-term regional stability.	Avoid. This is a risky policy with many potential pitfalls.
4	Select a country in the region and help to confer on it some sort of regional hegemony.	The U.S. establishment of puppet regimes in the region has never been terribly successful in bringing about stability.	Avoid. This is a risky policy with many potential pitfalls.
5	Craft an over-arching and clear set of policies for the region that is consistent both in its content and application.	This would alleviate some frustration from the region, but is unlikely to happen.	Recommended, but unlikely.
6	Improve U.S. policies toward the region by identifying key objectives and developing policies to work toward those.	This would be challenging for the U.S. to accomplish but may be well-received by the Middle East.	Recommended.

interests were most in line with its own and proceed to provide support for that group's acquisition and consolidation of power. The goal of the United States would be to maintain influence over the dominant religion and exert power through their governance of the region.

Strengths

This strategy could be beneficial to the United States in that it would ally it with countries in the region that belong to the sect. Allying with the dominant power(s) in the region would clearly serve U.S. interests. The alliance and the fact that the United States had assisted in the dominant sect's rise to power could potentially translate into increased U.S. influence over decision making within the rings of power in the region.

Weaknesses

In many ways, this is another crass national interest approach for foreign policy. There is no morally defensible argument that the authors can think of that would favor this approach. Though there is potential that it would increase stability in the region and improve U.S. influence there, it simply cannot be argued that it is the right thing to do.

On more practical bases, there are additional reasons to avoid this strategy. The United States has proven itself to be notoriously unable to back winning sides and then translate that into increased support for its policies from the victor. If the United States assisted in consolidating power within one faction in the region and it turned against the United States that would be a worst-case-scenario outcome for the United States.

Anti-U.S. sentiment in the region is already tied to a perception that the United States is against Islam. Choosing sides in the Shi'a-Sunni conflict would likely be portrayed as the United States attempting to stamp out the religion one sect at a time by using one against the other. This could exacerbate tensions in the region rather than alleviating them.

Conquer Recalcitrant States in the Region

U.S. military interventionism would be the hallmark of this policy. The U.S. presence in the region would expand and any major threat to U.S. interests there would be met with force. No state would be permitted to acquire a preponderance of power, nor would regional alliances that could become powerful be permitted to be formed.

Strengths

Defeating every state in the region that challenges the United States would be one way to further U.S. interests. This policy would permit the United States to act decisively when it felt that states posed a threat to its interests. It would likely require additional U.S. bases and troops to be permanently stationed in the region. This would permit rapid reaction at the first sign of belligerence from a regional power. It may also help the United States to enforce its will on a regular basis within the region.

Weaknesses

The United States has neither the military resources nor the national will to engage in such a major military undertaking successfully. It would be foolhardy in the extreme to believe that the country could dominate the region militarily. This would be exacerbated by the fact that this kind of U.S. activity in the region would likely turn additional countries in the region against the United States. In many ways, this strategy would be counterproductive to U.S. interests in the region rather than furthering them. Finally, the very idea that every state that confronts the United States should be met with military is objectionable.

Support Losing Sides in Regional Conflicts

This policy of flexible allegiances would allow the United States to shift its backing between states to prohibit any one state or bloc of states from dominating. In essence, the United States would guarantee the continued strife in the region in an effort to avoid any state from achieving sufficient power to challenge U.S. interests effectively. In its effect, this policy would have similarities to policy option 2.

Strengths

This would ensure that no state within the region became dominant. It would, in effect, freeze the region at its current level of instability. The United States would benefit from this situation because it both prevents regional hegemony by any one state and keeps a regional power bloc from developing. A major regional alliance could be threatening to U.S. interests in the region in that states could bind together to further their individual and regional interests rather than deferring to the United States.

Weaknesses

This has been a typical response to regional strife from the United States in the past. It arguably has not worked well. It has fed into the perception that the United States is an ally that cannot be trusted. No one believes that the United States will be there for them if the times get tough. It is obviously within the U.S. rights of sovereignty to behave in this manner and throw its support behind whichever competitor best suits U.S. national interests. However, it fails to build stability or lasting support for the United States in the region.

This option is also detrimental in that it is likely inhibiting economic growth and political stability in the region. So long as discord is fostered, Middle Eastern countries may feel compelled to expend disproportionate amounts on maintaining national security and military forces. This takes away funds that might otherwise be used for social programs and domestic economic development in these countries. It is likely that economic strength in the region would better serve U.S. interests by more closely tying national economies to the international economic system. This would theoretically result in greater willingness in region to compromise to maintain stability as well as making coercive economic mechanisms (sanctions) more effective in changing policies in the region when they do diverge from international norms. The United States might offset the negative implications of this policy option by forming an economic bloc in the region in which it was a participant.

Pick and Prep Our Preferred Regional Hegemon

This is the opposite of option 3. Under this policy proposal, the United States would select, groom and empower a state within the region to dominate it. Several states in the region have expressed a desire to exercise power there, Iran included. The United States would assist a state that would be favorable to its interests in the region and work to help it consolidate and wield power.

Strengths

If we could dominate the state that ruled the region, that would be an ideal solution for the United States. Its interests would be enforced by the regional hegemon without the need to commit U.S. troops or diplomatic personnel to protect them. Hegemony in the region would bring about stability as the states were governed by the overarching power. U.S. influence would be exercised indirectly (i.e. through the regional hegemon), allowing it to be somewhat shielded from any backlash from dissatisfied states, groups or individuals. It is likely, however, that the U.S. influence would be known and would create challenges for the regional hegemon in its relations with other states in the region.

Weaknesses

There is no state in the region that currently has the power and resources to be hegemonic. Furthermore, there is no state that would be an easy choice for the United States to empower to take the position. In fact, the state that is currently best-positioned to dominate the region would probably be Iran, and the United States is far from being able to exert its influence through Iran. It would not be easy for any state to consolidate power and rule the region because there is too much dissimilarity among the states and far too much factionalism. Becoming hegemonic would require a massive amount of resources as each state in the region would have to be coerced to bow to the ruling state. Few states in the Middle East would form natural alliances that would facilitate the consolidation of power. This would mean that the process of creating hegemony would require strife among the states in the region.

Furthermore, as mentioned previously, the United States has a poor track record for selecting victors. It would be detrimental to U.S. interests if the hegemon it empowered shifted preferences. It would also be problematic if the hegemonic state, once in the seat of power, abused the power and was found to be violating the rights of others in the region. A poor U.S. selection could result in a region that is actively working against U.S. interests there and had the power to do so on a regional scale.

Craft a Master Policy for the Middle East

The Master Policy concept would be one that declared U.S. policies toward the region and committed future administrations to upholding them. It would include (at a minimum) security, economic, political, human rights, and social priorities that the United States intended to enforce. It would also specify the regional conditions that would result in U.S. action, as well as what those actions would be.

Strengths

The creation of a master U.S. foreign policy for the Middle East would be a major achievement. It would benefit the United States by signaling the region that it takes matters there seriously, as well as that the United States is committed to improving relations with the states there. A consistent and declared policy toward the region would also be a step in the right direction of repairing our image of being unpredictable. Regardless of what the policy ended up being, it would be something that more clearly spelled out U.S. interests and reactions to behaviors than currently exists.

This policy would also have the benefit of clearly delineating U.S. preferences to states in other regions. It would allow for the world and international institutions to predict U.S. responses to various behaviors and activities...both good and bad. Even though some aspects of the coherent U.S. policy toward the Middle East would be objectionable to some states, it would still be appreciated that the U.S. position was known.

A consistent policy would also permit the U.S. military, intelligence, and diplomatic communities to plan better for the future of the region. As it currently stands, U.S. personnel do not know what interests in the region the United States will determine are worth fighting for or defending. It is startling to think that the U.S. military does not know what factors might cause the U.S. government to decide to invade Iran. Under what conditions will the United States deem the regional situation acceptable versus a reason to deploy troops? Currently no one, foreign or domestic, knows. A coherent policy would help the United States to plan for the future and appropriately equip and train our military forces and other entities.

Weaknesses

In many ways, this policy would detract from U.S. flexibility in dealing with unforeseen situations in the region. It would tie the hands of future presidents by committing them to policies that may not change sufficiently with the times. Clearly, there would be some ability to make change. However, committed funds in favor of the coherent policy would in some ways limit what could be done by future administrations.

A stated policy toward the region might also tempt states there to push to test U.S. limits. If we declared that action X would bring about U.S. military intervention, countries might try X-minus-1 to see if they could get away with it. This would be trying to the U.S. government and public. For example, a U.S. policy that military aggression against Israel was intolerable might result in increasing terrorism against the state; the United States did not say it would use military to suppress that.

Finally, it would be practically impossible for the United States to craft such a policy. There are too many variables and political pressures that would be brought to bear against the process. U.S. public opinion and those of its members of government are too fragmented to allow for the creation of a consistent policy. The drafting of such a policy would be so politically contentious that it would likely be so watered down by vague language and compromise that it would end up granting flexibility to future administrations that would be little improvement over the current situation. A 2004 Council on Foreign Relations Task Force on U.S.-Iran relations argued that such a "grand bargain" is not a realistic goal.[112]

Improve U.S. Policies toward the Region

This policy proposal would involve a higher level of consistency from the United States in the making of its policies toward the Middle East but would stop short of creating a Master Policy (option 5). It would involve the United States identifying a set of key strategic interests in the region and declaring what actions would be undertaken to ensure those interests.

Strengths

By selecting a subset of issues on which the U.S. policy will focus, this proposal limits the number of issues that must be tackled and may improve the possibility of arriving at a set of policies upon which agreement can be achieved. The United States would also be signaling which regional issues it finds most important, freeing it somewhat from concerns in other areas.

States in the region would be aware of the importance the United States has placed on these issues and may be willing to compromise some on these policies in exchange for U.S. concessions in areas deemed less important to U.S. interests. Countries would also be more clear on what types of behaviors would invoke U.S. action, whether it is rewards, sanctions, or military deployment.

By clarifying the U.S. positions on these key issues, international negotiations will be facilitated. The international system will be aware of the U.S. policy preferences and the importance it places on each of them. This would permit decision-makers around the world to anticipate U.S. responses and plan accordingly. This is not to say that all countries would be submissive to U.S. interests in these key policy areas. Rather, it suggests that states could make policies and negotiate with more certainty about U.S. response. Obviously some states would still engage in behaviors the United States would find objectionable. But they would do so knowing that the U.S. response will be negative. This would help to alleviate miscalculations by other states of U.S. intentions. An example of past miscalculations was the 1991 Gulf War, where Saddam Hussein perceived that the United States would not take a position on its decision to invade

Kuwait. It is possible that Hussein would not have taken this step if he were clear that the United States would mobilize its military in support of Kuwaiti interests.

Finally, this approach would facilitate U.S. planning in a variety of areas. U.S. military, intelligence, and diplomatic personnel would be working from the same overarching plan for the key areas and could be assured that, at least in these issue areas, U.S. responses would be predictable. This predictability would be beneficial to U.S. agencies, international organizations, and other states. The U.S. military could strategize, plan, train, and equip itself with the knowledge of which regional contingencies would require them to mobilize. Diplomatic representatives could negotiate with greater confidence of the U.S. government response to certain events. Intelligence personnel could better focus their attentions on the key areas so that the United States would be better prepared and informed about the region.

A similar recommendation was made in a 2004 document authored by a Council on Foreign Relations Task Force co-chaired by Zbigniew Brzeninski and Robert Gates. One of the Task Force's recommendations was that the United States could offer to engage Iran in a dialogue on specific issues relevant to regional stabilization. The Task Force argued that this would have more chances for success than the development of a more detailed plan for rapprochement.[113]

Weaknesses

In spite of selecting only a subset of issues on which to clarify U.S. policies, this would still be a very difficult policymaking exercise. Identification of which issues the United States would deem key to its interests would be a challenge in and of itself. Determining exactly what the U.S. responses would be in each case would further test U.S. policy-makers.

Leaving some issues off the U.S. regional agenda will likely be met with dissatisfaction from some states and domestic groups. Every organized issue area relevant to the region would fight to have its interests identified as one of those most important to the United States. Some would be outraged that the United States failed to elevate their issue to his level of importance while others would be angered that their issue is in the U.S. crosshairs.

By identifying which issues are most important to the United States, the government would also be identifying what issue areas were of less interest. This could encourage states in the region to engage in behaviors that were unanticipated by the U.S. policy-makers and not covered by the new policies but still threaten U.S. interests. In other words, this could drive opponents to be more aggressive in areas in which we have declared we will be less responsive.

Preferred Policy

Although there are clear disadvantages to the policy proposal, the best option for the United States to pursue in this area would be the development of coherent and clear policies in a key subset of issues. This policy option would permit the United States to prioritize its interests in the region. It would also facilitate planning for future contingencies with greater certainty within the United States and internationally.

This would allow the United States to prioritize expenditures on resources more effectively. The identified issue areas would receive more funding while fewer resources would be expended on issues deemed less important.

It will be very difficult for the United States to craft this policy and sell it to the world. However, the benefits associated with the clarity on these issues and the priorities being set by the United States would likely be worth the invested time and effort. If nothing else, this approach will facilitate others' relations with the United States because they will know our priorities.

Chapter 5

Iran: State Sponsor of Terror?

The United States and Iran have had long-standing disagreements on a variety of issues including terrorism and Iran's nuclear aspirations. The next two chapters take up these subjects in turn. Iran has consistently been listed as a state sponsor of terrorism by the U.S. Department of State since 1986. The U.S. justification for this label has traditionally been based on Iranian support for Hezbollah, the militant arm of Hamas and al Qaeda, which the United States has declared to be terrorist groups. Since the beginning of the 2003 war in Iraq, the United States has also accused Iran of providing support for the Iraqi insurgency movement. Table 5.1 compares the Iranian view of the groups to which it provides support with the American perspective.

Iran was linked to the 1988 bombing of Pan American Flight 103 over Lockerbie, Scotland.[1] The United States also had significant evidence that Iran provided support to the bombers of the Khobar Towers in Saudi Arabia in June 1996. The Towers housed U.S. Air Force personnel. Nineteen Americans were killed and 372 were wounded. It is believed that the attack was carried out by the Saudi Hezbollah group, which received support from Iran.[2]

Events in January 2002 brought the issue of Iran's alleged sponsorship of terrorism to the forefront. A ship (*Karine A*) was intercepted by the Israelis in the Red Sea. It was carrying over 50 tons of arms that were bound for the Gaza Strip and Palestinian Authority. The ship had been loaded in the Iranian port of Kish. This interdicted arms shipment raised international concerns about Iranian trafficking in arms to terrorists, in spite of the fact that clear evidence of Iranian government complicity in the transfer was not uncovered.[3] As with similar cases, both Iran and the

Table 5.1   State sponsorship of terrorism?

Iranian Perspective	U.S. Perspective
Hezbollah are legitimate fighters against Zionist Occupiers of the sacred al Qods territory.	The Iranian support for Hezbollah in Southern Lebanon is frequently cited as problematic by the U.S. government.
Both the United States and Israel should be designated state sponsors of terrorism.	The U.S. government has listed Iran as a state sponsor of terrorism since 1986.
Iran is concerned that the United States is planning to destabilize Iran, with the goal of regime change.	The U.S. government is concerned that Iran could potentially transfer WMD technologies to sub-national groups.

Palestinians denied they have been working together on this arms transfer project.[4]

Iran also helped to support the Palestinian cause after the 2009 Gaza conflict with Israel. In the wake of the fighting, Iran set up a Gaza Reconstruction Headquarters in Tehran. It was tasked with helping to build houses, schools, mosques, shops, a hospital and a university to help Gaza return to normal. It has also provided additional support to Hamas (discussed later in this chapter) so that organization can provide more assistance to Gaza's citizens.[5] In a rare instance where United States and Iranian actions are in concert, the United States has also pledged $900 million to help rebuild Gaza.[6]

Rogue groups have been supported by Iran as a force multiplier. It does so while giving the country deniability—assuming that the international system fails to tie Iran to the groups' actions directly.[7] It also helps to reinforce Iran's self-appointed position as a supporter of other Islamist revolutionary movements. Although Iran has supported a number of different organizations, it has been most closely tied with Hezbollah.

Lebanese Hezbollah

Hezbollah (meaning "Party of God") is a Shi'ite faction. It was formed in 1982 in response to Israel's invasion of southern Lebanon. They continue to operate in the Bekaa Valley, but have expanded with cells now in place around the world. Their primary goal was originally to liberate the territories occupied by Israel, but they have greatly expanded their power and scope since that time.[8] Their fight is primarily against Israel, but they are also against other Western countries that support the existence of the State of Israel. In particular, the group and its leadership have shown strong anti-U.S. sentiment, as evidenced in the following statement by its leader, Hassan Nasrallah:

> The main source of evil in this world, the main source of terrorism in this world, the central threat to international peace and to the economic development of this world, the main threat to the environment in this world, the main source of killing and turmoil, and civil wars and regional wars in this world is the United States of America.[9]

Since the founding of the group, Hezbollah is estimated to have participated in over 200 attacks and have killed over 800 individuals.[10] They were among the groups that brought about the popularization of suicide bombings as a tactic, but also train their members to be effective in assassinations, kidnappings, and other types of guerilla warfare.[11]

The group has broad influence in the Middle East. They are an umbrella group for Shi'ite groups in Lebanon and provide funding for a variety of radical groups in the region. One of the major reasons that the group has been so successful and receives so much support in Lebanon is that they have developed a social services arm. Although the group does not hesitate to use force against perceived enemies or threats, it is seen as a benefactor by common Shi'ite citizens. They are very involved in Lebanon's social programming and government. Hezbollah works with the Lebanese government in providing the people clean water, employment, assistance to farmers, housing, and even takes up collections for the poor families of martyrs.[12]

Because of its perceived benevolence and its power, the group has even become a functional aspect of Lebanese government through the electoral process. In the 2005 elections, Hezbollah gained 14 seats in the parliament of 128 members, as well as gaining ministerial positions for two of its members.[13]

In spite of its attempts to avoid direct links to Hezbollah, Iran has been identified as its main supporter and is unlikely to abandon its ties with the group. The attempts to distance itself from the group are founded in the Iranian desire to avoid the wrath of the United States and other states based on Hezbollah actions. However, Hezbollah has been identified as a "central part of [Iran's] 'Arab Strategy' for regional domination."[14]

Although Iran does not officially support Hezbollah beyond spiritually, the Supreme Leader in Iran is the head of the organization. In point of fact, the Iranian government was functional in the founding of Hezbollah. As early as 1979, Iran was establishing links with Palestinian groups and Shi'ite factions in southern Lebanon. "Iran initially began supporting radical groups, including many that embraced terrorism, after the 1979 Islamic

Revolution and quickly became the world's leading state supporter of terrorism."[15] Iranian dissidents and defecting members of a small Iranian peacekeeping force in Lebanon were training alongside Lebanese Shi'ite fighters. The Hezbollah organization was initiated as a branch of the Iranian Hizballah in Lebanon. As the group grew and intermingled with Lebanese civilians, family ties increased between Iran and Lebanon, further embedding the relationship between the group and country.

Iranians also utilized marriage to Lebanese Shi'ite women after the Lebanese civil war to acquire property in Lebanon. A great deal of property was damaged during the war. Iranian individuals could not acquire property in Lebanon, but if a man married a Lebanese woman he could buy her the property and then she could gift it back to him. In this way, the Iranian holdings of Lebanese property have expanded over time.

There are many different perspectives on the status of Hezbollah in the international system. The United States and many other countries have declared it a terrorist organization. However, Iran is joined by Lebanon, Syria, and Russia in portraying it as a resistance movement bent on removing Israeli occupation. There are also countries that differentiate among the branches of the organization and declare some of them terrorists and others freedom fighters.[16]

Iran is far and away, however, the group's most significant supporter. It has provided Hezbollah with significant funding over the years in support of its militant activities as well as of its social programming. Iran has utilized its Qods Force (tasked with supporting the Islamic revolution outside of Iran with funds, equipment, and training) to assist Hezbollah. Through the Qods Force, Iran funnels an estimated $100 million per year to Hezbollah.[17] The Iranian intelligence organization (Ministry of Intelligence and National Security—MOIS) provides Hezbollah with information. It is also believed that the IRGC has provided training and provisions for Hezbollah members.[18] To the best of its ability, Iran attempts to hide this activity from public view.

Direct support from Iran can be expected to continue:

> Hezbollah remains an asset for the Iranians as long as the Arab-Israeli conflict remains unresolved and good relations with Syria and Lebanon remain a priority for the Iranian regime. Furthermore, the relationship provides a counter-weight to US threats to Iran that stem from the military presence in Iraq and that could arise over charges of Iranian intervention or even the nuclear issue.[19]

The relationship between Hezbollah and the Iranian government is based in part on the concept of the *Islamic Ummah*, a belief in a community of believers in Islam and their need to be united. This ideology can bring together Shi'ites and Sunnis against forces believed to threaten Islam. Its application in the case of Hezbollah and Iran would indicate that the relationship is one that will be difficult to break. However, the relationship could shift from more conservative to more aggressive over time.

The relationship has not, however, been solely or even primarily based on religion. There is a significant geopolitical component to Iran's support of Hezbollah. "For Iran, supporting subversive movements became a way of weakening and destabilizing its neighbors as well as spreading its revolution and toppling what in the eyes of Tehran were illegitimate regimes."[20] In this way, Iran's support of radical organizations amounts to a unique form of power projection for the country. Iran's support for Hezbollah and other groups allows it to influence Lebanese governance indirectly and to counter U.S. policies in the region. In many ways, Hezbollah has served as a proxy for Iran in the ongoing Arab-Israeli conflict in the region. However, recent evidence indicates that Hezbollah's support for terrorism could hurt its image among supporters in the post-9/11 world and it has decreased its reliance on terrorism as a tactic.[21] Although Iran has formal relations with the Lebanese state and the two countries have diplomatic ties, Iran has also hosted a representative of Hezbollah in Tehran (Hossein Safieddin) who is treated as a diplomat.

Militant Arm of Hamas

Among the Palestinian groups to whom Iran has provided support, the most significant is the militant section of Hamas. The group was formed in 1987 out of the Muslim Brotherhood of Gaza. Its main goal has been the foundation of a Palestinian state in Israel. The Hamas charter actually commits Hamas to the destruction of Israel. Its attacks have been largely restricted to Israel, primarily in the West Bank and Gaza Strip.[22] The group has carried out a large number of kidnappings, suicide bombings, and mortar and rocket attacks. "Hamas is believed to have killed more than five hundred people in more than 350 separate terrorist attacks since 1993."[23]

Hamas was founded with three wings: political, intelligence, and military. It has since merged the intelligence and military wings.[24] The political faction raised international concerns when, in 2006, elections were held in the Palestinian Territories and Hamas emerged victorious. It has since refused to recognize the state of Israel and incurred economic sanctions.[25]

Like Hezbollah, Hamas operates an extensive social services network. The Hamas network focuses on improving the quality of life for Palestinians. It usurped this role from the Palestinian Authority (PA) after the First Gulf War. While Yasser Arafat threw his support behind Iraq's Saddam Hussein, Hamas's leadership called for both the United States and Iraq to withdraw their troops from Kuwait. This led to funding from Gulf States shifting from the PA to Hamas so it had the funds to take over the PA's welfare role.

The United States and the European Union emphasized their identification of Hamas as a terrorist organization during the Second Intifada. At the same time, Iran established itself as a major financial backer for Hamas.[26] Iranian-supported Hezbollah also provides moral, financial, and training support to the group. Most Iranian support is provided through unconventional means, paid from believers' charity money that is at the Iranian Supreme Leader's disposal. In addition to the Supreme Leader's office, there are several different Islamic Foundations (the bonyads discussed earlier) that are by no means answerable to the Iranian government and not monitored for their financial transactions. Part of the money spent by Iran could be transferred to groups through the bonyads. Also, several religious leaders in the holy city of Qom (which is comparable to the Vatican) have their private seminary schools that accept international students from Pakistan, Afghanistan, Malaysia, Indonesia, as well as from some African and Middle Eastern countries and Palestine. This connection could be another means through which radical Islamic groups in Iran are linked to Islamists elsewhere in the world. There is a clear potential for these types of relationships to affect and influence the Israeli-Palestinian conflict.

In October 2007, the United States enacted sanctions against the Iranian Bank Saderat and its branches for serving as a financing organization for both Hezbollah and Hamas. The U.S. State Department alleged that the bank had funneled millions of dollars to Hamas.[27] In full defiance, Iran has declared that sanctions against the Islamic Republic will not impede its nuclear progress.[28] On the other side, the United States has been challenged in convincing other countries to support its calls for tougher sanctions.[29] International circumstances are making alliance building more difficult. Of particular concern are China and Russia's relative lack of support for the sanctions. They have real potential to offset any pain that U.S. sanctions might inflict on Iran, thereby rendering the sanctions less effective.[30] Russian support came into question during its August 2008 invasion of Georgia. In response to U.S. support for Georgia and U.S. calls for the Russians to withdraw, Russia then openly stated that cooperation on the Iran effort will be much more difficult because of the U.S. lack of support for Russian actions.[31]

Al Qaeda

In addition to the above information about Iran's support for Hezbollah and Hamas, the U.S. government claims to have convincing evidence that Iran has provided support for al Qaeda in several of its major attacks. A U.S. National Intelligence Estimate in 1997 stated: "Iran and its surrogates, as well as terrorist financier Usama Bin Ladin [*sic*] and his followers, have stepped up their threats and surveillance of US facilities abroad in what also may be a portent of possible additional attacks on the United States."[32] Members of the 9/11 Commission, in particular, argued that many of the 9/11 hijackers who subdued the crews and passengers of the aircraft were in Iran for many months before the attack.[33] The 9/11 Commission Report declared that, "in late 1991 or 1992, discussions in Sudan between al Qaeda and Iranian operatives led to an informal agreement to cooperate in providing support—even if only training—for actions carried out primarily against Israel and the United States."[34] It is also known that senior managers in al Qaeda maintained contact with Iran and Hezbollah when they were in Sudan.[35] The Commission argued that there was evidence that senior al Qaeda operatives received explosives and other training in Iran in 1992 as well as receiving training from Lebanese Hezbollah in 1983.[36] The 9/11 Commission Report did conclude, however, that there was little evidence that Iran was actually aware of the nature of the impending attack or in any identifiable way participated in the attack itself.[37]

The Commission further reported that Iran had frequently allowed known members of al Qaeda to pass through their country—even to the point of ordering that certain passports not be stamped so that their entry into Iran could not be easily documented. Some of the transit of these individuals is believed to have allowed al Qaeda members to enter easily into training camps in Afghanistan in advance of the 9/11 attacks.[38] Other sources indicate that in 2001 between 200 and 250 al Qaeda members entered into Iran. There were rumors that they had already obtained permission to set up a military camp in the areas close to the Pakistan-Afghanistan borders. It is believed that bin Laden's family and his son, Saad bin Laden, joined them in 2002.[39]

Iran is ideally positioned in the Middle East to provide this kind of assistance. Its borders with both Pakistan and Afghanistan are rugged, mountainous, and relatively lightly inhabited. This facilitates undocumented and undetected travel between the states. In a separate case of terrorism from Bahrain, it was documented that Iran played a role. In that case, Bahraini investigators found that a cell of five terrorists met their al

Qaeda handlers in an airport in Tehran and then traveled with them to training sites in Afghanistan and fought against Coalition forces.[40]

Links were also established by the Commission between the perpetrators of the 1996 Khobar Towers attack in Saudi Arabia. In this case, there is evidence of al Qaeda involvement but "proof" was never uncovered. However direct ties between the IRGC and the Saudi Hezbollah organization that was deemed responsible for the attack were documented by the Commission.[41]

Iraqi Insurgents[42]

As mentioned above, the United States has accused Iran of providing support for the insurgency movement in Iraq. As early as 2004, Secretary of State Colin Powell and Secretary of Defense Donald Rumsfeld were complaining that Iran was providing financial support and weapons to the insurgents. The extent of the support was debated at the time.[43]

In August of 2006, U.S. brigadier general Michael Barbero stated that it was the Iranian government's goal to destabilize Iraq and increase the violence in the country. Barbero also said "I think it's irrefutable that Iran is responsible for training, funding, and equipping some of these (Shi'ite) extremist groups and also providing advanced IED technology to them."[44]

U.S. complaints were continuing when, in 2007, the United States captured members of the Iranian IRGC-Qods force in facilities in Iraq. The United States also found equipment in 2007, including shaped-charge armor-piercing munitions that it has identified as being of Iranian origin and smuggled into Iraq by Qods members for use against U.S. and Iraqi forces.[45] American General David Petraeus described the situation:

> In the past six months we have also targeted Shi'a militia extremists, capturing a number of senior leaders and fighters, as well as the deputy commander of Lebanese Hezbollah Department 2800, the organization created to support the training, arming, funding, and, in some cases, direction of the militia extremists by the Iranian Republican Guard Corps' Qods Force. These elements have assassinated and kidnapped Iraqi governmental leaders, killed and wounded our soldiers with advanced explosive devices provided by Iran, and indiscriminately rocketed civilians in the International Zone and elsewhere. It is increasingly apparent to both Coalition and Iraqi leaders that Iran, through the use of the Qods Force, seeks to turn the Iraqi Special Groups into a Hezbollah-like force to serve its interests and fight a proxy war against the Iraqi state and coalition forces in Iraq.[46]

Further evidence of Iranian assistance to Shi'a insurgents in Iraq was revealed by the U.S. government in August 2008. At that time, the U.S. government claimed that training was being conducted by Iran's Qods force and Lebanese Hezbollah inside Iran, including the locations of Qom, Tehran, Ahvas, and Mashad. It was the U.S. belief that these locations were providing special training on assassination to squads of Shia militants.[47]

Iran has consistently denied these allegations.[48] In spite of Iran's denials, what has happened in Iraq is that the Iraqi and Iranian Shi'ites have begun to unite, while the Iraqi Sunnis and Arabs are allying against them. This has been a major factor in the sectarian violence that has been occurring in Iraq. Iranian support for the Shi'ites has occurred through close relations between Iraqi Shi'ite political parties and religious leadership and the Iranian government. This led two scholars to comment: "it is Iran, not the United States, that is the most influential 'external' power in Iraq, with unparalleled ability to affect stability and security across most of the country."[49]

This engagement between members of Iran and Iraq's Shi'ite communities is of concern to many regional powers, especially those with Sunni majorities. They argue that this could result in the creation of a Shi'ite Crescent in the region. King Abdullah of Jordan said of the situation, "If Iraq goes to the Islamic Republic, then we have opened ourselves to a whole set of new problems that will not be limited to our borders."[50]

In a similar vein to the support for the Iraqi insurgency, reports in September 2008 indicated that Iran was also supplying weapons to the Taliban in Afghanistan to aid in its fight against U.S. troops, NATO forces, and the government of Hamid Karzai. These reports were provided by both Taliban members and British troops who reported intercepting some of the arms. There was some question about whether Iran was aware of the transfers or if they were being smuggled by sub-state actors. British troops and the Taliban indicated that both sources of supply were being used. This is particularly interesting considering Iran's support for the United States as it sought to bring down the Taliban at the beginning of the GWOT. Although relations between Iran and the Taliban have been strained in the past, it is possible that Iran is currently viewing the United States as a more significant threat than the Taliban and is therefore attempting to strengthen Talibani efforts.[51]

View from the United States

Iranian support for terrorist organizations has long been problematic for the United States. The groups that Iran has supported have proven to be direct threats to the United States and its allies, especially Israel. In particular, since the 1983 Marine barracks bombing in Lebanon, which was carried out by the Islamic Jihad faction of Hezbollah and is believed to have been aided by Iran, the United States has taken a tough stance against such support. It is certainly one of the reasons why Iran ended up on the U.S. Axis of Evil list in spite of the fact that it had recently been helpful to the United States in fighting in Afghanistan. The United States is not swayed by Iranian declarations that the groups that it allies with are nationalist or freedom fighter organizations.

Iran's alleged links to al Qaeda in the aftermath of 9/11 has further increased U.S. ire about the issue. That Iran would provide support (assuming that the U.S. position is correct and they are) for the organization responsible for the most significant terrorist attack in history...after it was known to have been the driving force behind the attack...is a major stumbling block for any attempt at improving relations between the United States and Iran.

The United States is concerned that Iran's support for terrorist and insurgent groups could translate into proliferation of WMD. Although there is no evidence that Iran has transferred such materials to date, the United States worries that it could do so either with existing chemical or biological agents or a forthcoming nuclear weapon. Some argue that this is unlikely. Daniel Byman (2008) listed three major reasons why Iran would not do this: (1) doing so would offer Iran few tactical benefits; (2) Iran has become more cautious in its support for terrorism in recent years; and (3) this would constitute a major escalation in the war on terrorism and incur U.S. and international wrath.[52]

Iran's support for the Iraqi insurgency has been somewhat limited by the strong U.S. presence there and Iran's desire to avoid angering the United States. However, it might end its relative restraint if: it looked like the United States was working to remove Iranian influence entirely; it seemed the United States will be in Iraq indefinitely; or if the United States hardened its position in other disputes with Iran, such as nuclear programs.[53]

U.S. Policy Options

It is unlikely that the United States will change its view that Iran is a state sponsor of terrorism. It is equally unlikely that Iran will change its position and renounce its support of certain groups and declare that the United States has been right all along. Therefore, it is important to evaluate potential policy alternatives available to the United States in dealing with the situation as it exists today. Table 5.2 provides U.S. policy options for addressing Iran's alleged state sponsorship of terrorism.

Military Action against Iran for Its Support for Terrorism

Because of the direct evidence of Iranian support for terrorist groups, the United States could conduct a military campaign similar to that under way in Iraq (option 1). The goals of the U.S. military would be replacing the existing Iranian regime with one that would not provide support for terrorism. It would also potentially provide the opportunity to intervene in Iran's burgeoning nuclear capabilities.

The United States could also mobilize resources already in the Middle East to engage in surgical strikes (option 2) against Iranian locations and infrastructure deemed to be instrumental in the Iranian support for terrorism. The U.S. government would have to mobilize its intelligence components first to identify appropriate targets. This might include suspected training sites, strategic border regions, and other targets of military significance.

Strengths

Decisive U.S. military action against Iran would demonstrate to other states that the United States was serious about punishing states that support terrorism. It would illustrate the U.S. resolve and power in the region. The actions could be a deterrent to others who are considering or currently supporting terrorism.

Weaknesses

Either of these U.S. actions could serve to mobilize the Iranian public in favor of support for terrorism rather than against it. Currently, there are few elites in Iran that have the means to provide financial assistance to terrorist organizations. U.S. military intervention could result in an Iranian public that was willing to make major sacrifices so that the government would have additional funds to provide support for terrorist groups.

The idea of surgical strikes in Iran to interfere in their support for terrorism borders is misguided. Although Iran does provide equipment and some training, the majority of its support comes in the form of funding. Unless the U.S. government were willing to bomb Iranian banks and civilians who provide funding, striking military targets would be unlikely to bring about positive change in Iran's behavior.

Table 5.2 U.S. policy options: State sponsorship of terrorism

Number	Policy Options	Impact / Probability	Authors' Views
1	Go to war with Iran over its support for terrorism, as is being done in Iraq.	Would be at least as difficult a battle to win as that which is currently being fought in Iraq.	Avoid.
2	Surgical strikes in Iran against suspected terrorism-supporting targets.	Public reaction would be negative in Iran, possibly consolidating opinion in favor of support for terrorism and nuclear weapons.	Avoid.
3	Turn a blind eye to Iranian support for terrorism, so long as it is primarily aimed toward others as it seems to be now.	A morally reprehensible position. But it could limit conflict with Iran to an extent.	Avoid.
4	Maintain and increase sanctions against individuals, corporations, and the Iranian Government when it can be proven that they are providing support for terrorists.	Can have a decidedly negative impact, but is probably preferable to deploying the U.S. military.	Avoid, unless option 5 fails.
5	Create incentives (market and political) for Iran to end its support for groups deemed to be terrorists.	This could bring around some of the pro-market Iranian elites and create pressures for new policies against supporting objectionable groups.	Recommend.

The United States is currently stretched so thin militarily that committing to another major front would be unwise. In fact, a 2007 *Congressional Research Service (CRS) Report to Congress* indicated that the United States is not currently capable of carrying out a successful invasion of Iran.[54]

Furthermore, Iran has consistently stated that it would engage in an aggressive counterattack in the event of an attack by the United States. In 2008, IRGC Commander General Mohammad Ali Jafari indicated that Iran would carry out missile attacks against Israel, blockade the Strait of Hormuz, and mobilize its ideological allies in the region against the United States in the event of a U.S. attack.[55]

Current U.S. actions may demonstrate an awareness of the threat U.S. military action would pose to regional security. In spite of direct evidence of Iranian support for Iraqi insurgents, the United States has not moved toward military retaliation.[56] This restraint may indicate that the United States is aware that it is already stretched thin and engaging in another military confrontation at this time would be unwise.

So Long as It's Not Us Approach

The United States could take the position that it would turn a blind eye to Iranian support for terrorism as long as it refrained from striking the United States or its assets around the world. This would include the territories of the United States as well as U.S. military bases and embassies located in other countries. The protection would not likely be extended to U.S. allies in the Middle East or elsewhere.

Strengths

This option would protect U.S. citizens and infrastructure from coming to harm at the hands of Iranian-supported terrorists. Iran's support of Hamas and Lebanese Hezbollah could be argued to be of little concern to the United States, as they tend to strike regionally (mostly against Israel) rather than against foreign targets such as U.S. territory. Its support for al Qaeda is of greater concern to the United States. It might be possible for the United States to broker a deal with Iran whereby its support for al Qaeda could be curtailed and the United States would complain less about their support for Hamas and Lebanese Hezbollah. This would be an action to protect the national interests of the United States.

Weaknesses

Aside from the obvious moral bankruptcy this kind of policy would demonstrate from the United States, there are additional negative implications of such a policy. The United States is currently conducting its GWOT in an attempt to uproot terrorists wherever they reside. Adoption of this policy option would undermine any activities in support of that effort. Furthermore, the option would abandon an ally in the region (Israel) that the United States has identified as being vitally important to its interests. This would send a message to the world that the United States cannot even be counted on to defend its most significant allies.

Continuation and Imposition of Sanctions for Support for Terrorism

The United States already has a number of sanctions in place against Iran and Iranian entities due to the state sponsorship of terrorism. This policy would involve maintenance and extension of the existing sanctions. It would be recommended that the sanctions be targeted at commodities and interests that would have a greater impact on elites. The sanctions would not restrict the trade in food, medical supplies or other commodities that would disproportionately impact the country's poor.

Strengths

U.S. foreign policy is based on the promise of carrots or the threat of sticks. The only sticks in the U.S. arsenal are sanctions and military action. This means that it is the only option available to the United States if it wants to be seen as doing something to punish the objectionable behavior of other states, but there is not public support for the use of the military, is sanctions. They provide the U.S. government the ability to impose penalties on countries without having to commit troops. This is not to argue that every country that angers the United States should be invaded. Rather, it is intended to argue that the United States needs to develop new and innovative carrots and sticks ... or some option in between ... so that we no longer have to rely on a policy tool known to have such negative impacts.

The U.S. government already has sanctions in place against organizations and individuals in Iran that it has identified as providing support for terrorists. Such sanctions apply penalties to U.S. and international entities that are found to be dealing with those under restrictions.

If sanctions alone are going to continue to be the U.S. policy toward Iran (whether for its nuclear activities or terrorism support) more needs to be done. The United States has to pressure other states to join actively into the sanctions efforts to make them more multilateral and comprehensive. The United States should work hardest to get other states within the region, the Russians, and the Chinese behind the U.S. sanctions activities to improve their chances for success.[57]

Weaknesses

It is exceedingly rare for sanctions to achieve their stated policy goals. At their worst, sanctions hurt domestic populations of the target countries and create humanitarian crises. Sanctions are applied to change the behavior of the targeted regime. They are intended either to inflict suffering on the regime until it changes its ways or to stimulate domestic uprisings so that the regime either alters its behavior or is overthrown. This first is rarely achieved because the elites who are part of the regime itself continue to have access to goods to fulfill their needs through the black market or through countries not party to the sanctions. The second rarely happens as well. Regimes against which sanctions are levied rarely care about public opinion or the general well-being of their citizens. The suffering of their citizens will not change their ways. Neither will some sort of public outcry, which is itself unlikely under an authoritarian regime.

Evidence of the typical success of sanctions is found in their application against Iraq from 1991 to 2003. Not only did the sanctions not bring about the removal of Saddam Hussein's authoritarian regime, they became a rallying point for Iraqi citizens who were convinced by the regime that the United States was using the sanctions to harm them. Sanctions come with a litany of negative impacts, including infliction of greater poverty on the target country's middle class and poor; stimulation of black market economies; dearth of staple items within the country; and a loss of market opportunity for the applying country.

To date, most countries of the world have proven to be reluctant to back U.S.-sponsored sanctions against Iran.[58] This means that the United States has been utilizing unilateral economic sanctions until the recent past, which are incredibly ineffective due to the fact that the rest of the world continues to trade with the target country. This has changed somewhat with the recent rounds of UN-sponsored sanctions. The United States continues to impose more sanctions on Iran than other countries or the international system.

There is a further complication with the use of sanctions against Iran. If the United States were to expand sanctions to a more comprehensive package and induce other governments to impose sanctions as well, that may provide better opportunity for the sanctions to be successful. However, doing so could damage the international economy. This is because sanctions that were successful would have to hurt Iran economically. To do so, it would have to impact Iran's trade in oil, which would have a concomitant impact on the international economy.[59]

An additional problem that may be experienced because of sanctions against Iran could be their unanticipated impact on the drug trade. Iran is currently working within and along its borders to help with international efforts to interrupt the flow of drugs coming out of Afghanistan. This cooperation has at times been reluctant, but has been received from Iran. This is in spite of the fact that Iranian interference with the transshipment of drugs sometimes results in the drugs being distributed in Iran itself. Iranian cooperation almost resulted in Iran and Afghanistan going to war in 1998 when a Taliban-controlled militia assassinated nine Iranian diplomats amidst drug violence along the Iranian-Afghani border.[60] The freezing of Iranian assets and limits on Iranian trade could affect its ability to continue these efforts. This could happen in one of two ways. First, the financial impact of the sanctions could compel Iran to reprioritize its budget, with less funding being made available for the drug interdiction mission. Second, the Iranians could decide that they do not have the will to continue to assist in this international activity in reaction to the sanctions.[61]

Incentivize Cooperation

This approach has been the preferred option for the EU for some time. It would entail the development and offer of various inducements to try and tempt Iran away from supporting terrorist organizations. It could not ask that Iran agree that the organizations to which it has provided support are indeed terrorists. As mentioned above, Iran does not believe that the groups it is supporting are terrorists. For the most part, they are fighters of foreign Zionist occupation in Israel. Others, such as al Qaeda, are seen by some as champions for Islam. Being compelled to call them terrorists could certainly create some dissatisfaction in the Iranian population. However, the United States and EU could work together to find the right combination of enticements. This would likely have to include the removal of sanctions, increased trade, expedited entry into the World Trade Organization (WTO), and other rewards for the preferred behaviors. Such incentives might convince the pragmatic Iran to curtail its support for terrorist organizations.

Strengths

There are many in Iran who are seeking improved economic performance for the country and better sharing of the wealth with the general population. If the United States could propose a package of benefits that was of interest to these people, it might help to sway public opinion. As it was argued above, Iran has no real direct grievance in the Israeli case. If the

United States could offer economic benefits and attractive political incentives, it may be able to change the course of Iranian activities.

Weaknesses

Increased U.S. investment in Iran and other financial benefits could provide the elites more committed to terrorism than economic development more funds to funnel into terrorist organizations. The United States would have to insist on the imposition of additional monitoring mechanisms of some sort to assure that this did not happen, as well as detailing penalties that would be imposed if Iran broke the agreement.

The United States would also have to work hard to convince the Israelis that this plan was in their best interests. The Israelis arguably have the most to lose in this situation. Getting them to agree to the incentive package as well as the monitoring and penalties would be important to the policy's success.

Preferred Policy

The best approach to the issue of Iranian support for terrorist groups for the United States to adopt would be a combination of sanctions and incentives. Sanctions alone have had little impact and will not solve the problem. The Supreme Leader himself directs where the funds should be expended and the sanctions have clearly not been successful in changing his beliefs about this behavior. However, sanctions against other global entities that are engaged in transactions with those known to be violating the incentive package agreement may be helpful.

An incentive package for Iran may help to strengthen and empower the elites who wish the government would focus on economic growth rather than regional conflicts. Policy statements that focused on the idea that money would be coming into the country, as well as funds not leaving the country to sponsor others' fights, may aid in persuading others in Iran that this is the correct course of action. Once the economic situation in Iran began to improve, it may become easier to convince others that this had been the appropriate path to take.

Chapter 6

Iran and Nuclear Power
(or Weapons?)

Recent relations between the United States and Iran have become increasingly contentious. A key dispute revolves around recent developments in Iran's nuclear industry. The two perspectives on the issue are presented on table 6.1.

At the heart of this international disagreement are issues of sovereignty. Iran argues that it has a sovereign right to generate nuclear energy. This is, indeed, its right. The United States, however, is within its sovereign rights to try and dissuade other countries from developing technologies it finds threatening. Therein lies the problem. Under the shadow of thirty years of mistrust and suspicion, the two sovereign states are pursuing mutually exclusive policy objectives. In such cases, only negotiations and compromise between the states can resolve the impasse, unless the states are willing to go to war to get their way. However, this argument is based on Iran having been truthful about its actions and intentions. There is evidence that this has not been the case.

Iran's nuclear facilities are spread through the country from north to south. Several of the sites have been declared and are under relevant IAEA safeguards. Among the most important of these are depicted on the map (figure 6.1) and described below:

- Bushehr nuclear reactor—the facility Iran is building with the Russians and is the point of the nuclear controversy with the United States because of the presence of heavy water reactors;
- Esfahan Nuclear Technology Center—believed to be the location of Iran's nuclear weapons program;

Table 6.1   The nuclear debate

Iranian Perspective	U.S. Perspective
Iran has consistently argued that its recent developments are focused on providing the country with increased access to nuclear power for civilian energy consumption. Its government has framed the issue as one of state sovereignty and nationalism.	The United States has been steadfast in its argument that Iran's insistence on acquisition of heavy water reactors can only be explained by a nuclear weapons aspiration. It has argued that alternatives exist for the heavy water reactors that provide nuclear energy without generating as much weapons grade material.
Iran's interpretation of the NPT is that it permits them the right to develop an indigenous fuel cycle, which the United States is denying it.	Many Western scientists believe that Iran does not need additional infrastructure to produce HEU for military purposes.
Iranians generally agree that an active nuclear program is in the country's best interest.*	The United States does not want Iran to gain access to the dual-use technology which, in addition to providing fuel for its power infrastructure, would also provide weapons-grade materials that Iran could use or sell.
Iran has argued that the United States is imposing a "second discrimination," first restricting its right to nuclear weapons and second attempting to prohibit it from having peaceful nuclear capabilities.**	The United States has worked through the UN Security Council to try and pressure Iran to turn back from this plan and make its nuclear program more transparent.
	Both U.S. unilateral and multilateral sanctions have been imposed and maintained in an attempt to influence Iran.

Notes: *Mehran Kamrava, "The United States and Iran: A Dangerous but Contained Rivalry," *The Middle East Institute Policy Brief*, No. 9, 2008.
**Wade Huntley, "Rebels without a Cause: North Korea, Iran, and the NPT," *International Affairs*, Vol. 82, No. 4, 2006, p. 733.

- Natanz Enrichment Plant—was kept secret by the Iranians until 2006 but was detected by the West in 2003—as of August 2008, reports indicated that Iran had confirmed the number of centrifuges at the Plant was 4,000, with 3,000 more being installed[1]; and
- Arak heavy water reactor—was kept secret by the Iranians until was revealed in 2002.[2]

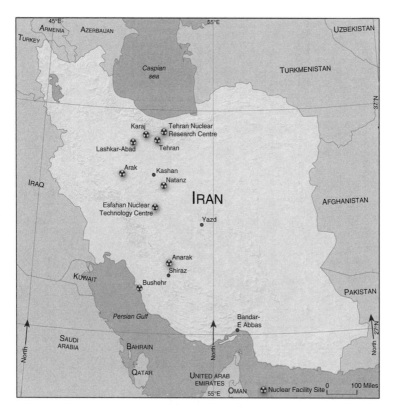

Figure 6.1   CRS known Iranian nuclear sites

Source: IAEA. Nuclear facility site locations are approximate. Map prepared by Congressional Cartography Program, 2006, as published in Hussein Hassan, "Iranian Nuclear Sites," *CRS Report for Congress*, November 13, 2006, RS22531, p. 4.

The majority of these facilities are situated in or around populated areas. The United States perceives this as part of Iran's desire to protect them from an attack comparable to that launched by Israel against Iraq's Osirak reactor in 1981.[3] It should be recognized that the impact of the attack on the Osirak reactor was not what had been intended. Saddam Hussein did not stop his activities after the attack, but rather sped up all Iraqi WMD programs.[4]

Table 6.2 presents a selected timeline of Iran's nuclear program. While the focus of this book is on U.S./Iran relations, it was felt that these key events were important to understanding the escalation of tensions about Iran's nuclear program. It is not the intention of table 6.2 to provide a comprehensive overview of Iran's activities. Instead, it is intended to identify points in time where Iran's covert program were brought to light and expanded, resulting in an intensifying

Table 6.2 Selected Timeline of Iran's nuclear program[a]

Date	Event	Importance
1968 + 1970	Iran signs NPT in 1968 and ratifies it in 1970[b]	Indicative of a desire to comply with international nuclear norms
1974	Iran establishes the Atomic Energy Organization of Iran	Signifies an increase in interest in developing nuclear technology
1985	Likely beginning point for Iran's enrichment program, when it began its gas centrifuge activities	Beginnings of the development of a new capacity
1988	Report of visits to Iran by A. Q. Khan, head of Pakistan's nuclear weapons program	Khan is known to have proliferated blueprints, materials, information, and centrifuge parts around the world
Late 1980s–1990s	Focus on Iran's nuclear ambitions is on fuel-cycle dealings with Russia and China	Concerns here that Russia and China are transferring technology
Mid-1990s	Pakistan sold Iran designs, technical schematics, and components for high-speed gas centrifuges used in uranium enrichment[c]	Clear evidence of proliferation
1995	Iran signs a deal with Russia to complete nuclear reactors at Bushehr[d]	Raises concerns about Iran's intentions as plans are for a heavy water reactor
1996	Building of Arak heavy water plant begins	Plant is still of concern
2001	Building of Natanz begins	Plant is home to Iran's enrichment program
August 14, 2002	Washington, DC office of the NCRI publicly reveals information about Iran's activities	Exposes Iran's activities to the world . . . and the fact that it has violated its NPT disclosure obligations
February 2003	IAEA inspections of Iran facilities; Khatami makes public other facilities that will complete the fuel cycle capability	Increasingly evident that Iran's program has been both extensive and secretive
August 2003	IAEA discovers traces of highly enriched weapons-grade uranium at Natanz facility; Iran argues this was contamination from Pakistani-supplied equipment	International concerns increase further

Date	Event	Commentary
October 2003	Iran declares its possession of a nuclear fuel cycle—"Full disclosure" of Iran's activities	Iran's open admission indicates its commitment to continue
November 2003	Iran shut down its enrichment facility	Some argue that this was done to allow Iran to work on troublesome aspects of its program with decreased scrutiny
June 2004	Iran notified IAEA that it would resume its operations under IAEA supervision	Perhaps a continuation of the ruse to allow Iran time to fix glitches in the process
February 2006	Iran suspended its adherence to the NPT Additional Protocol	Clear signal Iran is restarting its programs
July 31, 2006	UN Security Council (UNSCR 1696) is passed, demanding that Iran suspend enrichment and reprocessing activities with the potential for sanctions if it did not by August 31, 2006	Beginning of unity of action in the international system against Iran's program
December 9, 2006	President Ahmadinejad announced the installation of the first 3,000 centrifuges at Natanz	Clearly demonstrates Iran's unwillingness to suspend its activities
December 23, 2006	UN Security Council (UNSCR 1737) voted in favor of sanctions on Iran for its noncompliance	Initiation of sanctions by the international community
March 24, 2007	UN Security Council (UNSCR 1747) expanded sanctions due to Iran's failure to comply with UN actions	Expansion of economic sanctions. Intense negotiations were required to gain agreement
February 25, 2009	Iran tests its first nuclear power plant without radioactive rods, with the assistance of the Russians	Signals continued determination of Iran and lack of cooperation from Russia

Notes: [a]Timeline assembled by the Research Team from a variety of materials, including Yonah Alexander and Milton Hoenig, "Iran's Nuclear Ambitions: By Every Secret Means," *The New Iranian Leadership* (Westport, CT: Praeger Publishers, 2007), pp. 111–175. (note 11)

[b]Geoffrey Kemp, *U.S. Institute for Peace Special Report: Iraq and Its Neighbors,* November 2005, p. 3. (note 12)

[c]Kemp, p. 3. (note 13)

[d]Kemp, p. 3. (note 14)

U.S. response and imposition of UN sanctions. (The United States has also imposed additional unilateral sanctions against Iran.[5]) One of the important factors in the imposition and continuation of sanctions is Iran's response to them. The fact that Iran has withstood the sanctions and not given in implies that they are willing to take the pain instead of submitting. Rather than bowing to UN sanctions, in the 2006–2007 timeframe Iran actually expanded its activities. As it was stated in a recent article by Albright and Shire, "simply put, the history of Iran's efforts, the current scale of the enrichment program, and Iran's determination to continue enriching uranium in the face of overwhelming international economic and political opposition, raise serious questions about its intentions."[6] In fact:

> Iran has flatly ignored the call to suspend uranium enrichment, seemingly determined to have its centrifuges and run them too. It has flouted not only the Security Council, but also and, perhaps, more importantly the Bush Administration's determination that Iran not achieve a nuclear weapons capability.[7]

The nuclear program is fairly popular with the Iranian public. In a major survey of the Iranian population conducted by the Center for Public Opinion and Terror Free Tomorrow, 52 percent of respondents favored Iran developing nuclear weapons. However, the respondents also favored (70%) opening their facilities to full inspections and not possessing nuclear weapons in return for outside aid and investment.[8] It is not permitted for one to express openly an opinion against the country's uranium enrichment program in Iran. The capability is seen as a sovereign right for the country and to speak against it could be deemed treasonous.[9]

Iran entered into the Nuclear Nonproliferation Treaty (NPT) as a non-nuclear weapons (NNW) state. The NPT allows states that have entered into it with NNW status access to nuclear technologies for peaceful purposes.

> Affirming the principle that the benefits of peaceful applications of nuclear technology, including any technological by-products which may be derived by nuclear-weapon States from the development of nuclear explosive devices, should be available for peaceful purposes to all Parties to the Treaty, whether nuclear-weapon or non-nuclear-weapon States...[10]

and

> Article IV 1. Nothing in this Treaty shall be interpreted as affecting the inalienable right of all the Parties to the Treaty to develop research, production and use of nuclear energy for peaceful purposes without discrimination and in conformity with Articles I and II of this Treaty.[11]

Iran has argued that these clauses provide it the right to utilize the nuclear technologies it determines will best aid in achieving their nuclear power generation goals. In the Iranian case, this has been interpreted to mean that they should be permitted to employ heavy water reactors in their civilian nuclear power program. Iranian deputy foreign minister Saeed Jalili has, in the past, stressed that Iran has inalienable nuclear rights based on the NPT. He has also claimed that Western policies are "irresponsible," inconsistent and illogical with regard to Iran's peaceful nuclear weapons program.[12]

Iran claims that it requires nuclear power generation to meet its expanding energy needs and to allow the country to grow economically. For some examining the situation, this argument is untenable for a country with such major oil and natural gas reserves.

> Iran still claims that its massive investment in an extensive nuclear programme [sic] is for commercial and peaceful purposes only—despite the fact that Iran's oil reserves are the second largest in the world and its substantial gas reserves, believed to be the largest anywhere, are underdeveloped and lacking investment. Indeed, Iran annually vents off as much energy in natural gas as any programme [sic] of nuclear energy could generate.[13]

Under the terms of the NPT, Iran also retains the right to withdraw from the Treaty.[14] Iran argues that if it were pursuing nuclear weapons, it would withdraw from the Treaty (as North Korea did in 2003). Thus, its continued NPT membership is pointed to as evidence of its peaceful intentions.

It should be recognized that there is some validity to Iran's argument. While Iran has enormous reserves of oil and natural gas (second largest in the world in both cases), it is a net importer of natural gas. They are a major crude oil exporter, yet they have increasing domestic demand. The reason for this is that the Iranian infrastructure for refining and extracting these commodities are woefully outdated and inadequate to meet Iranian needs.[15] There is a reasonable argument to be made that Iran has to develop more energy production capacity to meet the future needs of the country.

Iran also argues that it needs to diversify the sources of its energy and industrial supply. Sanctions factor heavily into Iran's problems. Iran has suffered under sanctions since the 1979 Revolution. Because of these trade restrictions, Iran has been unable to acquire: spare parts for its commercial aircraft or military hardware; needed equipment replacements and upgrades for its energy sector; and other commodities. Iran has an understandable reluctance to rely on the West for the provision of equipment and supplies that could be cut off if a Western country decides it is unhappy with some aspect of Iran's conduct. It is fearful that its access to natural gas and oil, that are necessary to maintain their industrial capacity, could also be cut if the West were angered. Furthermore, Iran is concerned that it will develop greater capacity to produce nuclear power and then have its access to enriched uranium cut off by some actor in the international system. This is their rationale for developing an independent enrichment capacity. They do not want to have to rely on others for critical energy supply issues.

A major question in this debate, then, is whether Iran is simply trying to increase its energy production capacity or whether it is seeking nuclear weapons. There are a variety of motives identified in the literature for Iran's determination to develop nuclear weapons, if that is indeed what they are doing. First, the country has identified the threat posed by Israel and other countries in the region as a justification. Iran also feels the pressure of having Pakistan and India, two nuclear weapons states, nearby. Intensifying Iranian unease is the presence of American troops in Afghanistan and Iraq, as well as in bases throughout the region.[16] These justifications focus on nuclear weapons as a deterrent to aggression within the region. Given the instability of the region and the persistence of significant threats, it is understandable that Iran would wish to do what it could to defend itself.

A second major argument in favor of a nuclear weapons capacity is that with the weapons comes significant prestige and stature in the international system. Nuclear weapons are frequently portrayed in Iran as one additional way that the West denies other countries their rights in the international system. It is viewed as an imperial dictate that they not be permitted to have the weapons. Iranian leaders have frequently framed the nuclear weapons program with nationalistic jargon.[17] Developing a nuclear weapon would also have, therefore, important domestic political impacts. This strong appeal to Iranian nationalism makes it unlikely that the government would simply walk away from its programs. It has been suggested that Ahmadinejad's position on the nuclear weapons issue was designed to divert domestic public attention away from his failed economic policies.[18] These factors would suggest that Iran's nuclear program is as important symbolically as it is strategically, perhaps more so.

Some argue that Iran understands very well that a nuclear attack on Israel or another U.S. ally in the region would bring about harsh retaliation from the United States and would therefore be unlikely to use a nuclear weapon once it possessed it. This argument is that merely by acquiring the weapon Iran would improve its security position in the region and, in particular, versus nuclear-armed Israel.[19]

Two additional phenomena could be adding (albeit less substantially than those discussed previously) to Iran's motivation to acquire nuclear weapons. First, there has been a decrease in the childbirth rate in Iran since the Revolution. At the time of the Revolution, the birthrate for women of child bearing age was 6.5. Today that is estimated to have fallen to 0.66. This may be due, in part, to the creation of Islamic schools after the Revolution. Because there were now women-only schools, more women and girls are able to get an education and pursue jobs. Islamic law requires a woman to get her husband's permission to hold a job, so some women are not getting married so they can continue in their chosen careers. Another factor that may be influencing this phenomenon is the inflation rate in Iran. Young people in Iran (and their families) are complaining that the costs associated with getting married have become prohibitive. The ceremonies, dowries, and wedding feasts have become so expensive that even wealthier families are having trouble affording them.[20] The reduced birthrate is problematic to the traditional Iranian military strategy, which has focused on throwing wave after wave of Iranian soldiers at the enemy to compensate for inferior military forces and equipment.[21] Iran may be concerned that it cannot afford a traditional military force or its traditional tactics to defend its territories. It is thus trying to replace shear manpower with nuclear weapons.

The counterargument to this, however, is that Iran has a large population and compulsory military service at the age of 18. Iran rallied close to 650,000 troops to go to war with Iraq. It could potentially bring together close to a million troops, which would significantly exceed the numbers that Western countries could mobilize into the region.

A second phenomenon that was found discussed in the literature is somewhat ironic. The argument is that Iran has been constrained from acquiring most Western military equipment since the Revolution.[22] Because of this, it has had to turn to Russia, China, increased domestic development and clandestine acquisition for its military supplies. Iran has a continued perception that its military, in spite of its size, is inferior to those of its neighbors. Having a nuclear capacity would increase the Iranian deterrent capacity exponentially in the absence of a formidable and well-equipped military force.

Iran has demonstrated that it is dedicated to maintaining its enrichment facilities. This is in spite of some problems they have had in getting the centrifuges to operate efficiently. The Natanz facility is home to an underground enrichment plant that is intended to house 3,000 centrifuges in support of the Iranian program. However, currently there is little certain information about the progress being made by the Iranian program due to their denial of access to the IAEA of these facilities. In fact, a September 2008 report on the Iran situation from the IAEA declared that the situation was in gridlock and that there was "little else the IAEA [could] do in probing into Iran's nuclear program or, given the steady progress on the enrichment front reported, of checking it unless there is a breakthrough in the broader negotiations..."[23]

This enrichment capacity has been one of the sticking points in negotiating an end to the confrontation over the Iranian nuclear program. The United States consistently has made suspension of Iranian enrichment (either permanently or temporarily) a precondition to negotiations. Iran has been equally persistent in refusing.[24] It has continued to work on enrichment even after the Russians bowed to U.S. pressure in 2001 and terminated its cooperation with Iran on the development of a laser enrichment capacity for Iran.[25] This may have changed somewhat in July of 2008 when the U.S. Under-Secretary of State, William Burns, attended nuclear talks with Iran with no precondition attached. This is the highest-ranking diplomatic exchange between the two countries in over 30 years.[26]

However, elites in Iran can be divided into three categories regarding the nuclear program: those who advocate the program at all cost, those who wish to find ways to pursue it that will not hurt their diplomatic interests, and those who argue for the suspension of nuclear activities in favor of engagement with the international system.[27] In theory, this would mean that there are opportunities to turn Iran back from the development of nuclear weapons and its current programs.

As this manuscript was going to press, there was still great debate about how close Iran was to having a nuclear bomb. Admiral Mike Mullen, Chairman of the Joint Chiefs of Staff, declared that Iran had the capacity.[28] At the same time, U.S. Secretary of Defense Robert Gates stated that Iran was "not close to a weapon at this point. And so, there is some time" for diplomacy.[29] Iran dismissed the concerns.

European Negotiations

For more than the past six years, there have been efforts made by the EU and others to entice Iran into ending its enrichment aspirations and returning to negotiations. Beginning in October 2003, Britain, France, and Germany began working to put together an incentive package that would be acceptable to Iran. The goal of this activity was to encourage Iran to give up its enrichment program because the technology could be adapted to make weaponry. The packages included both promised incentives for compliance and threatened penalties if Iran failed to stop its program. From 2003 to 2006, Iran claimed that the packages offered by the three were insufficient incentive for them to stop enrichment activities. During this time, Iran also made threats to resume reprocessing at reactors that had been shut down, admitted conversion of uranium ore into gas uranium tetrafluoride, and its Parliament passed a resolution backing Iran's sovereign right to enrichment.[30] Not only were these European efforts unsuccessful, but there was an actual increase in tensions and Iranian activities while they were under way.

Since November 2004, the EU negotiations have included the requirement that Iran freeze its enrichment, submit to additional inspections from the IAEA and agree to the tagging and sealing of certain nuclear components to guarantee Iran was not using them. These measures were intended to provide confidence to the international community that Iran was not continuing its enrichment program.[31] The stated goal of the EU is to have Iran suspend activities during negotiations. However, the negotiations themselves will determine which aspects of Iran's program are permitted to be restarted and which are "sensitive" and should be permanently given up by Iran.[32] So the European temporary freeze could end up being permanent for some technologies.

August 2005 brought about another set of incentives that were again rejected by Iran. These called for Iran to permanently end uranium enrichment.[33] However, Iran has refused to suspend its activities, even if just for the European temporary suspension requirement for the duration of the negotiations.

In 2006, new efforts were undertaken by the EU. The incentives at this point included expedited talks about Iranian entry into the WTO, expanded university ties between the EU and Iran, political cooperation, support for the Iranian civilian nuclear program, and restoration of technical and economic assistance to Iran.[34] It did not include, however, a security guarantee from the EU to Iran. It also continued to insist that Iran terminate its enrichment program.[35] Some of the new incentives, however, included the possibility for security guarantees.[36] The forthcoming EU offer in 2006 drew the following message from Iran's Foreign Minister Manouchehr Mottaki: "pay attention that your proposals include the two basic conditions, that is recognizing Iran's definite rights and exercising these rights otherwise its fate will be like that of August [2005] package."[37]

By June 2008, the United States, Russia and China had joined with the EU participants to try and develop a package that would be acceptable to Iran. This became known as the 5+1, referring to the presence in the negotiations of the five permanent members of the UN Security Council plus Germany. (This name is quite confusing, as by the end of the negotiations the package was technically offered by the United Kingdom, France, Germany, the Russian Federation, China, the United States, the EU, and the UN.[38]) The 2008 package included the promise of U.S.

supply of nuclear technology to Iran if it ceases enrichment. The United States also offered to rescind some of the bilateral sanctions that it had imposed on Iran over the years. Europe continued to offer light-water reactor technologies to Iran.[39] The precondition in this case consisted of a six week suspension of Iranian enrichment activities while the negotiations were underway.[40] On June 14, 2008, EU foreign policy chief Javier Solana presented the new offer to Iran. However, Iran informally rejected the offer mere hours into Solana's visit. Again, the rejection was based upon the precondition. As stated by Gholam Hossein Elham, Iran's official government spokesperson: "Iran's stance is clear. The precondition of a halt and suspension of nuclear activities cannot be brought up...If it exists (a demand for suspension of enrichment) it cannot be considered at all. If the issue of suspension is relied upon, the (nuclear) issue will not change."[41]

This rejection was echoed by Iran's government through the media in a *Tehran Times* news article that included the text of the proposed package. The Editor's preface is included below because its tone is such a clear summary of the Iranian rejection:

> EU foreign policy chief Javier Solana released the 5+1 package to media on Saturday. There is no new point in the proposal. The package has tried to directly ask Iran to suspend its uranium enrichment program by asking Tehran to implement the UN 1803 Resolution.[42] The text, which also Solana claimed is a modified version of the 2006 package, tries to compromise Iran's legal nuclear rights in the form of offering economic incentives to the Islamic Republic.[43]

While these were both unofficial Iranian responses, they left little confusion about the status of an agreement. This Iranian rejection resulted in the EU approving new sanctions against Iran. These were put in place in addition to UN sanctions and U.S. sanctions that were continued and/or increased in response.

Iran stalled on its response through July 2008 and even filed an official request for clarification of the terms of the agreement with the EU during that time. Because of the delay, the 5+1 issued a deadline of August 3 for an Iranian response to the package. Still the response was not received until August 5. European and American diplomats had argued that the response amounted to stalling and obfuscation.[44]

Clearly, the Iranians remain unimpressed with the packages in spite of the additional signatories and the EU offers. Interestingly, the proposal included the willingness to offer the "reaffirmation of Iran's right to nuclear energy for exclusively peaceful purposes in conformity with its obligations under the NPT."[45] This passage highlights the fact that the two sides still have fundamental disagreements. Iran has consistently argued that it is engaged in nuclear technology development for peaceful purposes and is compliant with the NPT requirements. The major powers even concede this point, but argue that Iran has lost the confidence of the international community and therefore must make some concessions to rebuild what has been lost.[46]

Another sign of the Iranian recalcitrance has been the selection and treatment of its representatives to the nuclear negotiations. In 2007, former nuclear negotiator Hossein Mousavian was arrested and charged with espionage. It was interesting that at the time of the arrest Ahmadinejad announced that his country would not retreat "even an iota" on its nuclear activities.[47] While little has been reported about the specifics of the espionage charge, there is some belief that the arrest was related to his insufficiently aggressive stance in the negotiations during his tenure. Later in 2007, Ali Larijani, the chief Iranian nuclear negotiator, resigned from his post. This was seen as symbolic of divides in Iran over the nuclear issue and evidence of Ahmadinejad's trying to consolidate control over nuclear policy. This resignation was preceded by public spats between Larijani and Ahmadinejad and an increasing encroachment by Ahmadinejad on Larijani's areas of responsibility. It was anticipated that his resignation would allow Ahmadinejad to replace him with someone who was more defiant.[48] Ahmadinejad commented on the nuclear talks at about this time. He said "some losers go and tell [the West] they want to negotiate, and the enemies, because they are trapped in a deadlock, welcome them."[49] Larijani was replaced by Jalili Saeed, who was seen as a close friend to Ahmadinejad and potentially unqualified to fill such a lofty position.[50]

However, there is an Iranian counterargument to the U.S. and EU position in this case as well. In July of 2008, Iran reportedly submitted an alternative plan for the negotiations. Its proposal included preliminary talks, start of talks, and negotiations. These would take place among increasingly high-ranking officials from the countries involved. In all, the suggested process would involve four to six meetings among the ministers. According to the Iranian plan, at the start of talks phase the states would rescind multilateral and unilateral punishments of Iran. There was no clear reciprocal concession from the Iranians. Instead, the document stated that the parties involved in the start of talks would refrain from discussing divergent issues that could derail the negotiations. However, there were references to "the Islamic Republic of Iran [continuing] to cooperate with the agency" (which agency is unclear) and Iran's eventual [implementation] of the agreed action (again with a lack of clarity).[51] The Iranian proposal failed to even address the key Western demand of its ending enrichment.[52] At the time, Iran apparently hoped that there would be a mutual and simultaneous response from Iran on the 5+1 proposal and from the 5+1 on the Iranian proposal.[53] It is not clear whether a response was forthcoming from the 5+1, but it may be that this was what resulted in confusion and the Iranian "non-response."

View from the United States

The U.S. position on Iran's nuclear aspirations is founded on the belief that Iran is seeking enrichment capacity and heavy water reactors (at the Arak facility) in order to produce more highly enriched uranium (HEU) for a weapons program. In fact, Iran has informed the IAEA that they intend to add a reprocessing facility at Arak to separate materials from spent fuel.[54] As mentioned previously, Iran denies these activities are for nuclear weapons applications.[55] In fact, Khamenei issued a *fatwa* (religious edict) stating that production of nuclear weapons violates Islamic law and is *haram* (forbidden).[56]

Two major factors reinforce the U.S. position. First, IAEA inspections have shown that Iran has been engaged in undeclared nuclear activities for over two decades.[57] Iran's continued violation of the terms of its nuclear agreements within the international system is truly troublesome. Second, there is little justification for acquiring heavy water reactors when light water reactors provide the same energy generation capacity without the extra HEU production.

Iran is, however, correct in its assertions that it has the sovereign right to perform the enrichment that it has done or building the facilities it has. What is problematic and against the NPT agreement is that Iran has done these things covertly and has not placed the facilities under IAEA safeguards as it should have ... until after they were detected.[58] The absence of international confidence in Iran is another factor that exacerbates the situation and undermines Iran's argument.

The IAEA has determined that Iran continues to violate its directives and decisions of the UN Security Council.

Contrary to the decisions of the Security Council, Iran has not suspended its enrichment related activities, having continued the operation of PFEP [Pilot Fuel Enrichment Plant] and FEP [Fuel Enrichment Plant] and the installation of both new cascades and of new generation centrifuges for test purposes. Iran has also continued with the construction of the IR-40 reactor.[59]

The United States has been struggling to determine what to do with Iran's recalcitrance. The Bush administration emphasized that this is a priority among its foreign policy issues. It worked with the UN and through the EU to try and resolve the situation, including offering Iran incentive packages to stop its actions. Both U.S. unilateral and multilateral sanctions have been levied against Iran for its actions. These sanctions have not seemed to have much effect. The Bush administration did not rule out the use of force to halt Iran's nuclear activities. "While making clear that a diplomatic solution is the preferred option, President Bush himself has stated that 'all options are on the table, including military force, to deal with the nuclear threat.'"[60]

One of the controversial efforts that the United States has undertaken is the blacklisting and application of sanctions on Iranian banks. This process was initiated in 2006 by Stuart Levey (then under-secretary for terrorism and financial intelligence at the Treasury Department), in an effort pressure international banks not to do business with Iran until it changes its behaviors.[61] If the United States believes that the banks are helping to fund Iranian missile developments or nuclear projects, the bank can be sanctioned. Banks internationally have tended to shy away from doing business with the sanctioned banks due to fears that the United States would expand sanctions to them if they were to do so.[62] The United States has sanctioned many of Iran's top banks, including Bank Saderat (2006), Bank Sepah (2007), Bank Melli (2007), and the Export Development Bank of Iran (2008).[63] Other countries such as Australia, Britain, France, Germany, Japan, and Italy have cut back on their business with the Iranian banks and some have placed their own sanctions on them. The sanctions have contributed to the economic problems Iran has suffered recently, leading some to argue that "for the first time in 30 years... Washington has found a tangible way to pressure Iran."[64]

The National Intelligence Estimate (NIE) from the United States in November 2007 is a U.S. policy document that must be addressed. The NIE indicated that the Iranians had halted their nuclear weapons program in 2003.[65] In spite of the findings, the Bush administration continued pressure on Iran to halt its nuclear program and on the UN to impose sanctions. However, the finding in the NIE decreased the Russian, Chinese, and Saudi Arabian commitment to the imposition of harsher sanctions on the Iranian regime.[66] The NIE may also have signaled (whether intentional or not) that the United States is not going to be willing to back its position on Iran's nuclear program with force. In fact, both Vali Nasr (2008) and the Swedish Defense Research Agency (2008) argued that the NIE significantly weakened the Bush administration's call for using military force to turn back Iran's nuclear weapons program.[67]

American public opinion about the Iranian nuclear threat was also not swayed by the NIE. In December 2007, a Gallup Poll indicated that 60 percent of Americans still thought that the Iranian nuclear program posed a threat—with 33 percent identifying it as a "very serious" threat. It is interesting to note, however, that 37 percent of Americans do not think that Iran's nuclear program poses a threat to the United States.[68]

Israel has also expressed its determination that Iran should not acquire a nuclear device. In particular, the inflammatory rhetoric of the current Iranian administration has led some to believe that Iran would use the bomb if it had one...and probably against Israel.[69] In 2006, acting Prime Minister Ehud Olmert said: "under no circumstances can Israel allow someone with hostile intentions against us to have control over weapons of mass destruction that can endanger our existence."[70] Israel truly believes that Iran poses a threat to its very existence.[71] Israel's fears could result in Israeli action against Iran whether the United States supported it or not. According to an August 2008 news report:

> Israel will not allow Iran to attain nuclear capability and if time begins to run out, Jerusalem will not hesitate to take whatever means necessary to prevent Iran from achieving its nuclear goals, the government has recently decided in a special discussion. According to the Israeli daily *Ma'ariv*, whether the United States and Western countries succeed in thwarting the Islamic Republic's nuclear ambitions diplomatically, through sanctions, or whether a US strike on Iran is eventually decided upon, Jerusalem has begun preparing for a separate, independent military strike.[72]

Israel's fears for its security in the region could translate into a major crisis for the United States, if neither Israel nor Iran becomes willing to back away from their current positions. At the time that Israel's planning was reported (late August–early September 2008), there were divergent reports (both from Israeli news outlets) about the U.S. reaction to Israel's actions. In some cases, it was reported that the United States had not approved Israeli requests for equipment in support of such an attack. This, it was thought, might indicate a divergence of U.S. and Israeli intentions.[73] In other news sources, however, it was reported that the United States was making plans of its own and an attack on Iran was imminent.[74]

Iranian Missile Tests

A concern related to the nuclear issue is the fact that Iran is expanding its long range missile capabilities at the same time as it is pushing its nuclear program. Iranian authorities believe that ballistic missiles can improve both their defensive and offensive capabilities. This will provide for deterrence against the United States and Israel, as well as other potential aggressors in the region. It is important to note that the missiles that are being developed have the potential to strike not only Israel, but other countries in the Middle East and Eastern Europe as well. This makes the missiles, which clearly cannot hit the United States, a significant threat to U.S. interests in the region. Furthermore, the United States may find it difficult to build coalitions against Iran within the Middle East if the countries fear that they will face the Iranian ballistic missiles in retaliation.

In the summer of 2008, Iran ran extensive launch tests on indigenous missiles. Among these was the Shahab-3 missile (a modification of the North Korean No-dong missile), which has a range of about 2,000 km and would allow Iran to hit targets in Israel, Turkey, Pakistan, and much of the Arabian peninsula.[75] They also tested the shorter-range Zelzal (400 km) and Fateh (170 km) missiles as part of military exercises.[76] On the same day as the testing started (July 9, 2008) the Iranian military warned the United States and Israel against attacking them. Iranian Revolutionary Guard official Ali Shirazi said, "The Zionist regime is pushing the White House to prepare for a military strike on Iran...If such a stupidity is done by them, Tel Aviv and the U.S. naval fleet in the Persian Gulf will be the first targets which will be set on fire in Iran's crushing response."[77]

The August missile test was of greater concern to the United States. At that time, Iran test launched a rocket that it claimed will be capable of carrying a satellite into orbit. Like many other of Iran's interests, however, this is a dual-use technology that could also be used to launch nuclear warheads. In fact, Iran has been working with both China and North Korea to develop its ballistic missile capabilities.[78] The United States argued that the missile test was inconsistent with Iran's UN Security Council obligations. Interestingly, in February 2007 an Iranian rocket launch managed to carry materials into space. The payload was described by Iran as being "research material for the ministries of science and defense."[79]

While these tests were not wildly successful, they are important nonetheless. They demonstrate the political will of the country and its government to produce missiles and further their domestic technology capabilities. Iran's missiles have proven to be "crude, inaccurate, and unreliable" and represent "military entertainment."[80] Therefore, the United States does not face a direct threat from Iranian missiles.[81] However, this is another example of Iran's willingness to defy the international system and saber rattle in its attempts to deter and dissuade U.S. and Israeli actions.

U.S. Policy Options

The United States is obviously very concerned about Iran developing a nuclear enrichment or eventual weapons capability. This is a move that it believes would destabilize the region and could potentially put Israel at risk from an Iranian nuclear attack. It should be noted, however, that there are real deterrents to an Iranian attack against Israel. Primary among these is the fact that any nuclear attack against Israel would also be likely to adversely impact (through the blast itself or the associated fallout) both the Palestinian population and potentially Lebanese Hezbollah that are nearby.[82] It may be more likely that Iran would use a nuclear weapon to threaten or coerce states within the region rather than bombing them. This is a fine distinction and in no way argues that the United States should therefore find the weapons program more tolerable. However, it should be noted in U.S. policymaking that Iran obtaining an independent enrichment capacity may have goals aside from the annihilation of regional competitors.

The United States has many options available to it as it attempts to address its concerns about Iran's nuclear energy and/or weapons. The range of policy alternatives is presented on table 6.3.

Military and Intelligence Options

The United States has a wide variety of overt and covert military options at its disposal to address the Iranian nuclear program. These generally would involve attacks against the Iranian nuclear infrastructure or the country more broadly in order to deter Iran from developing a nuclear weapons capacity. Attacks could range from targeting specific enrichment sites or reactors to an all-out U.S. military invasion in support of regime change. Options 1–5 on table 6.3 all involve this type of activity. Because the implications of each of these policy options were deemed to be similar by the authors, they are treated together here.

A U.S. campaign would be likely to involve conventional air attacks against important facilities in Iran's nuclear program. The U.S. actions may also involve strategic strikes from special operations forces and/or an economic blockade of the country.[83] A major factor in the relative success of any military action would be the extent to which the United States engaged in international consensus building in the period before an attack.[84] There are many in the international community who share the U.S. concerns about Iran's nuclear aspirations. If the United States were to attempt to go it alone, it may create resentment. However, if the United States were to engage in coalition building in advance of any military

Table 6.3 U.S. policy options: Iran's nuclear program

Number	Policy Options	Impact / Probability	Authors' Views
1	Mobilize American military might against Iran, with the intention of halting the nuclear program, replacing the existing government, or both.	These would likely have an impact that could be contrary to U.S. interests in Iran and the region.	Avoid.
2	Utilize surgical air strikes against the Iranian nuclear infrastructure.		
3	Support (tacitly or overtly) Israeli strikes against the nuclear infrastructure.		
4	Perform covert strikes on Iran's nuclear infrastructure.		
5	Engage in covert operations to undermine the Iranian government with the intention of replacing it with one that will abandon the nuclear program.	Depends on many factors for success—not all in U.S. control. The outcome cannot be predicted given the political system in Iran. Not quite probable.	Not recommended. Requires careful calculation based on sketchy data. Could end up with another, more objectionable regime.
6	Continue and/ or increase both multilateral and unilateral sanctions on Iran.	Could have tragic impacts on a population that is by far the most pro-American in the Middle East. Probable.	Poor policy. Recommended only if 7 and 8 should fail.
7	Continue to offer Iran multilateral packages of inducements to desist.	Could gradually reach a compromise. Probable.	Recommended.
8	Start a more open diplomatic dialogue with Iran on the nuclear issue.	Has been advocated for a long time by some. Could be a short cut to get positive results. A rational choice.	Highly recommended.

Note: There are a lot of different articles and sources that provide listings of the possible U.S. policy options. See, for example, Mark Fitzpatrick, "Is Iran's Nuclear Capability Inevitable," in Patrick Cronin (ed.) *Double Trouble* (Westport, CT: Praeger, 2007), p. 1. This list is the authors' synthesis of these lists and reflects their views about the most credible potential policies.

action and take a multilateral approach—even if the United States were to carry out the actual strikes on its own—it would be received better internationally.

Perceptions about the U.S. intentions may also have an impact on the opportunity for success. If it were internationally perceived that the United States was determined to build its own power in the region and exerting hegemony, the reaction will likely be disadvantageous. However, if the international and regional perceptions of the U.S. intent were that the goal was to restore the balance of power in the region, this might be more acceptable. However, this approach would likely require the strengthening of regional allies at the same time as the United States is attempting to curtail Iranian power expansion.[85]

Strengths

In the authors' opinions, there are few benefits associated with military invasion, strategic strikes against Iranian infrastructure or covert activities against Iran to undermine its nuclear program or government. The only identifiable benefits would be the potential to destroy relevant infrastructure or install a new government more friendly to Western desires. However, these activities bear such significant risks and little chance for successful outcomes (discussed later) that they are discouraged.

Weaknesses

There are many reasons why the top five options above should be avoided. Not only would these policies not achieve their goals, but they would likely have the opposite impact as intended... they could increase the Iranian public support for developing nuclear weapons and increase public support of their government. Many in Iran would see U.S. military actions against their country as proof that Ahmadinejad's rhetoric about U.S. imperialism is correct. Furthermore, Ahmadinejad's successful domestic linking of the nuclear program with Iranian nationalism would intensify the negative public reaction. A U.S. attack or a U.S.-supported attack would create a rally-round-the-flag effect, intensify anti-U.S. sentiments in the country and perhaps in the region, and result in an Iranian public willing to make major sacrifices for a nuclear weapons capacity.

Vali Nasr put forth four possible Iranian government reactions to a U.S. military intervention in Iran: diversion of U.S. attention by increasing conflicts in Afghanistan and Iraq; asymmetric conflict against the U.S. Navy in the Persian Gulf and countries that host U.S. troops; symbolic terrorism combined with a propaganda war aimed at increasing anti-American sentiment in the Middle East, Africa, and Southeast Asia; and adoption of domestic strategies to defend Iran against regime change, domestic unrest or U.S. invasion.[86]

In a similar vein, Paul Pillar argued in 2007 that:

> No one can accurately predict the exact consequences of any US military strike or offensive against Iran. But there are good grounds for assessing the risks of any such action. Based on what we know about Iran, the Middle East, and perceptions of the United States in that region and around the world, the risks of major damage to US interests from such action are substantial, and the probability that such damage would occur is high.[87]

This dire warning is appropriate to the risks that would be associated with U.S. military action against Iran.

These views were also upheld by a study by the Swedish Defense Research Agency, which said that while it was difficult to predict with certainty what Iran would do, its range of strategic choices could be provided. As it was put by one of the authors of the study, "the most likely Iranian response would be asymmetric in character."[88] The study concluded that Iran could use ballistic missiles, paramilitary operations or increased support to proxies abroad. It also determined that targets for Iran's aggression could include U.S. forces in Iraq or elsewhere in the region, and oil infrastructure or telecommunications lines in the Gulf.[89] If the United States were to decide that military action was the only option available to it, plans should be made to defend U.S. troops, installations, and allies in the region. The U.S. military presence in the Middle East is substantial. Those forces would have to be prepared for increased Iranian strikes against U.S. assets and increased activity by Iraqi insurgents, Lebanese Hezbollah and Hamas, and perhaps al Qaeda as well.

It would also be difficult for the United States to strike against Iran's WMD programs without creating unintentional consequences for the Iranian populace. The Iranian facilities were intentionally built around population centers. Attacks against the sites would certainly have implications for civilians.

Covert actions make little sense, whether they are intended to destabilize the government or to strike infrastructure. Anyone familiar with public opinion toward the United States in the region is aware of the problem. It is not uncommon in the Middle East for any negative event to be blamed on the United States...crops fail, livestock dies, stock market fluctuates, it rains or it does not...all misfortune is the fault of the United States. If a covert attack on Iranian nuclear infrastructure happened, no one would doubt that the United States was responsible, regardless of how well its tracks were covered. Similarly, if the Israelis attack the Iranian infrastructure, the United States will be blamed or identified as responsible in some way. It has been argued that Israel has the capacity to attack Iran's infrastructure "with at least as much confidence as it had in the 1981 Osirak strike."[90] However, the Iranians have reportedly already begun blaming the United States, United Kingdom, and CIA for incidents that have occurred within their borders.[91] According to Air Force colonel Sam Gardiner, "this is the ultimate for the Iranians—to blame the CIA...It rallies support for the regime and shows the people that there is a continuing threat from the 'Great Satan.'"[92]

In the domestic political realm, Iran's most likely response to the U.S. attack would be radicalization. There are many factions in Iran. A U.S. strike against Iranian infrastructure would not be likely to result in reformists or moderates gaining power. Rather, the more radical, nationalistic, militaristic, and isolationist factions would likely seize the opportunity to once again paint Iran as a victim of U.S. aggression and imperialism.[93] Furthermore, Iran has rarely seen more domestic cohesion than when it has been faced with an outside foe. U.S. strikes against Iran would likely consolidate the radical factions into a powerful coalition that would wield significant power.

Any of these events may cause the Iranian public to rally around their leadership. It could easily be portrayed as another attempt by the United States to deny Iran its sovereign rights to nuclear power. The popular dedication to sacrifice to assure that Iran gained a nuclear device could be galvanized by U.S. actions. As it was put by Christopher Hemmer, "the idea that the Iranian people would react to a military strike by advocating the overthrow of the existing regime is delusional. Instead the likely outcome of any direct military incursion would be the bolstering of the current regime."[94]

Legally, the United States would be on shaky ground in mounting such attacks (though it must be admitted that this has not stopped U.S. actions at times in the past). International law prohibits countries from using military force to get their way in international disputes. The only way such a U.S. strike would be consistent with international law would be if they were mandated by the UN Security Council or if the U.S. attacks met the criteria for preemptive (or anticipatory) self-defense. The United States would likely find it very difficult (as it did in 2003) to convince the UN Security Council to approve of the attacks. At a minimum, China, Russia and France would be likely to object...and all that is needed is one veto. Meeting the criteria for preemptive self-defense would be a challenge under the current circumstances. Although the United States has used the concept of attacking in self-defense more aggressively since 9/11, its application has already been challenged.[95] The United States has simply been unable (and would likely be unable in this case) to convince the international system that threats were imminent.

Furthermore, the U.S. military is stretched too thin for invasion to be a credible threat. Given the wars in Afghanistan and Iraq and the continuing GWOT, the United States would have great difficulty mobilizing enough troops and equipment to be successful in a military invasion of Iran. In addition to these deterrents to military action (whether covert or overt) the United States must keep in mind that its military forces in Iraq and elsewhere in the region are very vulnerable to Iranian retaliatory strikes. While Iran's new missiles could not reach the territory of the United States, they could certainly hit U.S. military installations in Iraq and elsewhere in the region.

The U.S. economy could also be adversely affected by military confrontation with Iran. A major fear in this regard would be the Iranian disruption of the oil supply impacting energy markets.[96] This would hurt the global economy as well as that of the United States. According to James Fallows, while the global economy would eventually recover from such an oil shock, it would take a longer time than it took the U.S. stock market to adjust to the Great Depression.[97] In June of 2006, Ayatollah Khamenei issued a warning to the West that any attempts to punish Iran could jeopardize energy shipments from the region. He added that Iran would not initiate a war. However, other Iranian officials have ruled out the use of oil as a weapon in the past.[98]

The decision to use the "oil weapon" may be unlikely for Iran. While it clearly would impose significant costs on the United States for the attack, it would also hurt other countries internationally with which Iran has had improving relations. Furthermore, Iran is very dependent on oil revenues, which means that interfering with the international flow of oil would be very hurtful to Iranian economy itself. Even a partial cut in the flow of oil or natural gas could cause significant damage to the Iranian economy.[99]

There are others, however, that argue that an attack would have limited impact on the international economy. The direct impact on Iran itself and on the global economy, according to this argument, would be limited because Iran (and the Middle East more generally) is relatively isolated from the international economy. In fact, by some measures Iran is consistently rated as one of the least globalized countries in the world.[100] However, even those who make this argument admit that Iran's response to the U.S. attacks would determine the extent of the economic impact. Iran's reaction will influence both the intensity and the duration of the conflict. The longer the conflict lasts and the more aggressively Iran strikes at oil infrastructure or other strategic targets, the worse the economic impacts are likely to be.[101]

In addition to the above-stated reasons, it must be recognized that a strike against the Iranian nuclear infrastructure would be likely to stall their progress toward nuclear weapons (if that is their intent) rather than stop it. A 2008 study by the Swedish Defense Research Agency listed four possible outcomes from a military attack on Iran's nuclear infrastructure: it ends Iran's program; it stalls or delays the program; the program is unaffected; or it is accelerated.[102] It is difficult to conceive of a way in which a U.S. attack on the Iranian infrastructure would leave the program completely unchanged. Ending the Iranian program through such a strike is also unlikely. As stated by Albright and Shire:

> The survivability of an Iranian nuclear weapons program does not rest entirely on those sites [that might be struck by the United States]—knowledge and experience are transferrable, centrifuges are replicable. Iran could rapidly reconstitute its gas centrifuge efforts elsewhere at smaller, secret sites if it has not already begun to do so…Moreover, rather than possibly delaying or making it impossible for Tehran to carry out a final decision to make nuclear weapons, an attack might force the Iranian leadership's hand.[103]

What this means is that while destroying Iran's infrastructure may delay the country's efforts, it will not cause them to unlearn what they already know. The international system cannot take back Iran's acquired knowledge and capacities. Iran could also use U.S. strikes as a rationale to remove its sites from IAEA inspections, withdraw from the NPT, and move its facilities underground until it needs to test. This would result in increased Iranian dedication to developing nuclear capacities and even less oversight of its activities by the international community. This could potentially speed up Iranian developments. It could also increase the chance of a nuclear arms race developing in the region as Iranian withdrawal from the NPT and IAEA inspections would send a clear signal to other regional powers that Iran was dedicated to developing a weapon.[104]

Sanctions

As discussed above, the United States and UN have already imposed a variety of sanctions against Iran and its interests in attempts to compel Iran to curtail its enrichment activities. Sanctions could be continued and/or intensified by the United States and through international organizations. As with the preceding discussion of sanctions in the terrorism chapter, it would be recommended that the U.S. sanctions be targeted so that they penalize the Iranian elites while hurting the common man as little as possible.

Strengths

Again, the benefit of sanctions is that they allow the U.S. government to express its outrage at another government's actions without having to commit U.S. military troops. Furthermore, the imposition of sanctions allows the U.S. government to respond to public demands that something be done about a negative situation without making a major military commitment to every bad situation in the world.

Weaknesses

As discussed previously in the terrorism chapter (option 4), sanctions (option 6 in this chapter) are at best a weak policy tool. Because the terrorism chapter goes into some detail about the potential negative impacts of sanctions, this chapter will focus more on the U.S. sanctions that have been put in place based on the U.S. perceptions of the Iranian nuclear program. Current U.S. sanctions in place against Iran because of their nuclear program:

- Stop countries from supplying materials and technology that could aid Iran's nuclear and missile programs;
- Prohibit any country from buying arms from Iran;
- Call on all countries to show "vigilance and restraint" in selling arms to Iran;
- Create a more extensive (in addition to those named in Resolution 1737) listing of individuals and organizations whose international assets have been frozen—to include Bank Sepah, Iran's fourth largest bank;
- Call on countries to voluntarily restrict the travel of those named in the sanctions listings; and
- Call for the suspension of the granting of new loans, grants or credits to Iran unless for humanitarian purposes.[105]

Working through the UN Security Council, the United States helped to guide the passage of three rounds of progressively tougher sanctions against Iran ("United Nations Security Council Resolution (UNSCR) 1969, adopted in August 2006; 1737, in December 2006; and 1747, in March 2007"[106]). The U.S. defense of the application of sanctions against Iran is summarized below:

> Iran is one of the greatest threats to international peace in the world today. Iran's attempts to create a nuclear weapons capability, its sponsorship of terrorist groups in the Middle East, and its atrocious human rights record

make it one of the most urgent concerns for American foreign policy. Sanctions are an expression of American resolve to isolate the Government of Iran, increase diplomatic pressure and convince Iran to reverse its nuclear ambitions.[107]

There is little evidence that any of these measures have been successful in changing the behavior of Iranian authorities. On the contrary, it has led them to be more confrontational and defiant. A direct result of this may be the advancement in their ballistic missile technology and war gaming to demonstrate their military might.

Inducement Package Offers and Dialogue

The United States could continue to try and arrive at an incentive package that would be acceptable to Iran. There have been multiple rounds of offers made in the past, many of which were rejected out of hand by the Iranians. From the U.S. perspective, in the most recent offer, Iran was slow to respond to the international system with a decision on the package and has been consistently petulant in this process. In particular, Iran has objected to the continued U.S. insistence that they suspend their enrichment program before talks can begin. Based on this, it would seem that neither carrots nor sticks will sway Iran from its current path.[108]

While Iran has drug its feet on many package deals there are possibilities that an agreement could be achieved. It is likely that the U.S. position of no enrichment capability at all for Iran is not a policy that would be tolerable. However, there is some room for negotiations in which a certain level of capability would be deemed tolerable to the United States and acceptable to Iran. As it was put by The Stanley Foundation, "while the very existence of an enrichment capability is nonnegotiable for any realistic Iranian leader, the scope and final technological plateau of this capability is open for bargaining."[109]

Strengths

There are some that have argued that Iran has continued to drag its feet in this process in order to gain time to work on its nuclear weapons program. While negotiations were continuing, Iran has been able to work out some of the problems with its procedures and move its capacities forward.[110]

However, both members of the Iranian public (as discussed previously in this chapter) and its elites have argued that the country is giving up too much to gain a nuclear capacity. The sanctions that have been imposed and the inability of Iran to engage more fully in the international economy are keeping Iran's economy from achieving its potential. Some would rather reap the economic benefits of engagement rather than having the bomb.[111]

This means that there are at least some opportunities for improvement in the situation. Continued offering of inducement packages to Iran combined with increased U.S. engagement with the country may offer hope. A U.S. approach that focused on carrots rather than sticks could bolster the position of those who are pushing for economic engagement rather than nuclear. If nothing else, it would potentially decrease the power of Ahmadinejad's rhetoric. The only potential detriment of continuing engagement is that it could give Iran more time to develop its nuclear weapons program. The United States needs to work through the UN to push for continued IAEA access and to put pressure on the regime to be forthcoming.

Engagement (option 8) also would strengthen the U.S. position on the Iranian nuclear program with its international allies. In a 2006 statement before the U.S. House of Representatives, Under Secretary for Arms Control and International Security Robert Joseph stated that "the President has emphasized that all options are on the table to deal with the threat from Iran, but...our strong preference is to do so through determined diplomacy."[112] This seems to be contrary to some of the other rhetoric that came from the Bush administration that emphasized the unacceptability of Iran's obtaining a nuclear enrichment capacity. However, it would provide support for arguments in favor of this policy option.

China, Russia, and many states in the EU have disagreed with the U.S. position and also pushed for more extensive engagement with Iran. If the United States were less strident in its rhetoric about the situation and favored the language of engagement instead, it may improve relations with our allies and show a more united front to the Iranian administration.

Weaknesses

There are, however, significant potential disadvantages to these approaches. Most significantly, embracing engagement and offering lucrative inducement packages to Iran could be interpreted internationally (and would certainly be interpreted by Iran) as capitulation by the United States to Iran's position. This is not a perception that the United States can afford to have circulating internationally. Its implications would be that the closer a country gets to actually achieving a nuclear weapons capacity, the more leverage they will have to manipulate the United States. In many ways it could be seen as the United States rewarding Iran for defying international laws and breaking their treaty obligations.

Furthermore, Iran has seemed to be drawing-out negotiations with the international system. This has been interpreted by many as Iranian foot-dragging in order to gain time to further its technology developments. In August of 2008, the EU tightened sanctions on Iran due to what the EU claimed was insufficient response from Iran on a new package of incentives offered by the international system. The new EU sanctions deny public loans or export credits to companies trading with Iran and expand other existing sanctions.[113]

Preferred Option

As indicated on table 6.3, the authors believe that the best options for addressing Iran's nuclear program would be the establishment of a more open dialogue and continued offering of incentive packages to the country. Clearly this is not a risk-free option and it is also not likely to be a quick fix for the problem. However, the U.S. and Iranian governments are both facing possible impending regime changes. This will not provide a "clean slate" for the negotiations, but it could provide a new environment in which the two countries could have better relations. Both the Bush and Ahmadinejad governments took the hard line on negotiations. It is possible that more flexible regimes in both countries could achieve a negotiated settlement that eluded the preceding ones. Resolution of this issue could be a positive first step toward improving relations between the two countries more generally.

As of April 2009, the situation regarding Iran's nuclear program was still unclear. On April 8, the U.S. State Department declared that it would engage in direct talks with Iran regarding the program,[114] a step that was recommended by the authors. This is a positive sign from the Obama administration. However on April 9 Ahmadinejad declared that he was proud of his country's nuclear accomplishments, including the packaging of fuel for its reactors and successful centrifuge tests.[115] This may indicate continued recalcitrance from Iran under Ahmadinejad, in spite of American attempts to improve relations.

Chapter 7

Toward a More Comprehensive U.S. Foreign Policy for Iran

The relationship between the United States and Iran is clearly dysfunctional. It has been fractured by historical tensions and suffers from a variety of current policy impasses. However, it is not beyond repair. Iran and the Middle East are vitally important to U.S. interests. In fact, the authors believe that the relationship is too important to the United States for it to continue along its current path. A more constructive set of policies need to be put into place in order to create an environment that is more conducive to cooperation.

This book has examined the major hurdles that exist to the two countries improving relations. This chapter will provide a summary of those challenges. The book has also given the reader a range of policy alternatives available to the United States to confront each of the contentious points in the relationship. This chapter will put forth a recommended policy agenda for the United States to adopt in its future relations with Iran.

U.S.-Iran Relations

The United States and Iran have a checkered past during which both have violated trusts, caused the other distress, and violated the letter or intent of international agreements. Neither side is without blame. At the same time, each side has made overtures to the other at times in the past that have been rebuffed. This holds promise for the future as it demonstrates that each side places some value on improving relations. However, it also demonstrates the petulance each side has exhibited at times.

Unsurprisingly, U.S. and Iranian perspectives of historical events vary widely. Each side tends to paint itself as the victim and the other as the villain at important time periods. A less biased evaluation demonstrates that each has been both victim and villain in the relations.

The 1953 Coup was clearly a U.S./British attempt to consolidate power in the region and secure access to Iranian oil resources. Iranian sovereignty and government were violated by the U.S. action. That Madeleine Albright expressed regret for the U.S. role in the event demonstrates that even the U.S. government admits that this was imperialistic on the part of the United States. This is especially detrimental to the relationship due to the fact that the United States worked to overthrow a democratically elected regime. Now as the United States claims to be working to instill democratic norms and values throughout the Middle East, its intentions are understandably questioned. To this day, this incident has had the most profound negative impact on Iranian views of the United States.

Two major events in 1979 impacted relations. These were the Islamic Revolution and the Hostage Crisis. The Revolution alone would have destabilized relations between the two countries. Iran was making a break from a period of U.S. influence and attempting to isolate itself from the world. The Western interest in Iranian oil made that a frightening proposition for the United States. A more significant impact was felt in the United States from the Hostage situation. U.S. citizens were captivated by the daily coverage of the plight of the hostages. That the Iranian government did not act decisively to bring the situation to an end is, to many Americans, unforgivable. Interestingly, the fact that the United States again violated Iranian sovereignty in its rescue attempt does not seem to have resonated with the Iranians. This is perhaps because of the humiliating failure that the United States suffered in that endeavor.

The persistent U.S. pursuit of its own interests was also demonstrated in its reaction to the Iran-Iraq War. The U.S. inconsistency in its support of one side over the other coupled with its failure to react more aggressively to the Iraqi use of chemical weapons harmed its relations with Iran. In general, Iranians have felt betrayed by the entire international community based on the lack of international support for Iran's attempts to defend itself from Iraqi hostility.

Although the United States was initially officially neutral regarding the Iran-Iraq War, it became quietly pro-Iraq as the war progressed. Initially, Iraq made significant gains in Iran. However, it was not long before the Iranians had driven back Iraqi forces with wave after wave of soldiers. By 1982, Iraq's position had shifted to one of defending itself against the

Iranian onslaught. The U.S. position was still officially neutral. However, it did not feel that Iranian control of Iraq served U.S. interests in the region so it began providing arms to Iraq in secret. Only the eventual Iraqi use of chemical weapons pushed the United States back into a more neutral position, but even this did not warm the United States toward the Iranian position. The U.S. Department of State issued an official Condemnation of Iraqi Chemical Weapons Use in March of 1984 which stated that:

> While condemning Iraq's chemical weapons use…The United States finds that the present Iranian regime's intransigent refusal to deviate from its avowed objective of eliminating the legitimate government of neighboring Iraq to be inconsistent with the accepted norms of behavior among nations and the moral and religious basis which it claims.[1]

That the United States castigated Iran in the midst of this condemnation of Iraq was particularly insulting to many Iranians and further harmed relations.

The most recent incident to impact the relationship was the post-9/11 Axis of Evil speech. It is difficult to determine who was at fault in this incident. Iran had been assisting the United States in Afghanistan and felt that its inclusion in the Axis of Evil was a slap in the face. From the U.S. perspective, Iran had been and continued to be a state sponsor of terrorism that was pursuing a potentially threatening nuclear capacity and thus deserved to be on the list. Both sides can be argued effectively. What cannot be argued is that the U.S. inclusion of Iran on this list has damaged the relationship during a time that Iran seemed to be trying to push for improvement. It is hard to believe that the Bush administration could not have arrived at a State of the Union Address that both condemned Iranian misdeeds and praised it for its attempts to be more conciliatory. The outcome of grouping Iran with the two greatest villains in the international system should have been anticipated and could easily have been avoided.

Unfortunately, this is not a unique U.S. verbal blow to Iran. Since the Revolution, the United States has branded Iran with all sorts of negative labels, including pariah state and rogue state. Iran, for its part, has also been ready to use negative monikers to emphasize problems with the United States. There was only one instance (the Friday after 9/11 as mentioned earlier) where the "minister of slogan" at Friday Prayers did not invite believers to shout "Death to America" and "Death to Israel." It has also identified the United States as the Great Satan and Israel as occupiers of the Holy Qods.

This touches on another important factor in the relationship. In general, Americans have very little concept of the culture and government of

Iran. In many ways this may be due to the fact that the two cultures are so very different. Where the U.S. values separation of church and state, Iran has developed a system where religion and governance are inextricably linked. U.S. values such as participation in government, women's rights, freedom of speech and the press, and others are not universally shared among the Iranians. The idea that the Iranian seat of power is vested in the religious Supreme Leader rather than the elected president is difficult for many Americans to grasp. This is not meant to imply that either system of government is better or worse than the other. They are simply very different.

Both countries are currently suffering under the weight of the poorly performing international economy. This may be even truer in Iran than in the United States. Though it has enjoyed increasing oil wealth recently, the distribution of this windfall has been very limited. Only a handful of Iranian elites actually benefit directly. The rest have suffered from inflation, with government subsidies for necessary items failing to keep pace with the reduction in real wages. Ahmadinejad's government has suffered declining popularity due to its failure to follow through on promises of increased wealth for everyone. This decline is somewhat remarkable given that the administration entered with relatively low popular support.

Ahmadinejad has further upset some domestically by his continued attempts to pick fights with the United States and the international system. Although there is some support for his defense of Iranian interests, there are many who feel that he is hurting the country economically and politically. Where Khatami had sought to improve Iranian relations internationally as a means for integrating it more fully with the international economy with the intention of increasing the country's prosperity, Ahmadinejad has created a domestic crisis mentality that has resulted in less economic productivity.

Ahmadinejad's rhetoric has also impacted Middle East stability. Iran is seen by some of its neighbors as a loose cannon that is attempting to export its Islamic Revolution. His hosting of a Holocaust Denial conference and declarations that Israel should be wiped off the map serve to increase tensions in the region. Although persistent regional conflicts have seemed to fade into the background recently, Iran's sense of encirclement and its unique characteristics in the region make it a continuing source of concern. The United States and Iran obviously have differing levels of power in the international system—militarily, politically, and economically. They share, however, the mutually exclusive goal of dominating the Middle East. They also share the perception that the other is the most significant threat to regional stability. Interestingly, it is likely that the power of both states gives them each the potential to be a source of either stability or strife in the region. Both claim to be advocating for stability in the region. Each is also reluctant to give up their drive for regional status—the United States because it is a superpower and Iran because it is attempting to expand its regional influence. Perhaps if they could overcome their bilateral problems they could work together to bring about such stability. So long as they are competing, both are responsible for instability in the region.

A relevant issue to the Iranian role in regional instability is that of its close relations with Russia, China, Pakistan, and (less so) the EU. The United States is significantly concerned that Iran will ally closely with Russia or China in particular. As was discussed in detail earlier, there are motives for each country (Iran, Russia, and China) to work together. This complicates U.S. relations with each of these countries. A recent example was Russian statements (discussed earlier) that the U.S. position on its attack on Georgia might result in less Russian support for U.S.-sponsored sanctions against Iran. Among other issues, the United States is worried that Russia, China or Pakistan could provide Iran with improved conventional weapons or, perhaps more importantly, assistance on the Iranian nuclear weapons program. Furthermore, the U.S. goal to isolate Iran to change its behavior is significantly undermined if it has such powerful and industrial states to turn to for its trade and diplomatic relations.

Iran's sponsorship for terrorist organizations is one of its most clear contributions to regional instability. It is probable that its inferiority to the United States and others in the region leads it to utilize this tactic. It would be significantly challenged to compete with the United States without resorting to asymmetric warfare. Not only is this support well established through evidence held by the United States and others in the international community, Iran itself does not really deny its actions. Typically, it uses different terminology and claims that it is offering moral support to Hezbollah or Hamas. Certainly, it attempts to keep them out of the spotlight to avoid unnecessary attention. However, the issue here is one of interpretation. Iran does not identify the groups it supports (Hamas, Lebanese Hezbollah, Iraqi insurgents, etc.) as terrorists. Therefore, any support it is providing is not, in its eyes, for terrorism. This amounts to international diplomatic splitting of hairs that is equally typical of the United States. This is likely to be a continued point of contention between Iran, the United States, and the international system long into the future; just as it has been in the past.

Similarly, Iran's nuclear program has been a source of instability. All of Iran's arguments that it is pursuing enrichment for domestic energy purposes are undermined by the fact that there are technologies available to it to do so without producing weapons-grade materials in large quantities. Its insistence that it be permitted to have heavy water reactors and a major uranium enrichment capacity are inconsistent with international agreements to which Iran is party, leading some to question Iran's peaceful intentions.

When Iran's nuclear enrichment program is considered in concert with its space and ballistic missile program, it gives the impression that Iran is striving to gain regional hegemony through a nuclear weapon. This challenges U.S. global power projection and influence in the same region. This comes to a peak when coalition building is restrained by the fact that some small and vulnerable Arab states feel reluctant to enter into a sound alliance or coalition with the United States. Iran's military and emerging missile system creates the image of a regional power that threatens those small states to the extent that they do not feel secure, even through alliance with the world's superpower. Clearly, Iran's missiles could reach these states before the U.S. power to protect them would be capable of intervening.

However, Iran is correct in that it has the sovereign right to develop technologies in its national interest. Its continued membership to the NPT, from which it could withdraw at any point, is a positive sign. However, its breaking of the letter and intent of that agreement continue to be of concern.

The United States has made Iranian cessation of its enrichment program a consistent precondition for negotiations between the two countries. Iran has refused to even do so temporarily with the option to resume should the negotiations fail. In some ways, the impasse may be due to the political administrations that have been in place on both sides. Both Bush and Ahmadinejad took a hard-line stance against the other administration. The rhetoric emanating from each actor was so aggressive as to cut off options for cooperation. Neither could be seen to be backing down from the other's continued challenges. Therefore, cooperation was unlikely under those regimes. The new Obama Administration has significant opportunities to improve relations. The outstanding question is whether Ahmadinejad or his successor will be open to improving relations or not.

In a move not witnessed since before the 1979 Revolution, Ahmadinejad issued a statement of congratulations to Barak Obama immediately after his election. The U.S. response to the statement was described as cautiously optimistic.[2] However, the chances for major change from Iran are questionable. Almost immediately after Ahmadinejad had congratulated him, Obama castigated Iran once again. He said, "Iran's development of a nuclear weapon, I believe, is unacceptable, and we have to mount an international effort to prevent that from happening. Iran's support of terrorist organizations, I think, is something that has to cease."[3] This was followed almost immediately by criticism from Ali Larijani, Iran's speaker of the Majlis. He complained that Obama was not changing strategies from the preceding administration, as had been expected.[4]

In spite of the fact that the Supreme Leader was Khamenei for both presidents Khatami and Ahmadinejad, the current regime has been confrontational while the preceding was more conciliatory. This could mean three things:

- Khamenei could have intended to move the country toward a more strident posture with the United States. If that was the case, it is unlikely that the next administration, whether it is a new president or a continuation of Ahmadinejad, will change its behavior considerably. There are signs that this is the case. First, Khamenei does not miss any opportunity to assault the United States in his speeches to either domestic or international audiences. Second, on several occasions Khamenei has strongly and explicitly supported Ahmadinejad in spite of criticism from his opponents. One is the Parliament's support of the three candidates proposed for Ministerial positions by Ahmadinejad based on Khamenei's support.[5] Another would be the previously mentioned recent statements from Khamenei telling Ahmadinejad to plan on another term in office.

- A second option would be that Khamenei selected Ahmadinejad as the next president and was then surprised by his aggressive international stance. If this were the case, there will likely be an opportunity for improvement in the relationship under the next regime, which would may or may not have Ahmadinejad as its president. Khamanei has also sent signals that there are boundaries to the behavior he will accept from Ahmadinejad and that he will not permit Ahmadinejad to accumulate excessive power. During the parliamentary elections of 2006, on the order of Khamenei, most of Ahmadinejad's supporters were banned from the election based on the Guardian Council's intervention. This is part of the power struggle between the two, but it does not necessarily mean that they have significant disagreement in their foreign policy tactics. On the contrary, it seems that Khamenei approves of Ahmadinejad's bluffs and rhetoric about Israel at least.

- A third possibility is that Khamenei knew what he was getting with Ahmadinejad but failed to understand the domestic and international backlash that would result. This scenario (which seems to best fit with the situation as it evolved) would also be likely to result in a new Iranian regime that would be more willing to work with the United States toward improved relations. However, this all depends on how much Khamenei himself fears the United States or wants engagement. It appears that the Spiritual Leader of Iran does fear the United States and its influence among the Iranian population. That is perhaps the reason he keeps the door open to a possible reconciliation.

However, in practice his fear of the United States prevents its materialization. This leads the authors to conclude that if the regime feels it will be secure, it may be more open to reconciliation.

General Policy Propositions

Iran is a pragmatic country in that it can be counted on to act in its own interest.[6] Kamrava argued that Iran's pragmatism means it is realistic and assesses the country's needs and capabilities as it formulates its foreign policy.[7] This rationality of action could be used to argue in favor of any U.S. policy alternative that impacts the Iranian cost / benefit analysis in favor of U.S. goals. Theoretically, deterrence, containment and incentive packages could work so long as this Iranian pragmatism persists. Because the United States and Iran are both rational and pragmatic, efforts to arrive at an agreement for improved future relations have the possibility of success. If better relations are both desirable and possible, what remains is to arrive at a set of American foreign policies which can be implemented in pursuit of this goal. To do so, the remainder of this chapter will recap, evaluate, and synthesize the policy proposals put forth earlier in the text.

The first general observation that can be made about the policy proposals is that in each case it is argued that U.S. military actions against Iran would likely be counter-productive. This is clearly influenced by the authors' firm belief that military action against Iran should be avoided. Chances for success are so slim and the possibilities for major negative repercussions (possibly including objections in the international community; Iranian retaliation against allies and strategic resources in the region; subsequent deterioration of U.S. relations with other states in the region and world; U.S. failure to reach its goals due to being over-stretched; the empowerment of the Iranian executive as he stood up to the United States; and a rally-round-the-flag effect among the Iranian population) make this a terribly risky and ill-advised option. In addition to this admission of bias, however, it should be recognized that no piece of literature reviewed for this book or expert opinion obtained was in disagreement with the authors' concerns.

A second broad observation is actually a set of issues that are interrelated. There is no quick fix for the problems with the U.S.-Iran relationship. It has taken the countries over 60 years to get the relationship (and at least thirty years of negative and unproductive experiences) to this point and it will take a long time to overcome all the preconceived notions and socialized biases on both sides. Any policy or set of policies that propose to remedy this situation will have to look long into the future and emphasize patience. Both sides will have to be committed to this long path for there to be any hope of success. The Bush and Ahmadinejad administrations were not able to do this. Neither was committed to improvement. Both were dedicated to achieving the others' capitulation. The first step in moving forward will be waiting for both sides to get new governments in place that may be more amenable to reconciliation. Because the U.S. election is more than six months in advance of the Iranian, that means the U.S. administration will have more options in had by the time the Iranian counterpart takes office. It is therefore recommended that the United States begin work on this (perhaps creating an Iranian policy task force) to look into these options ahead of time. A second activity will require direct contacts between the two countries' government and security elites. These individuals will have to be convinced that there are benefits associated with cooperation and that this is the right path for their country to follow. Without a buy in from the elites, little progress will be made. The third step will involve some method(s) to start to build trust among the countries again. This will be a major undertaking that will require activity among elites and the common man alike.

Another theme across the policy issue areas was that the United States needs to start talking to Iran (directly, covertly, and indirectly) if it hopes to improve relations. Ignoring or dealing indirectly with U.S. problems with Iran have not worked. When a policy fails it is generally inappropriate to continue it. Instead, the United States should focus on engagement. Even if Iran proves to be reluctant, the United States would come out ahead in the international community for having made the overtures.

In addition to these general policy characteristics there is another that lies beneath them. The U.S. government and society need to learn more about Iran's culture, government, religion, and people. We cannot hope to put together packages of incentives to offer the Iranians unless we understand what they value. Similarly, it will be impossible to craft policy punishments that will change Iran's behavior until we know more about the way they receive and respond to such coercive tactics. An example of this is the imposition of sanctions. Iran's government has, in many ways, used American sanctions to rally the general population against the United States. If the United States did not anticipate that this would happen, it should have. There is ample historical precedent. The United States needs to develop a policy that will serve both its interests and Iran's. It cannot do that without a better understanding of Iran.

Specific Policy Proposals

On the basis of preceding discussions, the authors have arrived at some more specific recommendations for American foreign policy toward Iran. With the exception of the last option, which should only be pursued if all else fails, the others should be treated as a coherent policy package. No one policy is likely to resolve the long-standing issues between the countries. Instead, the United States has to be working this issue from all angles. Again, it is anticipated that these are long-term programs that will evolve over time. However, the Obama administration has the opportunity to lay the ground work for a more constructive future relationship with Iran. It is vitally important that it make the most of that opportunity.

The selected policy proposals were chosen because they offer more opportunities for success at less cost to the United States than other alternatives. As mentioned previously, military options were deemed inappropriate. It should be noted that the threat of the use of military force or commenting that it remains "on the table" are not included on the list below. It is not useful to threaten to use violence if one is not willing or able to follow through. If the costs of military action are too high for the United States to bear (which is likely true at this time), it should not threaten its use or its bluff might be called. No benefits are likely to be gained through such threats and their costs could be significant.

The time gap in normal diplomatic relations between the two states is significant and must be overcome. Both countries have suffered from a lack of information about the other during this period. Neither has a good grasp of the realities of politics and society within the other's borders. Though many Iranians have immigrated to the United States over time, many of these have elected to stay in the United States rather than return to Iran. They obviously cannot contribute to the U.S. information base about current affairs in Iran as they are devoting their time to trying to integrate into U.S. society. At times this immigrant population can even be the source of misinformation. The only way to bridge the gap in information is to take calculated cultural measures that can contribute to new understandings on both sides. This idea will be elaborated on further later in these conclusions.

For the reasons mentioned previously, it is important for the United States to become more knowledgeable about Iran. Even if this were initiated under a "know thy enemy" rubric, it would start a process that will likely be beneficial for the future. In some aspects, this began after 9/11. There are already increasing opportunities for U.S. citizens to learn more about a variety of Middle Eastern countries, languages, and issues. U.S.

colleges, universities and even high schools are offering more courses in Arabic than they have in the past. A concerted effort to increase the focus on the Persian language (which is spoken in Iran, Afghanistan, Tajikistan, Uzbekistan, and by portions of populations in other states of the region) and other aspects of life in Iran would build for the United States a team of experts who could help to guide decision making regarding Iran better than it has been in the past. It should be recognized that this strategy is not without risk. As was pointed out to one of the authors recently by Thomas Walker of the University at Albany-State University of New York, the risk with getting to know each other better is that we may find that we like each other less. This observation is not meant, by the authors or by Walker, to malign either state. It is merely intended to acknowledge that, as with any relationship, getting to know one another better does not presuppose increased amity.

A second important policy for the United States will be to develop a consistent and coherent policy toward Iran, if not in relation to the entire Middle East. If the policies listed on table 7.1 are selected for implementation, there should be a governmental commitment to seeing them through. If nothing else, the United States should make clear to the world what its priorities in the region are and what it intends to do to pursue them. This will make it much easier for others to predict and respond to U.S. policy decisions. It will also alleviate the concerns that many nations hold that they cannot anticipate U.S. responses to their activities. Furthermore, it would decrease the complaints from many countries that the United States cannot be trusted as an ally because its policies change so easily and with such frequency. Finally, such a policy would make policymaking in the United States easier and more reliable if relevant agencies (Defense, State, Commerce, etc.) were able to predict U.S. policy preferences with greater certainty.

As mentioned previously, the next Iranian presidential election should be in 2009. This election is of incredible importance for U.S. interests, as it will likely dictate the path of U.S. relations with Iran for the following four years and potentially for eight. The United States should be preparing for the impending elections in two ways. First, if at all possible, the United States should use allies, international organizations, and even direct diplomacy to assure Khamenei that it is serious about improving relations. These communications could clearly not hope to determine the next president of Iran. However, they might influence Khamenei and the Guardian Council to select presidential candidates that would be more open to improving relations. The United States should attempt to assure Khamenei and the Guardian Council that, although it has no intention of pushing for regime change in Iran, it would react favorably to the election of a less

Table 7.1 U.S. policy recommendations

Proposed Policies	General Benefit
There has been a thirty-year disconnect in diplomatic relations with Iran. This gap has to be filled with some solid and healing relations that can bridge the past with the present.	Consistent diplomatic relations are very important. After a gap of this length, the lack of knowledge of each partner can create political and cultural impediments on both sides. There is bound to be a lack of confidence and questioning of intentions. This has to be overcome.
Increase educational efforts for the U.S. military, diplomatic corps, and other government agencies regarding the government, economy, language, culture, and society of Iran.	Improved U.S. policies toward Iran; better understanding and predictability for Iranian actions; formation of a foundation for long-term improved relations.
Create a more consistent and coherent U.S. foreign policy toward Iran.	Consistent U.S. policies into the future; greater clarity for Iran about U.S. preferences; improved capacity for U.S. entities to plan for the future.
Attempt to influence the selection of the next President of Iran while preparing to develop more positive relations regardless of who is selected.	Selecting the next Iranian President would be nice, but may not be likely. Being prepared to deal with whatever new administration might be put into place will allow the United States to respond to the new administration positively and immediately.
Engage in one-on-one direct diplomacy.	Talking directly to Iran offers the best opportunity to get a better idea of exactly what are their goals and aspirations internationally and to influence those choices.

Indirect diplomacy through the EU, UN, and others.	This offers another path through which the United States could influence Iran with the added benefit that it can be depicted as if it were coming from elsewhere.
Increase backchannel diplomatic efforts.	Has the benefit of allowing for more sensitive issues to be discussed outside of the public eye. This might facilitate the initial phases of rapprochement.
Implement track-two diplomacy programs.	Track-two diplomacy could help to rebuild trust and relationships among U.S. and Iranian elites. These will be vital to the long term success of any normalization of relations.
Develop multilateral packages of inducements to offer Iran in exchange for compliance with international will.	This positive tool for convincing Iran will be more likely to bear fruit than any punishment. Iran's reticence to accept previous packages may merely mean we need to find better packages or that Ahmadinejad and / or Bush were the hindrance.

IF ALL ELSE FAILS

Work with the international community to develop more comprehensive multilateral sanction targeting Iran's elites.	Using multilateral and more targeted sanctions provides more opportunity for success than the current barrage of US unilateral sanctions combined with some multilateral measures.

bellicose and anti-Western president. However, as mentioned previously, news as of August 2008 seems to indicate that Khamenei does believe that Ahmadinejad will have a second term[8]...and as has been shown, Khamenei's beliefs are very important to Iranian elections.

If the current state of affairs was Khamenei's intent, nothing is lost in the attempt. If, instead, the current situation were unanticipated by Khamenei and he had ulterior motives for reassuring Ahmadinejad about a second term, there may be an opportunity here. However, it would seem that Khamenei is leaning toward more constructive relations with the West. "Subtle but real signals are now being sent by Supreme Leader Khamenei's inner circle, while traditional 'establishment' conservatives are closing ranks between themselves (and even some reformists) to foil President Ahmadinejad's radical populist objectives of a new 'revolution within the revolution.'"[9] In fact, it has been argued that Khamenei wishes to be seen as controlling the process of developing détente with the West and is quite concerned about reformists in general and Ahmadinejad's rhetoric in particular.[10]

One-on-one direct diplomacy between the United States and Iran has been lacking for a long time. This is unfortunate, as it probably offers major opportunities for the United States and Iran to understand each-others' views better and rebuild trust. The United States should begin the process of reinitiating direct diplomacy between the two states. Although it will be a long time before we are able to open and staff a new embassy there, this does not mean that we could not begin to have one-on-one discussions held by neutral, third-party hosts. Reopening these lines of communication will be one of the most important steps in laying the groundwork for a better future. It should be expected that both sides will defect from negotiations on occasion. Persistence and patience will be required from both parties.

Indirect diplomacy in which the EU, UN, or other entity acts as a go-between for Iran and the United States could also be continued. Although the outcomes of such indirect negotiations can be disappointing and can take a long time, it is the path that the United States has followed for years. Little harm could come from continuing to use this channel of influence. In fact, it could provide additional pressure on Iran because it would bring other countries into the discussion and demonstrate greater international interest in its outcome. Furthermore, these negotiations would benefit Iran because any agreement made would be with the EU, UN or others rather than with the United States. This may be more palatable to the Iranian public while animosities continue to exist between the two states. Turkey has been suggested as a country that might be useful in the conduct of indirect diplomacy with Iran. This is because Turkey has friendly relations with both Tehran and Tel Aviv, which is fairly unusual in the international system.[11]

Backchannel diplomacy could be going on at the same time as all other efforts. These secret meetings will likely be more candid than those held in front of the media. Using the backchannel diplomacy in combination with indirect diplomacy would: start building relationships among elites, introduce both countries' populations to the notion of cooperation between the states, allow for open and honest expression, permit debate, and demonstrate to the world that both sides are committed to improvement. Sensitive issues could be debated outside of the public eye to avoid backlash on either side. The governments could then also decide on the appropriate rate of information to be shared with the general public.

In addition, the United States should engage in a new round of track-two diplomacy meetings. Security elites as well as those from other sectors of society could begin sharing ideas and information in workshops and conferences. This would add another dimension to the process. Not only would members of government be building relations, but now elites in other areas would be networking. Too often diplomatic activities are restricted to governments. It then can sometimes become difficult to demonstrate to the general public that there are benefits to the agreements that reach them. This can result in public or even governmental rejection of the agreed-upon policy solution. By incorporating a broader section of the elites in the process, it will be easier to see that there are wide-reaching benefits to greater cooperation. For example, Iranian physicians could gain more access to the cutting edge procedures being developed in the United States. This creates an environment in which more and more citizens can be made aware of the advantages offered through cooperation. It will also more easily demonstrate the purpose and benefits achieved from government concessions during the negotiations. (Sure, we may have given up this, but look what we got in return...) The Stanley Foundation suggested that trilateral parliamentary meetings among the United States, Turkey, and Iran as well as the United States, Turkey and Israel would be another track-two effort that could improve relations among the participating countries.[12]

As the United States gains greater understanding of Iran, it may be possible to put together inducement packages that will be more enticing to the Iranian government. Although the use of carrots rather than sticks may be controversial, they offer more opportunity for success. The United States (likely in collaboration with other international actors) will have a challenge in selling the package to Iran as well as to their domestic populations.

The authors would advocate for the use of incentives with pressures rather than preconditions, as discussed earlier. Conditions lead to self-defeating negotiations and are otherwise counterproductive. Applying pressure on Iran by being conciliatory, appealing to the international system for assistance, securing the backing of both U.S. and Iranian allies, offering attractive incentives packages, and engaging the country diplomatically would be preferable. It allows Iran to enter into negotiations as an equal rather than as the child who had to be scolded before joining the adults at the dinner table. Removing conditions does not change Iranian behavior in any way. They will not likely step up their nuclear efforts, for instance, merely because we do not make their suspension a precondition to negotiation. The United States is therefore no further behind by not imposing conditions it is well aware will not be met. The United States would gain the benefit of demonstrating to the international system (Iran included) that it is serious about negotiating with Iran. It would also allow the Iranians to save face domestically and facilitate their engaging in the process. Providing Iran with a face-saving solution to this impasse is highly important. During the past 30 years, the United States has been referred to as the Great Satan. Iran must adjust this portrayal themselves. The nuclear issue in particular has been tied to Iranian nationalism and patriotism. For Iran to step back from this will require calculated adjustments of nationalistic rhetoric and an incentives package that is carefully considered. U.S. concession in this area would apply great pressure on Iran to enter negotiations and be less obstructionist.

Finally, the discussion turns again to the issue of sanctions. It should be clear to the reader by now that the authors are not advocates for the imposition of economic sanctions. However, it is possible that the United States will attempt to move the relationship with Iran to a more productive position and be rebuffed by Iran in all regards. This would effectively tie the U.S. hands for the improvement of relations as that will require both sides to be dedicated to warming. If Ahmadinejad were reelected in 2009 or someone equally or more combative were to be put into office, the United States would have little choice but to rely on sanctions. Sanctions that are currently in place are hurting the Iranian economy and its mass population. For that reason, if a more conciliatory administration were put into place in 2009 the United States should be poised to take advantage of it. It should not miss another opportunity (as it did with Khatami) to remedy the problems between the two countries.

If the United States is put in the position where sanctions are necessary, its approach still must change. The pain of the existing sanctions has not proved to be sufficient to bring about change. This is due to the following facts: the masses are suffering rather than the elites; other countries continue to trade with Iran, allowing elites continued access to markets and commodities; and the Iranian government has used the pain of sanctions to appeal to Iranian nationalism. Many of these factors can be overcome by changing the nature of the sanctions and the way they are being imposed. The United States should move toward using more multilateral sanctions and decreasing its reliance on unilateral ones. It should also attempt to craft sanctions that target individuals, organizations, and elites more effectively.

The U.S. goal is to change elite behavior. Therefore, the elites should be the ones who suffer the impacts from any sanctions. The Iranian system is designed in a way in which elites directly benefit from increased oil prices while the grassroots suffer from the increasing inflation rate. Sanctions only make the poor poorer and the rich richer. This is further complicated by the flight of rich Iranians to other countries. These individuals take their wealth with them in cash, resulting in the loss of capital in Iran. The individuals who are immigrating enjoy higher standards of living. Because it is an authoritarian regime, punishing the masses will not result in grass-roots movements to change policy, a mass uprising or revolution. Instead, it results in mass poverty and suffering. Grassroots activities could only be possible if the U.S. messages regarding the sanctions were publicly disseminated, which they are not. Rather, the Iranian government's messages blaming their plight on the United States are broadcast giving the administration another tool to increase anti-U.S. sentiment. Targeting sanctions and applying them multilaterally provides an improved opportunity for them to be successful. Targeting increases the chances for success in that the sanctions are specifically designed to penalize the elites rather than the poor. They are put in place on items that are disproportionately consumed by the wealthy. Multilateral sanctions increase the rate of success because the targeted country cannot merely turn to another country to supply the desires of the rich.

Notes

1 INTRODUCTION

1. Ali Ansari, *Confronting Iran: The Failure of American Foreign Policy and the Next Great Crisis in the Middle East* (New York: Basic Books, 2006), p. 2.
2. See testimonies delivered before the Subcommittee on National Security and Foreign Affairs, Committee on Government Oversight and Reform, U.S. House of Representatives on October 30, November 7, and November 14, 2007.
3. U.S. Department of State, "State Sponsors of Terrorism" downloaded from http://www.state.gov/s/ct/c14151.htm on November 20, 2007.
4. See, for instance, U.S. Department of State, "Chapter 3: State Sponsors of Terrorism," *Country Reports on Terrorism* (Washington, DC: Government Printing Office, April 2007).
5. See, for example, Lolita Baldor, "General: Iran Training Shiite Insurgents," *WashingtonPost.com,* August 23, 2006 and Thom Shanker and Steven Weisman, "Iran Is Helping Insurgents in Iraq, US Officials Say," *The New York Times,* September 20, 2004.
6. "Vice President's Remarks to the World Affairs Council of Dallas/Fort Worth," downloaded from www.whitehouse.gov/news/releases/2007/11/print/200711002-13.html on November 21, 2007.
7. Shanker and Weisman.
8. Director General of the IAEA, "Implementation of the NPT Safeguards Agreement in the Islamic Republic of Iran," August 30, 2007 and "Iran Generally Honest on Nuclear Program, IAEA Inspectors Say," *Global Security Newswire,* November 15, 2007.
9. Ayatollah Kashani, "Ayatollah Kashani: N-bomb Production Religiously Forbidden," *Islamic Republic News Agency,* November 9, 2007.
10. "Iran's Statement at IAEA Emergency Meeting," *Mehr News Agency,* August 10, 2005.
11. Sharon Squassoni, "Iran's Nuclear Program: Recent Developments," *CRS Report to Congress,* March 8, 2007, p. 2.
12. "Ahmadinejad Boasts of Iran's Nuclear Gear," *United Press International* online, November 7, 2007 and Sean Yoong, "Ahmadinejad: Destroy Israel, End Crisis," *The Washington Post,* August 3, 2006.

13. Homeira Moshirzadeh, "Discursive Foundations of Iran's Nuclear Policy," *Security Dialogue*, Vol. 38, No. 4, 2007, p. 522.

14. Anthony Cordesman, *Iran's Military Forces in Transition* (Westport, CT: Praeger, 1999), pp. 365–366.

15. Kenneth Katzman, "Iran: US Concerns and Policy Responses," *CRS Report for Congress*, August 6, 2007, pp. 13–16.

16. Patrick Clawson, "Role of the Regime," in James Dobbins, Sarah Harting, and Dalia Dassa Kaye (eds.), *Coping with Iran: Confrontation, Containment, or Engagement: A Conference Report* (Santa Monica, CA: RAND Corporation, 2007), p. 4.

17. See, for example, Katzman, and Col. Lawrence Wilkerson (ret.) *Testimony before the Subcommittee on National Security and Foreign Affairs of the Committee on Oversight and Government Reform* (Washington, DC: Government Printing Office, November 14, 2007).

18. Dalia Dassa Kaye and Fredric Wehrey, "A Nuclear Iran: The Reactions of Neighbours," *Survival*, Vol. 49, No. 2, 2007, pp. 112–119 and James Dobbins, Sarah Harting, and Dalia Dassa Kaye (eds.), *Coping With Iran: Confrontation, Containment or Engagement: A Conference Report* (Santa Monica, CA: RAND Corporation, 2007), p. xiii.

19. Mansour Farhang, "The Enigma of President Ahmadinejad," in Michel Korinman and John Laughland (eds.), *Geopolitical Affairs* (Middlesex, UK: Valentine Journal Academic, 2007), pp. 178–179.

20. Karim Sadjadpoour, "Ayatollah Ali Khamenei, Iran's Nuclear 'Carpet,' and Iraq," in Dobbins, Harting, and Dassa Kaye (eds.), *Coping with Iran: Confrontation, Containment or Engagement: A Conference Report* (Santa Monica, CA: RAND Corporation, 2007), pp. 3–5 and Mehdi Moslem, *Factional Politics in Post-Khomeini Iran* (Syracuse, NY: Syracuse University Press, 2002).

21. For an excellent discussion of the Neo-Kantian argument, see Hans Binnendijk and Richard Kugler, *Seeing the Elephant: The US Role in Global Security* (Washington, DC: National Defense University Press, 2006).

22. Patrick Disney, "Washington, Tehran Complicate Prominent Iranians' Travel to US," National Iranian American Council Web site, August 21, 2008, downloaded from www.niacouncil.org/index.php?option=com_context&task=view&id=1203&Itemid=2 on August 21, 2008.

23. Niusha Boghrati, "Iran: Crackdown on Intellectuals," *Worldpress.org*, April 24, 2007 downloaded from www.worldpress.org/Mideast/2764.cfm on November 20, 2007.

24. Downloaded from Fars News Agency at http://www.farsnews.com/newstext.php?nn=8705200775 on August 18, 2008.

2　Iran/U.S. Political History

1. Jeb Sharp, "The US and Iran Part I—The 1953 Coup," October 25, 2004, downloaded from www.theworld.org/?1=node/3566 on July 17, 2008.

2. Mostafa Elm, *Oil, Power, and Principle: Iran's Oil Nationalization and Its Aftermath* (Syracuse, NY: Syracuse University Press, 1992) pp. 7–10.
3. Stephen Kinzer, *All the Shah's Men* (Hoboken, NJ: Wiley, 2003) p. np.
4. Donald Wilber, *Clandestine Service History: Overthrow of Premier Mossadeq of Iran: November 1952-August 1953* (Washington, DC: CIA, 1954), p. iii.
5. Mark Gairowski and Malcom Byme *Mohammad Mossadeq and the 1953 Coup in Iran* (Syracuse, NY: Syracuse University Press, 2004), p. 231.
6. Sharp, np.
7. Wilber, pp. iii–iv.
8. Wilber, pp. vii–ix.
9. Stephen Kinzer, "The US and Iran Part I—The 1953 Coup," np.
10. Wilber, pp. xi–xiii.
11. "The Secret CIA History of the Iran Coup, 1953," *National Security Archive: Electronic Briefing Book No. 28* downloaded from www.gwu.edu/~nsarchiv/NSAEBB/NSAEBB28/index.html.
12. Digital History, "The Past Three Decades: Years of Crisis—Years of Triumph: No Islands of Stability," *Digital History,* 2006, downloaded from http://www.digitalhistory.uh.edu/database/article_display.cfm?HHID=403 on August 27, 2008.
13. "The US and Iran Part III—The Hostage Crisis," *TheWorld.org*, October 27, 2004, downloaded from www.theworld.org/?q=node/3569 on July 14, 2008.
14. Ali Ansari, *Confronting Iran: The Failure of American Foreign Policy and the Next Great Crisis in the Middle East* (New York: Basic Books, 2006), pp. 39–40.
15. Ansari, *Confronting Iran*, pp. 55–66.
16. Gary Sick, "The US and Iran Part II—The Shah and the Revolution," October 26, 2004, downloaded from www.theworld.org/?q=node/3566 on July 17, 2008.
17. Ansari, *Confronting Iran*, pp. 76–79.
18. Ansari, *Confronting Iran*, pp. 77–81.
19. Ansari, *Confronting Iran*, p. 81.
20. Transcript of "Interview with Jimmy Carter," *The Situation Room* October 10, 2007, downloaded from http://transcripts.cnn.com/TRANSCRIPTS/0710/10/sitroom.02.html on July 14, 2008.
21. Ansari, *Confronting Iran*, p. 89.
22. Ansari, *Confronting Iran*, p. 90.
23. Shaul Bakhash, "The US and Iran Part III—The Hostage Crisis," October 27, 2004, downloaded from www.theworld.org/?q=node/3566 on July 17, 2007.
24. Roger Howard, *Iran Oil* (London: I. B. Tauris, 2007), p. 10.
25. Ansari, *Confronting Iran*, p. 99.
26. "1979: Mob Destroys US Embassy in Pakistan," *BBC On This Day: 21 November*, downloaded from http://news.bbc.co.uk/onthisday/hi/dates/stories/november/21/newsid_4187000/4187184.stm on September 1, 2008.
27. The term Shi'a is an Arabic word that defines the group of Muslims who stayed true to Ali as an Imam and not a Caliph, the son-in-law and cousin

of the prophet Mohammad, believing that the three caliphs who preceded Ali (Abu Bakr, Umar, and Uthman) were not intended by Mohammad to be his immediate successors. Their belief is the starting phase of the emergence of a faction in Islam that believes in 12 Imams, the last of which disappeared in childhood and is expected to return...the 13th Imam, who Ahmadinejad has sometimes claimed to be. Shi'ite is the plural form of Shi'a. This form of writing emerged because of the ending letter of h (pronounced T) in Shi'a in Arabic, thus is a translation issue. Shi'ite means being related to Shi'a.

28. "Iran-Iraq War (1980–1989)," *Global Security*, downloaded from www. globalsecurity.org/military/world/war/iran-iraq.htm on July 9, 2008.

29. "Iran Iraq War 1980–1988," *Iran Chamber Society*, downloaded from http:// www.iranchamber.com/history/iran_iraq_war/iran_iraq_war1.php on July 7, 2007.

30. Ansari, *Confronting Iran*, p. 98.

31. Shaul Bakhash, "The Troubled Relationship: Iran and Iraq, 1930–80," in Lawrence Potter and Gary Sick (eds.), *Iran, Iraq, and the Legacies of War* (New York: Palgrave Macmillan, 2004), p. 22.

32. Nathan Gonzalez, *Engaging Iran* (Westport, CT: Praeger Security International, 2007), pp. 97–98.

33. Ray Takeyh, "Iran's New Iraq," *Middle East Journal*, Winter 2008, Vol. 62, No. 1, p. 19.

34. *Global Security*.

35. *Iran Chamber Society*.

36. Joost Hiltermann, "Outsiders as Enablers: Consequences and Lessons from International Silence on Iraq's Use of Chemical Weapons during the Iran-Iraq War," in Lawrence Potter and Gary Sick (eds.), *Iran, Iraq, and the Legacies of War* (New York: Palgrave Macmillan, 2004), pp. 151–166.

37. Nasser Hadian, "The US and Iran Part IV—Hostile Relations," October 28, 2004, downloaded from www.theworld.org/?q=node/3566 on July 17, 2008, np.

38. Ansari, *Confronting Iran*, p. 100

39. *Global Security*.

40. Committee to Investigate Covert Arms Transactions with Iran, *Report of the Congressional Committees Investigating the Iran-Contra Affair* (Washington, DC: U.S. Government Printing Office, 1987), pp. 155–281.

41. Further Continuing Appropriations Act, Pub. L. No. 97–377, §793, 96 Stat. 1830, 1865 (1982).

42. Stephen Engelberg, "downing of Fight 655: Questions Keep Coming," *The New York Times*, July 11, 1988, downloaded from http://query.nytimes.com/ gst/fullpage.html?res=940DE1DD103EF932A25754C0A96E948260&scp= 39&sq=USS+vincennes&st=nyt on September 2, 2008.

43. Shapour Ghasemi, "Shooting down Iran Air Flight 655 [IRR655]" *Iran Chamber: History of Iran*, 2004, downloaded from www.iranchamber.com/history/articles/shootingdown_iranair-flight655.php on September 2, 2008, p. 7.

44. Ghasemi, p. 4.

45. Geoffrey Kemp, "Iran and Iraq: The Shia Connection, Soft Power, and the Nuclear Factor," *United States Institute of Peace Special Report*, November 2005, p. 7.

46. Robert Litwak, *Rogue States and US Foreign Policy* (Washington, DC: Woodrow Wilson Center Press, 2000), pp. 158–198.

47. Hossein Alikhani, *Sanctioning Iran: Anatomy of a Failed Policy* (London: I. B. Tauris, 2000), p. 398.

48. Sick, p. 10.

49. Sick, p. 12.

50. Alikhani, *Sanctioning Iran*, p. 398.

51. Alikhani, *Sanctioning Iran*, p. 398.

52. Ansari, *Confronting Iran*, p. 181.

53. David Hastings Dunn, " 'Real Men Want to go to Tehran': Bush, Pre-emption and the Iranian Nuclear Challenge," *International Affairs*, Vol. 83, No. 1, 2007, p. 22.

54. Barbara Starr and Elaine Quijano, "Iran Gen.: Our Finger Is Always on the Trigger," *CNN.com* downloaded from www.cnn.com/2008/WORLD/meast/07/09/iran.missiles/index.html on July 9, 2008.

55. "Johnny Depp: US Is Like a Stupid Puppy," *CNN.com*, September 2003, downloaded from www.cnn.com/2003/SHOWBIZ/Movies/09/03/depp.us.reax.reut on August 18, 2008.

56. Michael Slackman, "Talks Signal Mideast Shift," *New York Times*, July 18, 2008, A1, and Elaine Sciolino and Sheryl Gay Stolberg, "US Considers Opening a Diplomatic Post in Iran," *The New York Times*, July 18, 2008, A11.

57. Elaine Sciolino, "Nuclear Talks with Iran end in a Deadlock," *The New York Times*, July 20, 2008, A1.

58. R. Nicholas Burns, Under Secretary for Political Affairs, "Michael Stein Address on US Middle East Policy at The Washington Institute's Annual Soref Symposium," May 11, 2006, downloaded from www.state.gov/p/us/rm/2006/68321.htm on March 4, 2008, p. 2.

59. Dennis Ross, "Diplomatic Strategies for Dealing with Iran," *CNAS Iran Strategy Working Paper #1*, June 2008, p. 19.

60. Ross, p. 20.

61. Dalia Dassa Kaye, *Talking to the Enemy: Track Two Diplomacy in the Middle East and South Asia* (Santa Monica, CA: RAND Corporation, 2007), pp. xi–xiv.

62. Kenneth Timmerman, "Iran Back Channel Backfires," *Insight on the News— World*, June 20, 2003, downloaded from www.kentimmerman.com/news/2003_06_20irantalks.htm on August 25, 2008.

63. Marc Perelman, "Book Reveals Details of Iran's Diplomatic Outreach to Israel," *Forward.com*, August 8, 2007, downloaded from www.forward.com/articles/11350/ on August 25, 2008.

64. Dassa Kaye, p. xii.

65. Dassa Kaye, pp. xiii–xiv.

66. Secretary of State Madeleine Albright, "Press Briefing on American-Iranian Relations," March 17, 2000, as released by the Office of the Spokesman, U.S. Department of State, downloaded from www.fas.org/news/iran/2000/000317a.htm on August 11, 2008.

67. James A. Baker, III, and Lee H. Hamilton, *The Iran Study Group Report* (New York: Vintage Books, 2006), p. 51 as related in Gawdat Bahgat, "Iran and the United States: The Emerging Security Paradigm in the Middle East," *Parameters*, Summer 2007, p. 17.

68. John Limbert, "Negotiating with the Islamic Republic of Iran: Raising the Chances for Success—Fifteen Points to Remember," *United States Institute of Peace: Special Report*, January 2008, Special Report 199, p. 1.

69. Limbert, p. 6.

3   MODERN IRANIAN POLITICS

1. Gholam-Abbas Tavassoli, "Islamic Movements in Iran," *WeltTrends*, Vol. 44, No. 12, 2004, p. 38.

2. Alexander Aghayan, "Leadership," *Iran Yearbook*, April 27, 2007, downloaded from www.aghayan.com/faghih.htm on August 26, 2008.

3. Kenneth Timmerman, "Iran's Sparring Ayatollahs," *The Wall Street Journal Interactive Edition*, December 9, 1997, downloaded from http://web.payk.net/mailingLists/iran-news/html/1997/msg01778.html on August 26, 2008.

4. Heidar Ali Balouji, "The Process of National Security and Decision Making in Iran: The Signing of the Additional Protocol," in Shannon Kile (ed.), *Europe and Iran: Perspectives on Non-Proliferation* (Solna, Sweden: Oxford University Press for SIPRI, 2005), p. 81.

5. Majlis Web site, August 26, 2008, downloaded from http://mellat.majlis.ir/archive/1382/05/12/newsdiplomatic.htm on August 26, 2008, translated from Farsi by an author.

6. Ali Ansari, "Iran under Ahmadinejad," *Adelphi Papers*, Vol. 47, No. 393, pp. 23–24.

7. Ansari, "Iran under Ahmadinejad," p. 12.

8. Ansari, "Iran under Ahmadinejad," p. 17

9. Ansari, "Iran under Ahmadinejad," p. 46.

10. Ken Ballen, "What Iranians Really Think," *The Wall Street Journal Online*, July 11, 2007, p. A14.

11. Ansari, "Iran under Ahmadinejad," p. 28.

12. "Iran Loser Blasts 'Illegal' Poll," *BBC News*, June 25, 2005 downloaded from www.news.bbc.co.uk/1/hi/world/middle_east/4622955.stm.

13. Ansari, "Iran under Ahmadinejad," p. 41.

14. Shayerah Ilias, "Iran's Economy," *CRS Report for Congress*, June 12, 2008, pp. 5–8.

15. Gonzalez, pp. 96–97.

16. Ansari, "Confronting Iran," p. 70.

17. Ansari, "Iran under Ahmadinejad," p. 80.

18. Ansari, "Iran under Ahmadinejad," p. 45.

19. Ilias, p. 15.

20. Ilias, p. 3.

21. Paul Riflin, "Iran's Energy Vulnerability," *The Middle East Review of International Affairs*, Vol. 10, No. 4, December 2006, p. 1.
22. Riflin, p. 9.
23. Roger Howard, *Iran Oil* (London: I. B. Tauris, 2007), pp. 134–135.
24. Riflin, p. 1.
25. Howard, p. 49.
26. Howard, p. 70.
27. Bill Samii, "Iran: New Foreign Policy Council Could Curtail Ahmadinejad's Power," *Radio Free Europe/Radio Liberty*, June 29, 2006 as cited in Gawdat Bahgat, "Iran and the United States: The Emerging Security Paradigm in the Middle East," *Parameters*, Summer 2007, p. 7.
28. Balouji, p. 82.
29. Jalil Roshandel, "No Real Change in Policy," *Bitterlemons-international.org* Middle East Roundtable Online Forum, Vol. 25, No. 4, July 6, 2006, downloaded from www.bitterlemons-international.org/inside.php?id=567.
30. "Ahmadinejad: The Big Powers are Going Down," *CNN.com*, downloaded on July 29, 2008.
31. Karim Sadjapour, "Iran's Political/Nuclear Ambitions and US Policy Options." *International Crisis Group*, May 18, 2006, downloaded from www.crisisgroup.org/home/index.cfm?id=4143&1=1 on July 18, 2008.
32. Wilfried Buchta, *Who Rules Iran? The Structure of Power in the Islamic Republic* (Washington, DC: Washington Institute for Near East Policy and the Konrad Adenauer Stiftung, 2000), p. 67.
33. Kenneth Katzman, *The Warriors of Islam: Iran's Revolutionary Guard* (Boulder, CO: Westview Press, 1993), p. 51.
34. Ilias, p. 10.
35. Ilias, pp. 10–12.
36. Anthony Cordesman, *The Military Balance in the Middle East* (Westport, CT: Praeger, 2004), p. 264.
37. Anthony Cordesman and Khalid Al-Rodhan, *Gulf Military Forces in an Era of Asymmetric Wars (Vol. 2)* (Westport, CT: Praeger, 2006, np.
38. U.S. Department of State, Office of the Coordinator for Counterterrorism, "Terrorist Safe-Havens: Strategies, Tactics, and Tools for Disrupting or Eliminating Safe-Havens," *Country Reports on Terrorism*, April 30, 2008, downloaded from http://www.state.gov/s/ct/rls/crt/2007/104103.htm on July 23, 2008.
39. Cordesman and Al-Rodhan, np.
40. Gonzalez, p. 89.
41. Ilias, p. 9.
42. "Report: Iranian Supreme Leader Backs Ahmadinejad's Second Term," *Xinhuanet.com*, August 25, 2008, downloaded from http://news.xinhuanet.com/english/2008–08/25/content_9709661.htm on August 25, 2008.
43. The Stanley Foundation, "Getting through the Next Six to Twelve Months with Tehran," *Policy Memo*, August 15, 2008, downloaded from www.stanleyfoundation.org on August 18, 2008.

44. The Stanley Foundation.
45. Greg Morsbach, "Chavez Tour Piques US Interest," *BBC News*, July 24, 2006, downloaded from http://news.bbc.co.uk/2/hi/americas/5205770.stm on August 28, 2008.
46. Joseph Carroll, "Public: Iran's Nuclear Program Poses Threat to U.S.," *Gallup Poll Report,* December 20, 2007. www.gallup.com/poll/103402/Public-Irans-Nuclear-Program-Poses-Threat-US.aspx, np.
47. Lydia Saad, "Americans Want a Restrained Iran Strategy," *Gallup Poll Report*, November 6, 2007.
48. Vali Nasr, "The Implications of Military Confrontations with Iran," *CNAS Iran Strategy Working Paper #2*, June 2008, p. 3.
49. Daniel Dombey and Stephanie Kirchgaessner, "Fresh Ways of Turning the Screw on Iran," *Financial Times*, October 22, 2007, as quoted in Ilias, p. 34.
50. U.S. Department of State, "International Religious Freedom Report: Iran," downloaded from www.state.gov/p/nea/ci/75227.htm on March 4, 2008.
51. U.S. Department of State, "Trafficking in Persons Report: Iran (Tier 3)" downloaded from www.state.gov/p/nea/ci/75147.htm on March 4, 2008.
52. U.S. Department of State, "International Narcotics Control Strategy Report," downloaded from www.state.gov/p/nea/ci/82330.htm on March 4, 2008.
53. Ilias, pp. 10–12.
54. Hormoz Rashidi, "Amnesty International Condemns Iran for Youth Execution," National Iranian Council Web site, August 21, 2008, downloaded from www.niacouncil.org/index.php?option=com)content&task=view &id=1202&Itemid=2 on August 21, 2008.
55. U.S. Department of State, "Country Report on Human Rights Practices," downloaded from www.state.gov/p/nea/ci/82004.htm downloaded on March 4, 2008.
56. Elham Gheytanchi and Babak Rahmi, "Tehran's Web of Silence," *The New York Times*, August 24, 2008.
57. Remarks by McCain to CPAC on February 7, 2008, downloaded from http://www.johnmccain.com/Informing/News/Speeches/b639ae8b-5a9f-41d5-88a7–874cbefa2c40.htm on August 11, 2008.
58. John Isaacs, "In a Nutshell: McCain vs. Obama on National Security," July 1, 2008 downloaded from the Center for Arms Control and Non-Proliferation Web site at: http://www.armscontrolcenter.org/policy/iraq/articles/070108_mccain_obama_national_security/ on August 11, 2008, p. 2.
59. Isaacs, p. 2.
60. "The Democrats' First 2008 Debate" *The New York Times*, April 27, 2007, downloaded from http://www.nytimes.com/2007/04/27/us/politics/27debate_transcript.html?_r=1&oref=slogin on August 11, 2008.
61. Iran Policy Committee, "US Policy Options for Iran," February 10, 2005.
62. David Hastings Dunn, "'Real Men Want to Go to Tehran': Bush, Preemption and the Iranian Nuclear Challenge," *International Affairs*, 2007, Vol. 83, No. 1, p. 34.
63. The Stanley Foundation.
64. Dennis Ross, "Diplomatic Strategies for Dealing with Iran," *CNAS Iran Strategy Working Paper #1*, June 2008, pp. 14–17.

4   IRAN, THE UNITED STATES, AND
MIDDLE EAST STABILITY

1. Stephen Kinzer, "The US and Iran Part I—The 1953 Coup," October 25, 2004, downloaded from www.theworld.org/?q=node/3566 on July 17, 2008.
2. U.S. Central Intelligence Agency, "Iran," *World Fact Book*, 2008, downloaded from www.cia.gov/library/publications/the-world-factbook/print/ir.html on 6/30/2008 on June 30, 2008.
3. This last from Nathan Gonzalez, *Engaging Iran* (Westport, CT: Praeger Security International, 2007), pp. 103–104.
4. Anthony Cordesman and Khalid Al-Rodhan, *Gulf Military Forces in an Era of Asymmetric Wars (Vol. 2)* (Westport, CT: Praeger, 2006), np.
5. Anonymous, "Larijani Raps 'Irresponsible' Comments," *Gulf Daily News Online*, February 24, 2009, downloaded from http://www.gulf-daily-news.com/Story.asp?Article=243864&Sn=BNEW&IssueID=31341 on March 2, 2009.
6. Dalia Dassa Kaye and Frederic Wehrey, "A Nuclear Iran: The Reactions of Neighbors," *Survival*, June 2007, Vol. 49, No. 2, p. 119.
7. Firas Hassan, Magnus Normark, and Magnus Norell, "Security Policy Consequences for the Gulf Region," in John Rydqvist and Kristina Zetterlund (eds.), *Consequences of Military Actions against Iran: Final Report* (Stockholm: Swedish Defense Research Agency, 2008), pp. 61–63.
8. Robert Lowe and Claire Spencer, *Iran, Its Neighbors and the Regional Crises: A Middle East Programme Report* (London: Chatham House, 2006), pp. 11–12.
9. Gonzalez, p. 95.
10. Sharam Chubin, *Iran's Nuclear Ambitions* (Washington, DC: Carnegie Endowment for International Peace, 2006), p. 15.
11. Gonzalez, p. 87.
12. Vali Nasr, "The Implications of Military Confrontations with Iran," *CNAS Iran Strategy Working Paper #2*, June 2008, p. 4.
13. Gonzalez, p. 105.
14. Dennis Ross, "Diplomatic Strategies for Dealing with Iran," *CNAS Iran Strategy Working Paper #1*, June 2008, p. 4.
15. Mehran Kamrava, "The United States and Iran: A Dangerous but Contained Rivalry," *The Middle East Institute Policy Brief*, No. 9, 2008, p. 1.
16. Kamrava, p. 2.
17. Gawdat Bahgat, "Iran and the United States: The Emerging Security Paradigm in the Middle East," *Parameters*, Summer 2007, p. 13.
18. Yossi Klein Halevi, "Israel, Iran Practically at War," *CBS News*, March 12, 2008, downloaded from www.cbsnews.com/stories/2008/03/12/opinion/printable3930010.shtml on August 25, 2008, p. 1.
19. Halevi, p. 1.
20. Halevi, p. 2.
21. Emily Landau, "Regional Reactions and Responses," *bitterlemons-international.org*, March 14, 2007, downloaded from www.bitterlemons-international.org/pervious.php?opt=1&id=172 on August 20, 2008.

22. Landau.
23. Jalil Roshandel, "New Wave of Nuclear Development," *bitterlemons-international.org*, March 14, 2007, downloaded from www.bitterlemons-international.org/pervious.php?opt=1&id=172 on August 20, 2008.
24. Roshandel, "New Wave of Nuclear Development."
25. Bernard Gwertzman, "Kissinger: Don't Exclude Military Action against Iran if Negotiations Fail," *Council on Foreign Relations Interview*, July 14, 2005, downloaded from www.cfr.org/publication/8255/kissinger.html on September 2, 2008.
26. Yossef Bodansky, "Pakistan's Islamic Bomb," *Freeman Center for Strategic Studies*, July 1998, downloaded from www.freeman.org/m_online/jul98/bodansky.htm on August 20, 2008.
27. Bodansky.
28. Roshandel, "New Wave of Nuclear Development."
29. John Rydqvist and Kristina Zetterlund (eds.), *Consequences of Military Actions against Iran* (Stockholm: Swedish Defense Research Agency, 2008), p. 10.
30. Vali Nasr, "The Implications of Military Confrontations with Iran," *CNAS Iran Strategy Working Paper #2*, June 2008, pp. 17–19.
31. Kamrava, p. 7, citing *ABC News* blog at http://blogs.abcnews.com/theblotter/2007/05/bush_authorizes.html and Seymour Hersh, "Preparing the Battlefield," *The New Yorker*, July 7, 2008 downloaded from <http://www.newyorker.com/reporting/2008/07/07/080707fa_fact_hersh on 6/30/2008>, np.
32. Hersh, np.
33. Ray Takeyh, "Iran's New Iraq," *Middle East Journal*, Vol. 62, No. 1, Winter 2008, pp. 13–14.
34. Takeyh, p. 20.
35. Takeyh, p. 26.
36. Takeyh, "Iran's New Iraq," p. 23.
37. See, for example, Takeyh, "Iran's New Iraq," p. 24 and Geoffrey Kemp, "Iran and Iraq: The Shia Connection, Soft Power, and the Nuclear Factor," *United States Institute of Peace Special Report*, November 2005, p. 3.
38. Takeyh, "Iran's New Iraq," p. 23.
39. Ray Takeyh, "Iran's Iraq Policy," *Payvand's Iran News…*, May 5, 2004, downloaded from www.payvand.com/news/04/may/1030.html on August 21, 2008, p. 2 of 3.
40. Takeyh, "Iran's New Iraq," p. 25.
41. Takeyh, "Iran's Iraq Policy," p. 1 of 3.
42. Takeyh, "Iran's Iraq Policy," p. 1 of 3.
43. Lionel Beehner and Greg Bruno, "Iran's Involvement in Iraq," *CFR Backgrounder,* March 3, 2008, downloaded from www.cfr.org/publication/12521/ on August 21, 2008.
44. The Dawa party is comprised of primarily Shi'ite intellectuals.
45. The SCIRI party started in Iran during the Iran-Iraq War. It has a military branch (Badr Brigade) and continues to receive support from Iran in the form of training, funding, weapons, and intelligence.
46. Beehner and Bruno.

47. Ted Galen Carpenter, "Iran's Influence in Iraq," *CATO Institute*, March 10, 2008, downloaded from www.cato.org/pub_display.php?pub_id=9258 on August 21, 2008.
48. Beehner and Bruno.
49. Kemp, p. 10.
50. Beehner and Bruno; and Kemp, p. 9.
51. Kemp, p. 8.
52. Hassan, Normark, and Norell, p. 53.
53. Takeyh, "Iran's New Iraq," p. 26.
54. Takeyh, "Iran's New Iraq," *Middle East Journal*, Vol. 62, No. 1, Winter 2008, p. 24.
55. Takeyh, "Iran's New Iraq," p. 24.
56. Beehner and Bruno.
57. Takeyh, "Iran's New Iraq," p. 14.
58. Takeyh, "Iran's New Iraq," p. 22.
59. Beehner and Bruno; and "Baghdad Forms a Committee to Evict MKO Terrorist Group from Iraq," *Iranian Students News Agency*, August 20, 2008, downloaded from http://www.isna.ir/ISNA/NewsView.aspx?ID=News-1183613&Lang=E on August 21, 2008.
60. Kemp, p. 5.
61. According to the U.S. State Department (*Country Reports on Terrorism 2007* [Washington, DC: U.S. Department of State, 2008], p. 292–294) among the other names for the MKO are: Mujahadin-e Khalq (MEK—Iranian government's name for the group); Sazman-e Mojahedin-e Khalq-e Iran; National Liberation Army of Iran (NLA); Organization of the People's Holy Warriors of Iran; People's Mujahedine Organization of Iran (PMOI); Muslim Iranian Student's Society; National Council of Resistance (NCR); and National Council of Resistance of Iran (NCRI).
62. U.S. Department of State, *Country Reports on Terrorism 2007*, p. 292.
63. U.S. Department of State, *Country Reports on Terrorism 2007*, p. 292.
64. Federation of American Scientists, "Mujahedeen-e Khalq (MEK)," *FAS Intelligence Resource Program* downloaded from www.fas.org/irp/world/para/mek.htm on August 21, 2008.
65. U.S. Department of State, *Country Reports on Terrorism 2007*, p. 292.
66. U.S. Department of State, *Country Reports on Terrorism 2007*, p. 293.
67. U.S. Department of State, *Country Reports on Terrorism 2007*, p. 294.
68. U.S. Department of State, *Country Reports on Terrorism 2007*, p. 294.
69. Federation of American Scientists.
70. Amin Tarzi and Darby Parliament, "Missile Messages: Iran Strikes MKO Bases in Iraq," *The Nonproliferation Review,* Summer 2001, pp. 126, 133.
71. Tarzi and Parliament, p. 127.
72. Massoud Khodabandeh, "Bulgarians to Dismantle Iranian Terrorist Group MKO in Iraq," *Terrorism Monitor*, Vol. 4, No. 3, February 9, 2006, p. 1.
73. Khodabandeh, p. 1.

74. Islamic Republic News Agency, "Hakim: Americans Prevent MKO Expulsion from Iraq," *Global Security*, downloaded from www.globalsecurity.org/wmd/library/news/iraq/2007/11/iras-071111-irna01.htm on August 21, 2008, p. 1.

75. Islamic Republic News Agency, p. 1.

76. "Iraqi Cabinet Wants MKO Expulsion from Iraqi Territory," *ArabicNews.com*, June 23, 2008, downloaded from www.arabicnews.com/ansub/Daily/Day/080623/2008062308.html on August 21, 2008.

77. "Special Unit Formed to Deal with MKO—Minister," *Iraq Updates*, August 8, 2008, downloaded from www.iraqupdates.com/scr/preview.php?article =34906 on August 21, 2008 and "MKO has 6 Months to Leave Iraq," *PressTV*, August 21, 2008, downloaded from www.presstv.ir/pop/print.aspx?id=67145 on August 21, 2008.

78. Ingmar Oldbert, "Iran from the Russian Perspective," in John Rydqvist and Kristina Zetterlund (eds.), *Consequences of Military Actions against Iran: Final Report* (Stockholm: Swedish Defense Research Agency, 2008), p. 80.

79. Robert Freedman, "Russian-Iranian Relations in the 1990s," *Middle East Review of International Affairs*, Vol. 4, No. 2, June 2000, p. 6.

80. Freedman, p. 1.

81. Oldbert, p. 84.

82. Anonymous, "Iran Tests Its First Nuclear Power Plant," *CNN.com*, February 25, 2009, downloaded from http://www.cnn.com/2009/WORLD/meast/02/25/iran.nuclear.plant/index.html?iref=newssearch on February 26, 2009.

83. Oldbert, pp. 80–81.

84. Freedman, p. 7.

85. Freedman, p. 5.

86. Rydqvist and Zetterlund, p. 10.

87. Oldbert, p. 93.

88. Modified from Barry Rubin, "China's Middle East Strategy," *Middle East Review of International Affairs*, Vol. 3, No. 1, March 1999, p. 3.

89. Richard Russell, "China's WMD Foot in the Greater Middle East's Door," *Middle East Review of International Affairs*, Vol. 9, No. 3, September 2005, p. 111.

90. Russell, "China's WMD Foot," p. 111.

91. Russell, "China's WMD Foot," p. 113.

92. Russell, "China's WMD Foot," p. 116.

93. Rubin, "China's Middle East Strategy," p. 48.

94. Russell, "China's WMD Foot," p. 116.

95. "Iran's Leader to Attend Shanghai Cooperation Organization Summit," Russian News & Information Agency, NOVOSTI, July 8, 2008, downloaded from http://en.rian.ru/world/20080807/115864571-print.html on August 21, 2008.

96. "Iran: Plans to Join Shanghai Group Seen as Bold Geopolitical Stroke," *IPR Strategic Business Information Database*, May 2006, downloaded from http://findarticles.com/p/articles/mi_hb6465/is_200605/ai_n25725173 on August 21, 2008.

97. "Europeans Eager to Improve Trade Relations with Iran," *Payvand's Iran News*, August 9, 2005, downloaded from www.payvand.com/news/05/aug/1099.html on August 22, 2008.

98. See, for example, Adam Tarock, "Iran-Western Europe Relations on the Mend," *British Journal of Middle Eastern Studies*, Vol. 23, No. 1, May 1999, p. 61.

99. Aylin Unver Noi, "Iran's Nuclear Programme: The EU Approach to Iran in Comparison to the US' Approach," *Perceptions*, Spring 2005, p. 84.

100. Unver Noi, p. 87.

101. Unver Noi, p. 88.

102. Nawab Khan, "EU-Iran Relations in the Last Two Years," *Payvand's Iran News...*, November 23, 2003, downloaded from www.payvand.com/news/03/nov/1139.html on August 26, 2008.

103. Khan.

104. Khan.

105. Abbas Maleki, "Iran-Pakistan-India Pipeline: Is It a Peace Pipeline," *MIT Center for International Studies*, September 2007, pp. 1–2.

106. Maleki, p. 2.

107. Harsh Pant, "India and Iran: An 'Axis' in the Making," *Asian Survey*, May-June 2004, Vol. 44, No. 3, pp. 369–383.

108. Reza Sayah and Saeed Ahmed, "Musharraf Says He Will Resign Pakistan Presidency," *CNN.com*, August 18, 2008, downloaded from www.cnn.com/2008/WORLD/asiapcf/08/18/musharraf.address/index.html on August 18, 2008. Anonymous, "Profile: Asif Ali Zardari," *BBC News* September 6, 2008, downloaded from http://news.bbc.co.uk/2/hi/south_asia/4032997.stm on February 26, 2009.

109. Maleki, p. 2.

110. A record of the recent IAEA actions against Iran is available at http://www.iaea.org/NewsCenter/Focus/IaeaIran/iran_timeline3.shtml on September 1, 2008.

111. Samuel Huntington, *Clash of Civilizations and the Remaking of World Order* (New York: Simon & Schuster, 1997), pp. 207–245.

112. Zbigniew Brzeninski and Robert Gates, Co-chairs, Suzanne Maloney, Project Director, "Report of an Independent Task Force for the Council on Foreign Relations," *Iran: Time for a New Approach* (New York: Council on Foreign Relations, 2004), p. 3.

113. Brzeninski, Gates, and Maloney, pp. 4–5.

5   Iran: State Sponsor of Terror?

1. National Commission on Terrorist Attacks upon the United States, *The 9/11 Commission Report: Final Report of the National Commission on Terrorist Attacks upon the United States* (New York: W.W. Norton, 2004) p. 75.

2. *The 9/11 Commission Report*, p. 60.

3. Roger Howard, *Iran Oil* (London: I. B. Tauris, 2007), p. 23.

4. Douglas Frantz and James Risen, "A Nation Challenged: Terrorism; A Secret Iran-Arafat Connection Is Seen Fueling the Mideast Fire," *The New York Times*, March 24, 2002, downloaded from http://query.nytimes.com/gst/fullpage.html?res=9D02E0DD143BF937A15750C0A9649C8B63&sec=&spon=&pagewanted=all on August 18, 2008.

5. Damien McElroy, "Iran Vows to Pay for Gaza Aid as Children Return to UN Schools," *Telegraph.co.uk* January 24, 2009 http://www.telegraph.co.uk/news/worldnews/middleeast/israel/4330561/Iran-vows-to-pay-for-gaza-aid-as-children-return-to-UN-schools accessed on February 26, 2009.

6. Anonymous, "US to Donate '$900m in Gaza Aid'" *BBC News* February 24, 2009 downloaded from http://news.bbc.co.uk/2/hi/middle_east/7907483.stm on February 26, 2009.

7. Daniel Byman, "Iran, Terrorism, and Weapons of Mass Destruction," *Studies in Conflict & Terrorism*, 2008, Vol. 31, p. 172.

8. "Hizballah (Party of God)," *GlobalSecurity.Org*, July 16, 2006, downloaded from www.globalsecurity.org/military/world/para/hizballah.htm on April 19, 2007.

9. As quoted in Ely Karmon, *"Fight on All Fronts": Hizballah, the War on Terror, and the War in Iraq* (Washington, DC: Washington Institute for Near East Policy, 2003), p. 8.

10. Council on Foreign Relations, "Hezbollah," downloaded from http://www.cfr.org/publication/9155/ on July 18, 2008.

11. "Hezbollah," *MIPT Terrorism Knowledge Base*, February 1, 2007 Memorial Institute for the Prevention of Terrorism, downloaded from www.tkb.org/Group.jsp?groupID=3101 on February 10, 2007.

12. Sonja Pace, "Hezbollah Wary; Ponders New Political Role in Lebanon," *Payvand's Iran News*, April 6, 2005, downloaded from www.payvand.com/news/05/apr/1033.htm on April 19, 2007.

13. Council on Foreign Relations, "Hezbollah," July 17, 2006, downloaded from www.cfr.org/publication/9155/#7 on April 19, 2007.

14. Mario Loyola, "Land of Cedars and Sorrow," *National Review*, 2007, pp. 34–38.

15. Byman, p. 170.

16. Karmon, p. 4.

17. "Hezbollah as a Strategic Arm of Iran," Intelligence and Terrorism Information Center at the Center for Special Studies. Iranian News Agency, 2006, p. 17.

18. Karmon, p. 4.

19. Geoffrey Kemp, "Iran and Iraq: The Shia Connection, Soft Power, and the Nuclear Factor," *United States Institute of Peace Special Report*, November 2005, pp. 11–12.

20. Byman, 170.

21. Byman, 173.

22. U.S. Department of State, "Chapter 6: Terrorist Groups: HAMAS," *The Terrorist Enemy*, downloaded from http://www.state.gov/documents/organization/45323.pdf on July 23, 2008, pp. 98–99.

23. Council on Foreign Relations, "Backgrounder: Hamas," June 8, 2007, downloaded from www.cfr.org/publication/8968 on July 24, 2008, np.

24. Ami Isseroff, "A History of the Hamas Movement," *MidEastWeb*, nd, downloaded from www.mideastweb.org/hamashistory.htm on July 24, 2008, np.

25. Council on Foreign Relations, "Backgrounder: Hamas."

26. Isseroff.

27. U.S. Department of State, "Terrorist Safe Havens: Strategies, Tactics, Tools for Disrupting or Eliminating Safe Havens," *Country Reports on Terrorism*,

April 30, 2008, downloaded from http://www.state.gov/s/ct/rls/crt/2007/
104103.htm on July 23, 2008, np.

28. "Iran N-Progress Unhindered by Sanctions," *Press TV*, August 15, 2008,
downloaded from http://www.presstv.ir/detail.aspx?id=66660&sectionid=35
1020104 on August 18, 2008.

29. Richard Cowan, "US Senate Panel Approves New Iran Sanctions," *Reuters
Online*, downloaded from http://www.reuters.com/article/latestCrisis/
idUSN17419147 on August 18, 2008.

30. Peter Hirschberg, "Georgia's Israeli Arms Point Russia to Iran," *Asia Times
Online*, August 14, 2008, downloaded from http://www.atimes.com/atimes/
Middle_East/JH14Ak02.html on August 18, 2008.

31. Scott Peterson, "Russian Support for Iran Sanctions at Risk amid Georgia
Rift," *The Christian Science Monitor*, August 14, 2008.

32. *The 9/11 Commission Report*, p. 342.

33. *The 9/11 Commission Report*, pp. 240–241.

34. *The 9/11 Commission Report*, p. 61.

35. *The 9/11 Commission Report*, p. 240.

36. *The 9/11 Commission Report*, p. 61.

37. *The 9/11 Commission Report*, pp. 240–241.

38. *The 9/11 Commission Report*, p. 169.

39. Lawrence Wright, "The Master Plan: For the New Theorists of Jihad, Al
Qaeda Is Just the Beginning," *The New Yorker*, September 11, 2006, downloaded from http://www.newyorker.com/archive/2006/09/11/060911fa_fact3
on August 6, 2008.

40. Matthew Levitt and Michael Jacobson, "Timely Reminder of Iranian Support
for Terrorism," *Policy Watch #1345: The Washington Institute for Near East
Policy*, February 22, 2008, downloaded from www.washingtoninstitute.org/
print.php?template=C05&CID=2721 on August 27, 2008, p. 2.

41. *The 9/11 Commission Report*, p. 60.

42. The authors recognize that there will be some disagreement with their discussing the Iraqi insurgency issue in a chapter on terrorism. It is acknowl-
edged that whether the insurgents are considered terrorists depends on the
definition of terrorism that one is applying. In this case, because the insurgents are sub-state actors engaged in violence against civilians (in some cases)
in an attempt to bring about social or political change and they are allegedly
receiving support from Iran, they were included with the discussion of Iranian
state sponsorship of terrorism. The MKO was discussed in the chapter on
Middle East security. This was due to the fact that they were a threat to Iran
and regional stability rather than being supported by Iran.

43. Thom Shanker and Steven Weisman, "Iran Is Helping Insurgents in Iraq, US
Officials Say," *The New York Times*, September 20, 2004, np.

44. Lolita Baldor, "General: Iran Training Shiite Insurgents," *Washington Post*,
August 23, 2006, np.

45. Yonah Alexander, "Iran's Nuclear Ambitions: By Every Secret Means," *The
New Iranian Leadership* (Westport, CT: Praeger, 2007), np.

46. As quoted in Andrew McCarthy, "Cognitive Dissonance," *National Review
Online*, September 11, 2007, downloaded from http://article.nationalreview.

com/?q=YTQyNjE0MmRlZTk2YTk3OTM1N2RiYmUwN2RiYzUwMm
M= on July 25, 2008.

47. "US Military: Iran Training Assassination Squads," *CNN.com*, August 15, 2008 downloaded from www.cnn.com/2008/WORLD/meast/08/15/iran. death.squads/index.html on August 15, 2008.

48. Shanker and Weisman.

49. Robert Lowe and Claire Spence (eds.), *Iran, Its Neighbors, and the Regional Crises* (London: Chatham House, 2006), downloaded from www.chatham-house.org.uk/pdf/research/mep/Iran0806.pdf, p. 20.

50. International Crisis Group, "Iran in Iraq: How Much Influence," p. 1.

51. Kate Clark, "Iran 'Sending Weapons to Taleban' " *BBC News*, September 15, 2008, downloaded from http://news.bbc.co.uk/go/pr/fr/-/2/hi/south_asia/7616429.stm on September 15, 2008.

52. Byman, p. 169.

53. Byman, pp. 174–175.

54. Kenneth Katzman, "Iran: US Concerns and Policy Responses," *CRS Report for Congress*, Updated August 6, 2007.

55. Farideh Farhi, "Tehran's Reaction to Military Threats," *Informed Comment: Global Affairs*, June 29, 2008 downloaded from http://icga.b.ogspot. com/2008/06/tehrans-reaction-to-military-threats.html on July 1, 2008.

56. David Hastings Dunn, " 'Real Men Want to Go to Tehran': Bush, Pre-emption and the Iranian Nuclear Challenge," *International Affairs*, 2007, Vol. 83, No. 1, pp. 33–34.

57. Dennis Ross, "Diplomatic Strategies for Dealing with Iran," *Center for a New American Iran Strategy Working Paper #1*, June 2008, pp. 12–14.

58. Hossein Alikhani, *Sanctioning Iran: Anatomy of a Failed Policy* (London: I. B. Tauris, 2000), p. 395.

59. Anthony Cordesman and Martin Keliber, *Iran's Military Forces and Warfighting Capabilities* (Westport, CT: Praeger, 2007), p. 20.

60. Kemp, p. 4.

61. "Sanctions May Hurt Iran's Drug War," *MSNBC.com*, June 24, 2008, down-loaded from www.msnbc.msn.com/id/25351006/print/1/displaymode/1098/ on August 19, 2008.

6 IRAN AND NUCLEAR POWER (OR WEAPONS?)

1. Ali Akbar Dareini, "Iran: New Strides in Uranium Enrichment," *Associated Press Online*, August 29, 2008, downloaded from http://www1.irna.ir/en/ news/view/line-203/0808298376181247.htm on August 29, 2008; "Iran Confirms Nuclear Component Production," *CNN.com*, August 29, 2008, downloaded from www.cnn.com/2008/WORLD/meast/08/29/iran.nuclear/ index.html on August 29, 2008; and "Attar: 4,000 Centrifuges Work at Natanz Enrichment Facilities," *Islamic Republic News Agency*, August 29, 2008, downloaded from http://www1.irna.ir/en/news/view/line-203/ 0808298376181247.htm on August 29, 2008.

2. Hussein Hassan, "Iranian Nuclear Sites," *CRS Report for Congress*, November 13, 2006, pp. 2–3.
3. Sanam Vakil, "The Persian Dilemma: Will Iran Go Nuclear," *Current History*, April 2005, p. 186.
4. Firas Hassan, Magnus Normark, and Magnus Norell, "Security Policy Consequences for the Gulf Region," in John Rydqvist and Kristina Zetterlund (eds.), *Consequences of Military Actions against Iran: Final Report* (Stockholm: Swedish Defense Research Agency, 2008), p. 45.
5. Vice President Dick Cheney, "Vice President's Remarks to the World Affairs Council of Dallas/Fort Worth," downloaded from www.whitehouse.gov/news/releases/2007/11/print/20071102.html on November 11, 2007.
6. David Albright and Jacqueline Shire, "A Witches' Brew? Evaluating Iran's Uranium-Enrichment Progress," *Arms Control Today*, November 2007, Vol. 37, No. 9, p. 14.
7. Albright and Shire, p. 6.
8. Center for Public Opinion, Terror Free Tomorrow, "Iranians Continue to Back Compromise, Better Relations with US and West, but Opposition to Developing Nuclear Weapons Drops; Support for Government Economic Policies increases," 2008, p. 4.
9. Ali Ansari, "Iran under Ahmadinejad," *Adelphi Papers*, Vol. 47, No. 393, p. 7.
10. International Atomic Energy Agency, *Treaty on the Non-Proliferation of Nuclear Weapons*, April 22, 1970.
11. International Atomic Energy Agency.
12. "Norway Urges Talks to Settle Iran's Disputed Nuclear Case," *Ettelaat*, June 29, 2007, downloaded from http://www.uni-graz.at/yvonne.schmidt/NAHOST_News_ARCHIVE_2007.html on September 1, 2008.
13. David Hastings Dunn, " 'Real Men Want to go to Tehran': Bush, Pre-emption and the Iranian Nuclear Challenge," *International Affairs*, Vol. 83, No 1, 2007, p. 25.
14. International Atomic Energy Agency.
15. Bengt-Goran Bergstrand, "Appendix 1. Background Data on Iranian Energy Developments," in John Rydqvist and Kristina Zetterlund (eds.), *Consequences of Military Actions against Iran* (Stockholm: Swedish Defense Research Agency, 2008), pp. 163–174.
16. Vakil, pp. 183–184.
17. Shahram Chubin, "Understanding Iran's Nuclear Ambitions," in Patrick Cronin (ed.), *Double Trouble* (Westport, CT: Praeger, 2007), p. np.
18. Dennis Ross, "Diplomatic Strategies for Dealing with Iran," *Center for a New American Iran Strategy Working Paper #1*, June 2008, p. 6.
19. Gawdat Bahgat, "Iran and the United States: The Eemerging Security Paradigm in the Middle East," *Parameters*, Summer 2007, p. 15.
20. Roger Howard, *Iran Oil* (London: I. B. Tauris, 2007), p. 136.
21. See, for example, Martin Walker, "Walker's World: Iran's Baby Bust," *Spacewar.com*, November 19, 2007, downloaded from www.spacewar.com/reports/Walkers_World_Irans_baby_bust_999.html on November 21, 2007, np.

22. See, for example, Anthony Cordesman and Khalid Al-Rodhan, *Gulf Military Forces in an Era of Asymmetric Wars (Vol. 2)* (Westport, CT: Praeger, 2006), np.

23. Farideh Farhi, "IAEA Declares a Gridlock with Iran," *National Iranian American Council Policy Memo*, September 2008, p. 1.

24. Mark Fitzpatrick, "IS Iran's Nuclear Capability Inevitable?" in Patrick Cronin (ed.), *Double Trouble* (Westport, CT: Praeger, 2007), np.

25. Robert Joseph, Under Secretary for Arms Control and International Security, "Iran's Nuclear Program," Statement before the House International Relations Committee, Washington, DC, March 8, 2006, downloaded on March 4, 2008.

26. "Iran Sees 'Positive' Nuclear Talks with US," *CNNOnline.com* downloaded from http://www.cnn.com/2008/WORLD/meast/07/18/iran.talks.ap/index.html on July 18, 2008.

27. Karim Sadjadpour, "Iran's Political/Nuclear Ambitions and US Policy Options," *International Crisis Group* May 18, 2006, downloaded from www.crisisgroup.org/home/index.cfm?id=4143&1=1 on July 21, 2008.

28. Anonymous. "Iran Dismisses Concerns about Nuclear Material," *International Herald Tribune* March 2, 2009, downloaded from http://www.iht.com/articles/ap/2009/03/02/news/ML-Iran-Nuclear.php on March 2, 2009.

29. Jay Solomon, "Adm. Mullen Says Iran Has Material for Bomb," *Wall Street Journal Online*, March 2, 2009, downloaded from http://online.wsj.com/article/SB123593870238604043.html?mod=googlenews_wsj on March 2, 2009.

30. Lionel Beehner, Council on Foreign Relations, "Iran: Nuclear Negotiations," *Backgrounder*, May 16, 2005, downloaded from www.cfr.org/publication/7730/iran.html on August 18, 2008, p. 2 of 4.

31. Beehner, p. 3 of 4.

32. Beehner, p. 3 of 4.

33. "EU to Barter for Civilian Iran Nuclear Programme," *The Guardian*, May 15, 2006, downloaded from www.guardian.co.uk/world/2006/may/15/iran.eu/print on August 19, 2008.

34. Dan Bilefsky, "EU Plans 2nd Package of Incentives to Iran," *International Herald Tribune*, May 15, 2006, downloaded from www.iht.com/articles/2006/05/15/news/union.php on August 19, 2008 and "EU Prepared to Back Civilian Iran Program," *China Daily*, May 16, 2006, downloaded from www.chinadaily.com.cn/world/2006-05/16/content_590756.htm on August 19, 2008.

35. Bilefsky.

36. "EU to Barter for Civilian Iran Nuclear Programme," *The Guardian*, May 15, 2006, downloaded from www.guardian.co.uk/world/2006/may/15/iran.eu/print on August 19, 2008.

37. "EU Prepared to Back Civilian Iran Program."

38. Office of the Spokesman, U.S. Department of State, "P5+1 Updated Incentives Package," June 17, 2008, downloaded from www.state.gov/r/pa/prs/ps/2008/jun.105992.htm on August 19, 2008 and the text of UN Security Council Resolution 1803 (2008).

39. "Report: Incentive Package Includes US Giving Iran Nuke Technology," *USA Today*, June 6, 2008, downloaded from www.usatoday.com/news/world/2006-06-06-iran-nuclear_x.htm on August 19, 2008.

40. "Iran Nuclear Position 'Unchanged,'" *BBC News*, July 5, 2008, downloaded from http://news.bbc.co.uk/go/pr/fr/-/2/hi/middle_east/7491180.stm on August 19, 2008.

41. "EU's Solana Delivers Incentive Package to Iran," *Khaleej Times Online*, June 14, 2008, downloaded from http://www.khaleejtimes.com/DisplayArticleNew.asp?section=middleeast&xfile=data/middleeast/2008/june/middleeast_june274.xml on August 19, 2008.

42. UN Security Council Resolution 1803 (2008) essentially called on Iran to engage in confidence building and submit to the calls of the UN for it to suspend enrichment and imposed sanctions on Iran to which it expected all states to be party.

43. *Tehran Times*, Editor's Note, "Text of 5+1 Package to Iran," *Tehran Times*, June 16, 2008, downloaded from www.campaigniran.org/casmii/index.php?q=node/5295/print on August 19, 2008.

44. Hilary Leila Krieger and Herb Keinon, "US Threatens to Punish Iranian 'Delay,'" *Jerusalem Post, Online Edition*, August 5, 2008, downloaded from http://www.jpost.com/servlet/Satellite?cid=1215331199928&pagename=JPost/JPArticle/ShowFull on August 19, 2008.

45. Office of the Spokesman.

46. John Ward Anderson, "EU Backs Sanctions on Iran, Freezes Bank Assets," *Washington Post*, June 24, 2008, p. A08, downloaded from http://www.washingtonpost.com/wp-dyn/content/article/2008/06/23/AR2008062300491.html on August 19, 2008.

47. Nasser Karimi, "Iran Arrests Former Nuclear Negotiator," *The Boston Globe*, May 3, 2007, downloaded from http://www.boston.com/news/world/middleeast/articles/2007/05/03/iran_arrests_former_nuclear_negotiator/ on August 20, 2008.

48. Robin Wright, "Iran's Nuclear Negotiator Resigns: Ahmadinejad Seen Asserting Control," *WashingtonPost.com*, October 21, 2007, A16, downloaded from http://www.washingtonpost.com/wp-dyn/content/article/2007/10/20/AR2007102001259.html on August 20, 2008.

49. Wright, "Iran's Nuclear Negotiator Resigns."

50. Wright, "Iran's Nuclear Negotiator Resigns"; and "FACTBOX: Iran's New Atomic Negotiator Saeed Jalili," *Reuters Online*, October 23, 2007, downloaded from www.reuters.com/articlePrint?articleId=USL239329720071023 on August 20, 2008.

51. "The Modality for Comprehensive Negotiations," July 31, 2008, downloaded from www.campaigniran.org/casmii/index.php?q=node/5847/print on August 27, 2008.

52. Stanly Johny, "The Unending Iranian Nuclear Crisis," *Indian Institute for Defense Studies & Analyses Strategic Comments*, July 25, 2008, downloaded from www.idsa.in/publications/stratcomments/StanlyJohny250708.htm on August 27, 2008.

53. Edward Thomas, "Iranian Proposal for Negotiations," August 6, 2008.
54. See, for example, Whitney Raas and Austin Long, "'Osirak Redux?' Assessing Israeli Capabilities to Destroy Iranian Nuclear Forces," *International Security,* Spring 2007 for an excellent discussion of the technical aspects of US objections.
55. See, for example, Vakil, p. 183.
56. See, for example, Vakil, p. 184.
57. Sharon Squassoni, "Iran's Nuclear Program: Recent Developments," *CRS Report for Congress,* September 6, 2006, pp. 1–4.
58. Michael Brenner, corresponding with the Gulf Security 2000 blog on June 23, 2008 and Yonah Alexander and Milton Hoenig, "Iran's Nuclear Ambitions: By Every Secret Means," *The New Iranian Leadership* (Westport, CT: Praeger, 2007), pp. 111–175.
59. International Atomic Energy Agency Board of Governors, *Implementation of the NPT Safeguards Agreement and Relevant Provisions of Security Council resolutions 1737 (2006), 1747 (2007) and 1803 (2008) in the Islamic Republic of Iran,* GOV/2008/15, May 26, 2008.
60. Dunn, p. 20.
61. Robin Wright, "Stueart Levey's War," *The New York Times,* November 2, 2008.
62. Farah Stockman, "Bush Effort to Sanction Iran Banks Runs into Resistance," *The Boston Globe,* December 16, 2007.
63. Jeannine Aversa, "US Slaps Sanctions on Iran Bank," *The Boston Globe,* October 22, 2008 and Wright, 2008.
64. Robin Wright, "Stuart Levey's War."
65. U.S. National Intelligence Council, "Iran: Nuclear Intentions and Capabilities," *National Intelligence Estimate,* November 2007, p. 6.
66. Ross, p. 9.
67. Fredrik Lindvall, "United States: Drivers, Background, and the Attack Scenario," in John Rydqvist and Kristina Zetterlund (eds.), *Consequences of Military Actions against Iran: Final Report* (Stockholm: Swedish Defense Research Agency, 2008), p. 31, and Vali Nasr, "The Implications of Military Confrontations with Iran," *CNAS Iran Strategy Working Paper #2,* June 2008, p. 2.
68. Joseph Carroll, "Public: Iran's Nuclear Program Poses Threat to U.S.," *Gallup Poll Report,* December 20, 2007 via http://www.gallup.com/poll/103402/Public-Irans-Nuclear-Program-Poses-Threat-US.aspx, np.
69. Dalia Dassa Kaye and Frederic Wehrey, "A Nuclear Iran: The Reactions of Neighbors," *Survival,* June 1, 2007, Vol. 49, No. 2, p. 112.
70. George Jahn, "EU Drafts Iran Security Council Referral Resolution," *Boston Sun,* January 17, 2006, cited in Dunn, p. 21.
71. Dassa Kaye and Wehrey, p. 112.
72. JPost.com Staff, "Report: Israel Won't Allow a Nuclear Iran," *Jerusalem Post: Online Edition,* August 29, 2008, downloaded from http://www.jpost.com/servlet/Satellite?cid=1219913194872&pagename=JPost/JPArticle/ShowFull on September 1, 2008.

73. Leslie Susser, "US and Israel Diverge on Iranian Weapons," *Jewish Exponent*, August 28, 2008, downloaded from www.jewishexponent.com/article/16945 on September 2, 2008.

74. Stan Goodenough, "US Gearing Up to Attack Iran—Report," *Jerusalem Newswire*, September 1, 2008, downloaded from www.jnewswire.com/articles/print/2517 on September 2, 2008.

75. Michal Zippori and Shirzad Bozorgmehr, "Iran Test-Fires More Long-Range Missiles," *CNN.com* downloaded from www.cnn.com/2008/POLITICS/07/10/us.iran/index.html?iref=newssearch on July 10, 2008.

76. Barbara Starr and Elaine Quijano, "Iran Gen.: Our Finger Is Always on the Trigger," *CNN.com* downloaded from www.cnn.com/2008/WORLD/meast/07/09/iran.missiles/index.html on July 9, 2008.

77. "Iranian Military Warns US, Israel against Attack," *CNN.com* downloaded from www.cnn.com/2008/WORLD/meast/07/08/iran.military.ap/index.html?iref=newssearch on July 9, 2008.

78. Lee Kass, "Iran's Space Program: The Next Genie in a Bottle," *The Middle East Review of International Affairs*, Vol. 10, No. 3, September 2006, pp. 1–4.

79. "Iran Test Fires Rocket, Says State Media," *CNN.com*, August 17, 2008, downloaded from www.cnn.com/2008/WORLD/meast/08/17/iran.rocket/index.html on August 18, 2008.

80. The Stanley Foundation, "Getting through the Next Six to Twelve Months with Tehran," *Policy Memo*, August 15, 2008, downloaded from www.stanleyfoundation.org on August 18, 2008.

81. The Stanley Foundation.

82. The Stanley Foundation.

83. John Rydqvist and Kristina Zetterlund (eds.), *Consequences of Military Actions against Iran* (Stockholm: Swedish Defense Research Agency, 2008), p. 8.

84. Fredrik Lindvall, "Some Consequences from a US Perspective," in John Rydqvist and Kristina Zetterlund (eds.), *Consequences of Military Actions against Iran* (Stockholm: Swedish Defense Research Agency, 2008), pp. 110–111.

85. Lindvall, "Some Consequences," p. 111.

86. Nasr, p. 11.

87. Paul Pillar, "Regional and Global Consequences of US Military Action in Iran," *Statement to the Subcommittee on National Security and Foreign Affairs, Committee on Government Reform and Oversight, House of Representatives*, November 14, 2007, p. 1.

88. Lindvall, "Some Consequences," p. 113.

89. Rydqvist and Zetterlund, p. 9.

90. Raas and Long, p. 1.

91. Seymour Hersh, "Preparing the Battlefield," *The New Yorker*, July 7, 2008 downloaded from <http://www.newyorker.com/reporting/2008/07/07/080707fa_fact_hersh on 6/30/2008>, np.

92. Quoted in Hersh, np.

93. Nicklas Norling, "Domestic Consequences in Iran," in John Rydqvist and Kristina Zetterlund (eds.), *Consequences of Military Actions against Iran: Final Report* (Stockholm: Swedish Defense Research Agency, 2008), p. 68.

94. Christopher Hemmer, "Responding to a Nuclear Iran," *Parameters*, Autumn 2007, p. 44.

95. Bengt-Goran Bergstrand, "US Military Attacks on Iranian Nuclear Facilities and International Law," in John Rydqvist and Kristina Zetterlund (eds.), *Consequences of Military Actions against Iran* (Stockholm: Swedish Defense Research Agency, 2008), p. 138, pp. 147–150.

96. See, for example, The Stanley Foundation; and Hemmer, p. 43.

97. James Fallows, "The Nuclear Power Beside Iraq," *The Atlantic Monthly*, may 2006, p. 32.

98. Robert Lowe and Claire Spencer (eds.), *Iran, Its Neighbors and the Regional Crises: A Middle East Programme Report* (London: Chatham House, 2006), p. 13.

99. Hassan, Normark, and Norell, p. 49.

100. Johannes Malminen, "Iran—Global Economic Consequences of an Attack," in John Rydqvist and Kristina Zetterlund (eds.), *Consequences of Military Actions against Iran* (Stockholm: Swedish Defense Research Agency, 2008), pp. 115 + 118–119.

101. Duration argument from Malminen, p. 125.

102. Rydqvist and Zetterlund, p. 10.

103. Albright and Shire, pp. 10–11 (sidebar).

104. Hassan, Normark, and Norell, p. 45.

105. Yonah Alexander and Milton Hoenig, "Iran's Nuclear Ambitions: By Every Secret Means," in *The New Iranian Leadership* (Westport, CT: Praeger, 2007) citing UN Security Council Resolutions 1747 and 1737.

106. Kamrava, p. 7.

107. U.S. Department of State, "Iran Sanctions and Activities of Privately Funded Actors in Iran: Department of State Establishes Policy to Encourage Non-Governmental Organizations to Apply for an Office of Foreign Assets Control License to Work in Iran," June 23, 2006, downloaded from www.state.gov/g/drl/rls/69445.htm on March 4, 2008.

108. See, for instance, Albright and Shire, p. 14.

109. The Stanley Foundation.

110. Patrick Clawson and Michael Eisenstadt, "Forcing Hard Choices on Tehran: Raising the Costs of Iran's Nuclear Program," *The Washington Institute for Near East Policy: Policy Focus #62*, November 2006, p. v.

111. Clawson and Eisenstadt, p. 3.

112. Joseph.

113. "EU Tightens Iran Nuclear Sanctions," *CNN.com*, August 11, 2008, downloaded from http://www.cnn.com/2008/WORLD/meast/08/08/iran.eu.sanctions.ap/index.html?iref=newssearch on August 11, 2008.

114. Charley Keyes, "US to Join Nuclear Talks with Iran, State Department Says," *CNN.com*, April 8, 2009, downloaded from http://www.cnn.com/2009/POLITICS/04/08/us.iran.nuclear/index.html on April 9, 2009.

115. Anonymous, "Iran President 'Proud' of Nuclear Progress," *CNN.com*, April 9, 2009, downloaded from http://www.cnn.com/2009/WORLD/meast/04/09iran.nuclear/index.html?iref=newssearch on April 13, 2009.

7 Toward a More Comprehensive
U.S. Foreign Policy for Iran

1. As cited in, Joyce Battle (ed.), "Shaking Hands with Saddam Hussein: The US Tilts toward Iraq, 1980–1984," *The National Security Archive*, February 25, 2003, downloaded from www.gwu.edu/~nsarchiv/NSAEBB/NSEBB82/index2.htm on August 25, 2008.

2. "Ahmadinejad Welcomes Obama Change," CNN.com, November 6, 2008, downloaded from www.cnn.com/2008/WORLD/meast/11/06/iran.obama/index.html on November 7, 2008.

3. Barak Obama, "Transcript: 'I'm Going to Confront this Economic Crisis,' Obama Says," *CNN.com*, November 7, 2008, downloaded from www.cnn.com/2008/POLITICS/11/07/obama.conference.transcript/index.html?iref=newssearch on November 10, 2008.

4. Shirzad Bozorgmehr, "Iran Blasts Obama's Nuclear Criticism," *CNN.com*, November 8, 2008, downloaded from http://www.cnn.com/2008/WORLD/meast/11/08/iran.obama/index.html?iref=newssearch on November 10, 2008.

5. Farideh Farhi, "Iran's Majlis Confirms All Three of Ahmadinejad's Ministerial Candidates," *Informed Comment: Global Affairs*, August 5, 2008, downloaded from http://icga.blogspot.com/2008/08/irans-majles-confirms-all-three-of.html on August 22, 2008.

6. Christopher Hemmer, "Responding to a Nuclear Iran," *Parameters*, Autumn 2007, p. 48 and Mehran Kamrava, "The United States and Iran: A Dangerous but Contained Rivalry," *The Middle East Institute Policy Brief*, No. 9, 2008, pp. 8–9.

7. Kamrava, p. 9.

8. "Report: Iranian Supreme Leader Backs Ahmadinejad's Second Term," *Xinhuanet.com*, August 25, 2008, downloaded from http://news.xinhuanet.com/english/2008–08/25/content_9709661.htm on August 25, 2008.

9. The Stanley Foundation, "Getting through the Next Six to Twelve Months with Tehran," *Policy Memo*, August 15, 2008, downloaded from www.stanleyfoundation.org on August 18, 2008.

10. The Stanley Foundation.

11. The Stanley Foundation.

12. The Stanley Foundation.

Glossary of Persian and Arabic Words

Arvand Roud	Arvand River—a contentious river and border region in the Middle East—referred to as the Shatt al-Arab by Arabs
Ayatollah	Sign of God—a high-ranking Shia scholar
Ba'athist Party	A political party that blends Islam and socialism in both Syria and Iraq.
Basij	Militia of the Masses
Bonyads	Foundations—Charitable Islamic foundations that play a significant role in Iranian life
Dawa	An Iraqi political party that was exiled in Iran during Saddam Hussein's reign
Fadayeen Khalgh	Radical Marxist-Leninist group in Iran in the 1970s
Fatwa	Religious edict
Firman Moloukaneh or Firman	Royal decrees
Haram	Forbidden
Imam Jome'h	Friday Prayer Leader
Majlis	Assembly, also general term for Iranian Parliament
Majlis-e Khobregan	Assembly of Experts
Majlis-e Shura-ye Eslami	Formal name of Iranian Parliament
Mujahedin Khalgh	Radical Islamist group in Iran in the 1970s
Ostan	Province

Qods	(also sometimes spelled Quds) Elite arm of IRGC (Also the Persian word for Jerusalem and the al Aqsa mosque.)
Qom	A holy city in Iran, 80 miles from Tehran, famous for its seminary schools, including the one that Khomeini attended
SAVAK	(Sazeman-e Ettela'at va Amniyat-e Keshvar) National Intelligence and Security Organization in Iran
Shatt al-Arab	River of the Arabs—a contentious river and border region in the Middle East—referred to as the Arvand Roud by Iranians
Shura-ye negahban	Guardians Council of the Constitution
Tudeh or Tudeh Party	People's Party (cover name for the Communist Party in Iran)
Ummah	Overarching Islamic Nation

Bibliography

Aghayan, Alexander, "Leadership," Iran Yearbook, April 27, 2007 www.aghayan. com/faghih.htm

Ahmed, Saeed and Reza Sayeh, "Musharraf Says He Will Resign Pakistan Presidency" via *CNN.com*, August 18, 2008 http://www.cnn.com/2008/ WORLD/asiapcf/08/18/musharraf.address/index.html

Albright, David and Jacqeline Shire, "A Witches' Brew? Evaluating Iran's Uranium Enrichment Progress," *Arms Control Today*, November 2007, Vol. 37, No. 9

Albright, Madelaine, "Press Briefing on American Relations," via *U.S. Department of State*, March 17, 2000 http://www.fas.org/news/iran/2000/000317a.htm

Alexander, Yonah and Milton Hoenig, "Iran's Nuclear Ambitions: By Every Secret Means," in *The New Iranian Leadership* (Westport, CT: Praeger, 2007)

Alikhani, Hossein, *Sanctioning Iran: Anatomy of a Failed Policy* (London: I. B. Tauris, 2000)

Al-Rodhan, Khalid and Anthony Cordesman, *Gulf Military Forces in an Era of Asymmetric Wars (Vol. 2)* (Westport, CT: Praeger, 2006)

Anonymous, "1979: Mob Destroys US Embassy in Pakistan," *BBC on This Day: 21 November*, http://news.bbc.co.uk/onthisday/hi/dates/stories/november/21/ newsid_4187000/4187184.stm on September 1, 2008

———, "Ahmadinejad Boasts of Iran's Nuclear Gear," via *United Press International* online, November 7, 2007

———, "Ahmadinejad Welcomes Obama Change," *CNN.com*, November 6, 2008 http://www.cnn.com/2008/WORLD/meast/11/06/iran.obama/index.html

———, "Attar: 4,000 Centrifuges Work at Natanz Enrichment Facilities," *Islamic Republic News Agency*, August 29, 2008 http://www1.irna.ir/en/news/view/ line-203/0808298376181247.htm

———, "Backgrounder: Hamas," via *Council on Foreign Relations*, June 8, 2007 http://www.cfr.org/publication/8968

———, "Baghdad Forms a Committee to Evict MKO Terrorist Group from Iraq," via *Iran Student News Agency*, August 20, 2008 http://www.isna.ir/ISNA/ NewsView.aspx?ID= News-1183613&Lang=E

———, "Director General of the IAEA: 'Implementation of the NPT Safeguards Agreement in the Islamic Republic of Iran,'" *Global Security Newswire*, August 30, 2007

———, "EU Prepared to Back Civilian Iran Program," via *China Daily*, May 16, 2006 http://www.chinadaily.com.cn/world/2006-05/16/content_590756.htm

Anonymous, "EU's Solana Delivers Incentive Package to Iran," via *Khaleej Times Online*, June 14, 2008 http://www.khaleejtimes.com/DisplayArticleNew.asp?section=middleeast&xfile =data/middleeast/2008/june/middleeast_june274.xml

———, "EU Tightens Iran Nuclear Sanctions," via *CNN.com*, August 11, 2008 http://www.cnn.com/2008/WORLD/meast/08/08/iran.eu.sanctions.ap/index.html?iref=newssearch

———, "EU to Barter for Civilian Iran Nuclear Programme," via *The Guardian*, May 15, 2006 http://www.guardian.co.uk/world/2006/may/15/iran.eu/print

———, "Europeans Eager to Improve Trade Relations with Iran," via *Payvand's Iran News*, August 9, 2005 http://www.payvand.com/news/05/aug/1099.html

———, "FACTBOX: Iran's New Atomic Negotiator Saeed Jalili," via *Reuters Online*, October 23, 2007 www.reuters.com/articlePrint?articleId=USL23932 9720071023

———, "Hakim: Americans Prevent MKO Expulsion from Iraq," via *Islamic Republic News Agency*, August 21, 2008 http://www.globalsecurity.org/wmd/library/news/iraq/2007/11 /Iraq-071111-irna01.htm

———, "Hezbollah," via *Council on Foreign Relations*, July 17, 2006 http://www.cfr.org/publication/9155/#7

———, "Hezbollah," via *Memorial Institute for the Prevention of Terrorism: Knowledge Base*, February 1, 2007 http://www.tkb.org/Group.jsp?groupID=3101

———, "Hezbollah as a Strategic Arm of Iran," *Intelligence and Terrorism Information Center at the Center for Special Studies*, Iranian News Agency, 2006

———, "Hizballah (Party of God)," via *GlobalSecurity.org*, July 16, 2006 http://www.globalsecurity.org/military/world/para/hizballah

———, "Iran Confirms Nuclear Component Production," via *CNN.com*, August 29, 2008 http://www.cnn.com/2008/WORLD/meast/08/29/iran.nuclear/index.html

———, "Iran Dismisses Concerns about Nuclear Materials," via *International Herald Tribune Online*, March 2, 2009 http://www.iht.com/articles/ap/2009/03/02/news/ML-Iran-Nuclear.php on March 2, 2009

———, "Iran Generally Honest on Nuclear Program, IAEA Inspectors Say," *Global Security Newswire*, November 15, 2007

———, "Iran in Iraq: How Much Influence," *International Crisis Group, Middle East Report*, No. 38. March 21, 2005, http://www.crisisgroup.org/home/index.cfm?id=3395&l=1 on August 10, 2008

———, "Iran Iraq War 1980–1988," via *Iran Chamber Society*, http://www.Iranchamber.com/history/iran_iraq_war/iran_iraq_war1.php on August 8, 2008

———, "Iran-Iraq War (1980–1989)," via *GlobalSecurity.org*, July 9, 2008 http://www.globalsecurity.org/military/world/war/iran-iraq.htm

———, "Iran Loser Blasts 'Illegal' Poll," via *BBC News*, June 25, 2005 http://www.news.bbc.co.uk/1/hi/world/middle_east/4622955.stm.

———, "Iran N-Progress Unhindered by Sanctions," via *Press TV*, August 15, 2008 http://www.presstv.ir/detail.aspx?id=66660&sectionid=351020104

———, "Iran Nuclear Position 'Unchanged'," via *BBC News*, July 5, 2008 http://news.bbc.co.uk/go/pr/fr/-/2/hi/middle_east/7491180.stm

———, "Iran Sees 'Positive' Nuclear Talks with US," via *CNN.com*, July 18, 2008 http://www.cnn.com/2008/WORLD/meast/07/18/iran.talks.ap/index.html

———, "Iran Test Fires Rocket, Says State Media," via *CNN.com,* August 17, 2008 http://www.cnn.com/2008/WORLD/meast/08/17/iran.rocket/index.html

———, "Iran Tests Its First Nuclear Power Plant," via *CNN.com*, February 25, 2009, http://www.cnn.com/2009/WORLD/meast/02/25/iran.nuclear.plant/index.html?iref=newssearch on February 26, 2009

———, "Iranians Continue to Back Compromise, Better Relations with US and West, but Opposition to Developing Nuclear Weapons Drops; Support for Government Economic Policies increases," *Center for Public Opinion: Terror Free Tomorrow*, 2008

———, "Iranian Military Warns US, Israel against Attack," via *CNN.com*, July 9, 2008 http://www.cnn.com/2008/WORLD/meast/07/08/iran.military.ap/index.html?iref=newssearch

———, "Iraqi Cabinet wants MKO Expulsion from Iraqi Territory," via *ArabicNews.com*, June 23, 2008 http://www.arabicnews.com/ansub/Daily/Day/080623/2008062308.html

———, "Johnny Depp: US Is Like a Stupid Puppy," via *CNN.com*, September 2003 www.cnn.com/2003/SHOWBIZ/Movies/09/03/depp.us.reax.reut

———, "Larijani Raps 'Irresponsible' Comments," via *Gulf Daily News Online*, February 24, 2009 http://www.gulf-daily-news.com/Story.asp?Article=243864&Sn=BNEW&IssueID=31341 on March 2, 2009

———, "MKO has 6 Months to Leave Iraq," via *Press TV*, August 21, 2008 http://www.presstv.ir/pop/print.aspx?id=67145

———, "The Modality for Comprehensive Negotiations (Non-Paper)" July 31, 2008 http://www.campaigniran.org/casmii/index.php?q=node/5847/print

———, "Mujahedin-e Khalq Organization (MEK or MKO)," via *FAS: Intelligence Resource Program*, August 21, 2008 http://www.fas.org/irp/world/para/mek.htm

———, "Norway Urges Talks to Settle Iran's Disputed Nuclear Case," *Ettelaat*, June 29, 2007 http://www.uni-graz.at/yvonne.schmidt/NAHOST_News_ARCHIVE_2007.html

———, "Profile: Asif Ali Zardari," *BBC News*, September 6, 2008 http://news.bbc.co.uk/2/hi/south_asia/4032997.stm, accessed February 26, 2009.

———, "Sanctions May Hurt Iran's Drug War," via *MSNBC.com*, June 24, 2008 www.msnbc.msn.com/id/25351006/print/1/displaymode/1098/

———, "The Secret CIA History of the Iran Coup, 1953," via *National Security Archive: Electronic Briefing Book No. 28* http://www.gwu.edu/~nsarchiv/NSAEBB/ NSAEB B28 /index.html

———, "'Special Unit Formed to Deal with MKO'-minister," via *IraqUpdates.com*, August 8, 2008 http://www.iraqupdates.com/scr/preview.php?article=34906

———, "Text of 5+1 Package to Iran," via *Tehran Times*, June 16, 2008 http://www.campaigniran.org/casmii/index.php?q=node/5295/print

Anonymous, *Treaty on the Non-Proliferation of Nuclear Weapons* (New York and Vienna: International Atomic Energy Agency, April 22, 1970)

————, "Iran President 'Proud' of Nuclear Progress," via *CNN.com*, April 9, 2009 http://www.cnn.com/2009/WORLD/meast/04/09iran.nuclear/index.html?iref=newssearch on April 13, 2009

————, "US Military: Iran Training Assassination Squads," via *CNN.com,* August 15, 2008 http://www.cnn.com/2008/WORLD/meast/08/15/iran.death.squads/index.html

————, "US to Donate '$900m in Gaza Aid' " via *BBC News* February 24, 2009 http://news.bbc.co.uk/2/hi/middle_east/7907483.stm on February 26, 2009

————, ["I Announce for the 1000th Time and Louder than Before that We Are Friends with All Peoples of the World Including the People of Israel"] *via Fars News Agency*, August 18, 2008 http://www.farsnews.com/newstext.php?nn=8705200775

————, "Report: Incentive Package Includes US Giving Iran Nuke Technology," via *USAToday*, June 6, 2008 www.usatoday.com/news/world/2006-06-06-iran-nuclear_x.htm

————, "Report: Iranian Supreme Leader Backs Ahmadinejad's Second Term," *Xinhuanet.com*, August 25, 2008 http://news.xinhuanet.com/english/2008-08/25/content_9709661.htm

Ansari, Ali, *Confronting Iran: The Failure of American Foreign Policy and the Next Great Crisis in the Middle East* (New York: Basic Books, 2006)

————, "Iran under Ahmadinejad," *Adelphi Papers*, Vol. 47, No. 393, 2007

Aversa, Jeannine, "US Slaps Sanctions on Iran Bank," via *boston.com*, October 22, 2008, http://www.boston.com/news/nation/washington/articles/2008/10/22/us_slaps_sanctions_on_iran_bank

Bahgat, Gawdat, "Iran and the United States: The Emerging Security Paradigm in the Middle East," *Parameters*, Summer 2007, p. 13

Baker, James A. III and Lee H. Hamilton, *The Iran Study Group Report* (New York: Vintage Books, 2006)

Bakhash, Shaul, "The Troubled Relationship: Iran and Iraq, 1930–80," in Lawrence Potter and Gary Sick (eds.), *Iran, Iraq, and the Legacies of War* (New York: Palgrave Macmillan, 2004)

————, "The US and Iran Part III-The Hostage Crisis," via *TheWorld.Org* October 27, 2004 http://www.theworld.org/?q=node/3566

Baldor, Lolita, "General: Iran Training Shi'ite Insurgents," *WashingtonPost.com,* August 23, 2006

Ballen, Ken, "What Iranians Really Think," *The Wall Street Journal Online*, July 11, 2007

Balouji, Heidar Ali, "The Process of National Security and Decision Making in Iran: The Signing of the Additional Protocol," in Shannon Kile (ed.) *Europe and Iran: Perspectives on Non-Proliferation* (Solna, Sweden: Oxford University Press for SIPRI, 2005)

Battle, Joyce (ed.), "Shaking Hands with Saddam Hussein: The US Tilts toward Iraq, 1980–1984," *The National Security Archive*, February 25, 2003 www.gwu.edu/~nsarchiv/NSAEBB/NSEBB82/index2.htm

Beehner, Lionel, "Iran: Nuclear Negotiations," via *Backgrounder*, May 16, 2005 http://www.cfr.org/publication/7730/iran.html

———, "Iran's Involvement in Iraq," via *Backgrounder*, March 3, 2008 http://www.cfr.org/publication/12521/

Bilefsky, Dan, "EU Plans 2nd Package of Incentives to Iran," via *International Herald Tribune*, May 15, 2006 http://www.iht.com/articles/2006/05/15/news/union.php

Binnendijk, Hans and Richard Kugler, *Seeing the Elephant: The US Role in Global Security* (Washington, DC: National Defense University Press, 2006)

Bodansky, Yossef, "Pakistan's Islamic Bomb," via *Freeman Center for Strategic Studies*, July 1998 www.freeman.org/m_online/jul98/bodansky.htm

Boghrati, Niusha, "Iran: Crackdown on Intellectuals," *Worldpress.org*, April 24, 2007 via http://www.worldpress.org/Mideast/2764.cfm on November 20, 2007

Bonato, Leo and Juan Carlos Di Tata, Nisreen Farhan, Rakia Moalla-Fetini, and Roman Zytek, *International Monetary Fund: Islamic Republic of Iran: Statistical Appendix* (Washington, DC: International Monetary Fund, February 9, 2007)

Bozorgmehr, Shirzad, "Iran Blasts Obama's Nuclear Criticism," *CNN.com*, November 8, 2008, http://www.cnn.com/2008/WORLD/meast/11/08/iran.obama/index.html?iref=newssearch on November 10, 2008

Bozorgmehr, Shirzad and Michal Zippori, "Iran Test-Fires More Long-Range Missiles," via *CNN.com* http://www.cnn.com/2008/POLITICS/07/10/us.iran/index.html?iref=newssearch on October 7, 2008

Brenner, Michael corresponding with the *Gulf Security 2000* blog on June 23, 2008

Brzeninski, Zbigniew, Robert Gates, and Suzanne Maloney, "Report of an Independent Task Force for the Council on Foreign Relations," *Iran: Time for a New Approach* (New York: Council on Foreign Relations, 2004)

Buchta, Wilfried, *Who Rules Iran? The Structure of Power in the Islamic Republic* (Washington, DC: Washington Institute for Near East Policy and the Konrad Adenauer Stiftung, 2000)

Burns, R. Nicholas, "Michael Stein Address on US Middle East Policy at The Washington Institute's Annual Soref Symposium," May 11, 2006, via http://www.state.gov/p/us/rm/2 006/68321.htm

Byman, Daniel, "Iran, Terrorism, and Weapons of Mass Destruction," *Studies in Conflict & Terrorism*, 2008, Vol. 31, p. 170

Byrne, Malcolm and Mark Gairowski, *Mohammad Mossadeq and the 1953 Coup in Iran* (Syracuse, NY: Syracuse University Press, 2004)

Carpenter, Ted Galen, "Iran's Influence in Iraq," via *CATO Institute*, March 10, 2008 http://www.cato.org/pub_display.php?pub_id=9258

Carroll, Joseph, "Public: Iran's Nuclear Program Poses Threat to U.S.," *Gallup Poll Report,* December 20, 2007 via http://www.gallup.com/poll/103402/Public-Irans-Nuclear-Program-Poses-Threat-US.aspx

Carter, Jimmy, transcript of interview with, *The Situation Room* October 10, 2007, via http://transcripts.cnn.com/TRANSCRIPTS/0710/10/sitroom.02.html

Cheney, Dick, "Vice President's Remarks to the World Affairs Council of Dallas/Fort Worth," via http://www.whitehouse.gov/news/releases/2007/11/print/20071102.html on November 21, 2007

Chubin, Sharam, *Iran's Nuclear Ambitions* (Washington, DC: Carnegie Endowment for International Peace, 2006)

Chubin, Sharam, "Understanding Iran's Nuclear Ambitions," in Patrick Cronin (ed.), *Double Trouble* (Westport, CT: Praeger, 2007)

Clark, Kate, "Iran 'Sending Weapons to Taleban," *BBC News*, September 15, 2008 http://news.bbc.co.uk/go/pr/fr/-/2/hi/south_asia/7616429

Clawson, Patrick, "Role of the Regime," in James Dobbins, Sarah Harting, and Dalia Dassa Kaye (eds.) *Coping with Iran: Confrontation, Containment, or Engagement: A Conference Report* (Santa Monica, CA: RAND Corporation, 2007)

Clawson, Patrick and Michael Eisenstadt, "Forcing Hard Choices on Tehran: Raising the Costs of Iran's Nuclear Program," *The Washington Institute for Near East Policy: Policy Focus*, No. 62, November 2006

Cordesman, Anthony, *Iran's Military Forces in Transition* (Westport, CT: Praeger, 1999)

——, *The Military Balance in the Middle East* (Westport, CT: Praeger, 2004)

Cordesman, Anthony and Martin Keliber, *Iran's Military Forces and Warfighting Capabilities* (Westport, CT: Praeger, 2007)

Cowan, Richard, "US Senate Panel Approves New Iran Sanctions," via *Reuters Online*, August 18, 2008 http://www.reuters.com/article/latestCrisis/idUSN17419147

Dareini, Ali Akbar, "Iran: New Strides in Uranium Enrichment," *Associated Press Online*, August 29, 2008 http://www1.irna.ir/en/news/view/line-203/0808298376181247.htm

Digital History, "The Past Three Decades: Years of Crisis—Years of Triumph: No Islands of Stability," *Digital History*, 2006, www.digitalhistory.uh.edu/database/article_display_printable.cfm?HHD=403 on September 27, 2008

Disney, Patrick, "Washington, Tehran Complicate Prominent Iranians' Travel to US," via *National Iranian American Council*, August 21, 2008 http://www.niacouncil.org/index.p hp?option=com_content&task=view&id=1203&It

Dobbins, James, Sarah Harting, and Dalia Dassa Kaye (eds.), *Coping with Iran: Confrontation, Containment or Engagement: A Conference Report* (Santa Monica, CA: RAND Corporation, 2007)

Dombey, Daniel and Stephanie Kirchgaessner, "Fresh Ways of Turning the Screw on Iran," *Financial Times*, October 22, 2007, as quoted in Ilias, p. 34

Dunn, David Hastings, " 'Real Men Want to go to Tehran': Bush, Pre-emption and the Iranian Nuclear Challenge," *International Affairs*, Vol. 83, No 1, 2007

Elm, Mostafa, *Oil, Power, and Principle: Iran's Oil Nationalization and Its Aftermath* (Syracuse, NY: Syracuse University Press, 1992)

Engelberg, Stephen, "Downing of Flight 655: Questions Keep Coming," *The New York Times*, July 11, 1988 http://query.nytimes.com/gst/fullpage.html?res=940DE1DD103EF932A25754C0A96E948260&scp=39&sq=USS+vincennes&st=nyt

Fallows, James, "The Nuclear Power beside Iraq," *The Atlantic Monthly*, May 2006

Farhang, Mansour, "The Enigma of President Ahmadinejad," in Michel Korinman and John Laughland (eds.), *Geopolitical Affairs* (Middlesex, UK: Valentine Journal Academic, 2007)

Farhi, Farideh, "IAEA Declares a Gridlock with Iran," *National Iranian American Council Policy Memo*, September 2008

———, "Tehran's Reaction to Military Threats," via *Informed Comment: Global Affairs*, June 29, 2008 http://icga.b.ogspot.com/2008/06/tehrans-reaction-to-military-threats.html

Fitzpatrick, Mark, "Is Iran's Nuclear Capability Inevitable?" in Patrick Cronin (ed.), *Double Trouble* (Westport, CT: Praeger, 2007)

Frantz, Douglas and James Risen, "A Nation Challenged: Terrorism; A Secret Iran-Arafat Connection Is Seen Fueling the Mideast Fire," via *The New York Times*, March 24, 2002, http://query.nytimes.com/gst/fullpage.html?res=9D0 2E0DD143BF937A15750C0A9649C8B63&sec=&spon=&pagewanted=all

Freedman, Robert, "Russian-Iranian Relations in the 1990s," *Middle East Review of International Affairs*, Vol. 4, No 2, June 2000

Ghasemi, Shapour, "Shooting Down Iran Air Flight 655 [IR655]," *Iran Chamber: History of Iran*, 2004, http://www.iranchamber.com/history/articles/shooting-down_iranair_flight655.php on September 2, 2008

Gheytanchi, Elham and Babak Rahimi, "Tehran's Web of Silence," *The New York Times,* August 24, 2008

Gonzalez, Nathan, *Engaging Iran* (Westport, CT: Praeger Security International, 2007)

Goodenough, Stan, "US Gearing Up to Attack Iran—Report," *Jerusalem Newswire*, September 1, 2008, http://www.jnewswire.com/articles/print/2517

Gwertzman, Bernard, "Kissinger: Don't Exclude Military Action against Iran if Negotiations Fail," *Council on Foreign Relations Interview*, July 14, 2005 www.cfr.org/publication/8255/kissinger.html

Hadian, Nasser, "The US and Iran Part IV—Hostile Relations," via *TheWorld.Org*, October 28, 2004 www.theworld.org/?q=node/3566

Halevi, Yossi Klein, "Israel, Iran Practically at War," via *CBS News,* March 12, 2008 www.cbsnews.com/stories/2008/03/12/opinion/printable3930010.shtml

Hassan, Hussein, "Iranian Nuclear Sites," *CRS Report for Congress*, November 13, 2006

Hemmer, Christopher, "Responding to a Nuclear Iran," *Parameters*, Autumn 2007

Hiltermann, Joost, "Outsiders as Enablers: Consequences and Lessons from International Silence on Iraq's Use of Chemical Weapons during the Iran-Iraq War," in Lawrence Potter and Gary Sick (eds.), *Iran, Iraq, and the Legacies of War* (New York: Palgrave Macmillan, 2004)

Hirschberg, Peter, "Georgia's Israeli Arms Point Russia to Iran," via *Asia Times Online*, August 14, 2008, http://www.atimes.com/atimes/Middle_East/JH14Ak02.html

Howard, Roger, *Iran Oil* (London: I. B. Tauris, 2007)

Huntington, Samuel, *Clash of Civilizations and the Remaking of World Order* (New York: Simon & Schuster, 1997)

Huntley, Wade, "Rebels without a Cause: North Korea, Iran, and the NPT," *International Affairs*, Vol. 82, No. 4, 2006

Ilias, Shayerah, "Iran's Economy," *CRS Report for Congress*, June 12, 2008

International Atomic Energy Agency Board of Governors, *Implementation of the NPT Safeguards Agreement and Relevant Provisions of Security Council resolutions 1737 (2006), 1747 (2007) and 1803 (2008) in the Islamic Republic of Iran*, GOV/2008/15, May 26, 2008

International Institute of Strategic Studies, *Military Balance, 2008* (Wales: Routledge)

Iran Policy Committee, "US Policy Options for Iran," February 10, 2005

Isaacs, John, "In a Nutshell: McCain vs. Obama on National Security," via *Center for Arms Control and Non-Proliferation*, July 1, 2008 http://www.armscontrolcenter. org/policy/I raq/articles/070108_mccain_obama_national_security/

Isseroff, Ami, "A History of the Hamas Movement," via *MidEastWeb*, www. mideastweb.org/h amashistory.htm on July 21, 2008

Jahn, George, "EU Drafts Iran Security Council Referral Resolution," *Boston Sun*, January 17, 2006, cited in Dunn, p. 21

Johny, Stanly, "The Unending Iranian Nuclear Crisis," *Indian Institute for Defense Studies & Analyses Strategic Comments*, July 25, 2008 www.idsa.in/publications/ stratcomments/StanlyJohny250708.htm

Joseph, Robert, "Iran's Nuclear Program," Statement before the *House International Relations Committee*, Washington, DC, March 8, 2006

JPost.com Staff, "Report: Israel Won't Allow a Nuclear Iran," *The Jerusalem Post: Online Edition*, August 29, 2008 http://www.jpost.com/servlet/Satellite?cid= 1219913194872& pagename=JPost/JPArticle/ShowFull

Kamrava, Mehran, "The United States and Iran: A Dangerous but Contained Rivalry," *The Middle East Institute Policy Brief*, No. 9, 2008, p. 1

Karimi, Nasser, "Iran Arrests Former Nuclear Negotiator," via *The Boston Globe*, May 3, 2007 http://www.boston.com/news/world/middleeast/articles/2007/05/03/ iran_arrests_for mer_nuclear_negotiator/

Karmon, Ely, *"Fight on All Fronts": Hizballah, the War on Terror, and the War in Iraq* (Washington, DC: Washington Institute for Near East Policy, 2003)

Kashani, Ayatollah, "Ayatollah Kashani: N-bomb Production Religiously Forbidden," *Islamic Republic News Agency*, November 9, 2007

Kass, Lee, "Iran's Space Program: The Next Genie in a Bottle," *The Middle East Review of International Affairs*, Vol. 10, No 3, September 2006

Katzman, Kenneth, "Iran: US Concerns and Policy Responses," *CRS Report for Congress*, August 6, 2007

———, *The Warriors of Islam: Iran's Revolutionary Guard* (Boulder, CO: Westview Press, 1993)

Kay, Joseph and Alex Lefebvre, "The Diplomacy of Imperialism: Iraq and US Foreign Policy," via *World Socialist Website*, March 19, 2004 http://www.wsws. org/art icles/2004/mar2004/iraq-m19.shtml

Kaye, Dalia Dassa, *Talking to the Enemy: Track Two Diplomacy in the Middle East and South Asia* (Santa Monica, CA: RAND Corporation, 2007)

Kaye, Dalia Dassa and Fredric Wehrey, "A Nuclear Iran: The Reactions of Neighbours," *Survival*, Vol. 49, No. 2, 2007

Keinon, Herb and Hilary Leila Krieger, "US Threatens to Punish Iranian 'Delay'," via *Jerusalem Post, Online Edition*, August 5, 2008 http://www.jpost.com/ servlet/Satellite?cid=12153 31199928&pagename=JPost/JPArticle/ShowFull

Kemp, Geoffrey, *Iran and Iraq: The Shia Connection, Soft Power, and the Nuclear Factor*, Special Report (Washington, DC: U.S. Institute for Peace, November 2005)

Kessler, Glenn, "In 2003, US Spurned Iran's Offer of Dialogue: Some Officials Lament Lost Opportunity," *Washington Post*, June 18, 2006, p. A16

Keyes, Charley, "US to Join Nuclear Talks with Iran, State Department Says," via *CNN.com*, April 8, 2009 http://www.cnn.com/2009/POLITICS/04/08/us. iran.nuclear/index.html on April 9, 2009

Khan, Nawab, "EU-Iran Relations in the Last Two Years," via *Payvand's Iran News*, November 23, 2003 http://www.payvand.com/news/03/nov/1139.html

Khodabandeh, Massoud, "Bulgarians to Dismantle Iranian Terrorist Group MKO in Iraq," via *Terrorism Monitor*, February 9, 2006 http://www.jamestown.org/ terrorism/news/article. php?articleid=2369895&printhis=1

Kinzer, Stephen, *All the Shah's Men* (Hoboken, NJ: Wiley, 2003)

Landau, Emily, "Regional Reactions and Responses," via *Bitterlemons-international.org*, March 14, 2007 http://www.bitterlemons-international.org/pervious.php?opt=1&id=172

Levitt, Matthew and Michael Jacobson, "Timely Reminder of Iranian Support for Terrorism," *PolicyWatch #1345: The Washington Institute for Near East Policy*, February 22, 2008 http://www.washingtoninstitute.org/print.php?template= C05&CID=2721

Limbert, John, "Negotiating with the Islamic Republic of Iran: Raising the Chances for Success—Fifteen Points to Remember," *United States Institute of Peace: Special Report*, January 2008, Special Report 199

Litwak, Robert, *Rogue States and US Foreign Policy* (Washington, DC: Woodrow Wilson Center Press, 2000)

Long, Austin and Whitney Raas, "'Osirak Redux?' Assessing Israeli Capabilities to Destroy Iranian Nuclear Forces," *International Security*, Spring 2007

Lowe, Robert and Claire Spencer, *Iran, Its Neighbors and the Regional Crises: A Middle East Programme Report* (London: Chatham House, 2006)

Loyola, Mario, "Land of Cedars and Sorrow," *National Review*, 2007

Maleki, Abbas, "Iran-Pakistan-India Pipeline: Is it a Peace Pipeline," *MIT Center for International Studies*, September 2007

McCain, John, Remarks to CPAC on February 7, 2008, via http://www. johnmccain.com/Informing/News/Speeches/b639ae8b-5a9f-41d5-88a7- 874cbefa2c40.htm

McCarthy, Andrew, "Cognitive Dissonance," via *National Review Online*, September 11, 2007 http://article.nationalreview.com/?q=YTQyNjE0MmRlZ Tk2YTk3OTM1N2RiYmUwN2RiYzUwMmM=

McElroy, Damien, "Iran Vows to Pay for Gaza Aid as Children Return to UN Schools," via *Telegraph.co.uk* January 24, 2009 http://www.telegraph.co.uk/ news/worldnews/middleeast/israel/4330561/Iran-vows-to-pay-for-gaza-aid-as- children-return-to-UN-schools on February 26, 2009

Morsbach, Greg, "Chavez Tour Piques US Interest," *BBC News*, July 24, 2006 http://news.bbc.co.uk/2/hi/americas/5205770.stm

Moshirzadeh, Homeira, "Discursive Foundations of Iran's Nuclear Policy," *Security Dialogue*, Vol. 38, No. 4, 2007

Moslem, Mehdi, *and Factional Politics in Post-Khomeini Iran* (Syracuse, NY: Syracuse University Press, 2002)

Nasr, Vali, "The Implications of Military Confrontations with Iran," *CNAS Iran Strategy Working Paper #2*, June 2008

National Commission on Terrorist Attacks upon the United States, *The 9/11 Commission Report: Final Report of the National Commission on Terrorist Attacks upon the United States* (New York: W.W. Norton, 2004), p. 75

Noi, Aylin Unver, "Iran's Nuclear Programme: The EU Approach in Comparison to the US' Approach," *Perceptions*, Spring 2005

Obama, Barak, "Transcript: 'I'm Going to Confront this Economic Crisis,' Obama Says," November 7, 2008, *CNN.com,* www.cnn.com/2008/POLITICS/11/07/obama.conference.transcript/index.html?iref=newssearch on November 10, 2008

Pace, Sonja, "Hezbollah Wary; Ponders New Political Role in Lebanon," *Payvand's Iran News*, April 6, 2005 www.payvand.com/news/05/apr/1033.htm

Pant, Harsh, "India and Iran: An 'Axis' in the Making," *Asian Survey*, Vol. 44, No. 3, May–June 2004

Parliament, Darby and Amin Tarzi, "Missile Messages: Iran Strikes MKO Bases in Iraq," *The Nonproliferation Review*, Summer 2001

Perelman, Marc, "Book Reveals Details of Iran's Diplomatic Outreach to Israel," via *Forward.com*, August 8, 2007 www.forward.com/articles/11350/

Peterson, Scott, "Russian Support for Iran Sanctions at Risk amid Georgia Rift," *The Christian Science Monitor,* August 14, 2008

Pillar, Paul, "Regional and Global Consequences of US Military Action in Iran," *Statement to the Subcommittee on National Security and Foreign Affairs, Committee on Government Reform and Oversight, House of Representatives*, November 14, 2007

Quijano, Elaine and Barbara Starr, "Iran Gen.: Our Finger Is Always on the Trigger," via *CNN.com* www.cnn.com/2008/WORLD/meast/07/09/iran.missiles/index.html on July 9, 2008

Riflin, Paul, "Iran's Energy Vulnerability," *The Middle East Review of International Affairs*, Vol. 10, No 4, December 2006

Roshandel, Jalil, "New Wave of Nuclear Development," via B*itterlemons-international.org*, March 14, 2007 http://www.bitterlemons-international.org/pervious.php?opt=1&id=172

———, "No Real Change in Policy," *Bitterlemons-international.org*, Middle East Roundtable Online Forum, Vol. 25, No. 4, July 6, 2006 www.bitterlemons-international.org/inside.php?id=567

Ross, Dennis, "Diplomatic Strategies for Dealing with Iran," *Center for a New American Iran Strategy Working Paper #1*, June 2008

Rubin, Barry, "Chin's Middle East Strategy," *Middle East Review of International Affairs*, Vol. 3, No 1, March 1999

Russell, Richard, "China's WMD Foot in the Greater Middle East's Door," *Middle East Review of International Affairs*, Vol. 9, No 3, September 2005

Rydqvist, John and Katrina Zetterlund (eds.), *Consequences of Military Actions against Iran: Final Report* (Stockholm: Swedish Defense Research Agency, 2008)

Saad, Lydia, "Americans Want a Restrained Iran Strategy," *Gallup Poll Report*, November 6, 2007

Sadjadpoour, Karim, "Ayatollah Ali Khamenei, Iran's Nuclear 'Carpet,' and Iraq," in Dobbins, James, Sarah Harting, and Dalia Dassa Kaye (eds.), *Coping with Iran: Confrontation, Containment or Engagement: A Conference Report* (Santa Monica, CA: RAND Corporation, 2007)

———, "Iran's Political/Nuclear Ambitions and US Policy Options." via *International Crisis Group*, May 18, 2006 www.crisisgroup.org/home/index.cfm?id=4143&1=1

Samii, Bill, "Iran: New Foreign Policy Council Could Curtail Ahmadinejad's Power," *Radio Free Europe/Radio Liberty*, June 29, 2006 as cited in Gawdat Bahgat, "Iran and the United States: The Emerging Security Paradigm in the Middle East," *Parameters*, Summer 2007

Sciolino, Elaine, "Mossadegh: Eccentric Nationalist Begets Strange History," via *The New York Times*, April 16, 2000 http://query.nytimes.com/gst/fullpage.html?res=9807E1D61631F 935A25 757 C0A9669C8B63&sec=&spon=&pagewanted=all

———, "Nuclear Talks with Iran End in a Deadlock," *The New York Times*, July 20, 2008, A1

Sciolino, Elaine and Sheryl Gay Stolberg, "US Considers Opening a Diplomatic Post in Iran," *The New York Times*, July 18, 2008

Shanker, Thom and Steven Weisman, "Iran Is Helping Insurgents in Iraq, US Officials Say," *The New York Times,* September 20, 2004

Sharp, Jeb, "The US and Iran Part I—the 1953 Coup," via *TheWorld*.org, October 25, 2004 http://www.theworld.org/?1=node/3566

Sick, Gary, "The US and Iran Part II—The Shah and the Revolution," via *TheWorld.org,* October 26, 2004 http://www.theworld.org/?q=node/3566

Slackman, Michael, "Talks Signal Mideast Shift," *The New York Times*, July 18, 2008, A1

Solomon, Jay, "Adm. Mullen Says Iran Has Material for Bomb," via *Wall Street JournalOnline*,March2,2009http://online.wsj.com/article/SB123593870238604043.html?mod=googlenews_wsj on March 2, 2009

Squassoni, Sharon, "Iran's Nuclear Program: Recent Developments," *CRS Report to Congress,* March 8, 2007

———, "Iran's Nuclear Program: Recent Developments," *CRS Report for Congress*, September 6, 2006

The Stanley Foundation, "Getting through the Next Six to Twelve Months with Tehran," *Policy Memo*, August 15, 2008 http://www.stanleyfoundation.org

Stockman, Farah, "Bush Effort to Sanction Iran Banks Runs into Resistance," via *boston.com*, December 16, 2007 http://www.boston.com/news/world/middleeast/articles/2007/12/16/ bush_effort_to_sanction_iran_banks_runs_into_resistance

Susser, Leslie, "US and Israel Diverge on Iranian Weapons," *Jewish Exponent*, August 28, 2008 http://www.jewishexponent.com/article/16945/

Tavassoli, Gholam-Abbas, "Islamic Movements in Iran," *WeltTrends*, Vol. 44, No. 12, 2004

Takeyh, Ray, "Iran's Iraq Policy," via *Center for American Progress*, May 5, 2004 http://www.payvand.com/news/04/may/1030.html

Takeyh, Ray, "Iran's New Iraq," *Middle East Journal*, Vol. 62, No. 1, Winter 2008

Tarock, Adam, "Iran-Western Europe Relations on the Mend," *British Journal of Middle Eastern Studies*, Vol. 26, No. 1, May 1999

Timmerman, Kenneth, "Iran Back Channel Backfires," *Insight on the News— World*, June 20, 2003 http://www.kentimmerman.com/news/2003_06_20 irantalks.htm

———, "Iran's Sparring Ayatollahs," via *The Wall Street Journal Interactive Edition*, December 9, 1997 http://web.payk.net/mailingLists/iran-news/html/1 997/msg01778.html

U.S. Central Intelligence Agency, "Iran," *World Fact Book*, 2008, via http://www. cia.gov/library/publications/the-world-factbook/print/ir.html on June 30, 2008

U.S. Government, Further Continuing Appropriations Act, Pub. L. No. 97-377, §793, 96 Stat. 1830, 1865 (1982)

U.S. House of Representatives, Committee to Investigate Covert Arms Transactions with Iran, *Report of the Congressional Committees Investigating the Iran-Contra Affair, with Supplemental, Minority, and Additional Views* (Washington, DC: Government Printing Office, November 1987)

U.S. National Intelligence Council, "Iran: Nuclear Intentions and Capabilities," *National Intelligence Estimate*, November 2007

U.S. State Department, "Chapter 3: State Sponsors of Terrorism," *Country Reports on Terrorism* (Washington, DC: Government Printing Office, April 2007)

———, "Chapter 6: Terrorist Groups: HAMAS," *The Terrorist Enemy*, http:// www.state.gov/ documents/organization/45323.pdf

———, "Country Report on Human Rights Practices," via www.state.gov/p/nea/ ci/82004.htm on March 4, 2008

———, "International Narcotics Control Strategy Report," via www.state.gov/p/ nea/ci/823 30.htm on March 4, 2008

———, "International Religious Freedom Report: Iran," www.state.gov/p/nea/ ci/75227.htm on March 4, 2008

———, "Iran Sanctions and Activities of Privately Funded Actors in Iran: Department of State Establishes Policy to Encourage Non-Governmental Organizations to Apply for an Office of Foreign Assets Control License to Work in Iran," June 23, 2006, via www.state.gov/ g/drl/rls/69 445.htm

———, "State Sponsors of Terrorism" via http://www.state.gov/s/ct/c14151.htm on November 20, 2007

———, "Terrorist Safe Havens: Strategies, Tactics, Tools for Disrupting or Eliminating Safe Havens," *Country Reports on Terrorism*, April 30, 2008, via http://www.state.Gov/s/ct/r ls/crt/2007/104103.htm

———, "Trafficking in Persons Report: Iran (Tier 3)" via www.state.gov/p/nea/ ci/75147.htm on March 4, 2008

———, Office of the Coordinator for Counterterrorism, "Terrorist Safe-Havens: Strategies, Tactics, and Tools for Disrupting or Eliminating Safe-Havens," *Country Reports on Terrorism*, April 30, 2008 http://www.state.gov/s/ct/rls/ crt/2007/104103.htm

————, Office of the Spokesman, "P5+1 Updated Incentives Package," June 17, 2008, via www.state.gov/r/pa/prs/ps/2008/jun.105992.htm

Vakil, Sanam, "The Persian Dilemma: Will Iran Go Nuclear," *Current History*, April 2005

Walker, Martin, "Walker's World: Iran's Baby Bust," via *Spacewar.com*, November 19, 2007 www.spacewar.com/reports/Walkers_World_Irans_baby_bust_999.html

Wilber, Donald, *Clandestine Service History: Overthrow of Premier Mossadeq of Iran: November 1952–August 1953* (Washington, DC: CIA, 1954)

Wilkerson, Lawrence, *Testimony before the Subcommittee on National Security and Foreign Affairs of the Committee on Oversight and Government Reform* (Washington, DC: Government Printing Office, November 14, 2007)

Wright, Lawrence, "The Master Plan: For the New Theorists of Jihad, Al Qaeda Is Just the Beginning," via *The New Yorker*, September 11, 2006 http://www.newyorker.com /archive/2006 /09/11/060911fa_fact3

Wright, Robin, "Iran's Nuclear Negotiator Resigns: Ahmadinejad Seen Asserting Control," via *WashingtonPost.com*, October 21, 2007, A16, http://www.washingtonpost.com/wp-dyn/content/article/2007/10/20/AR2007102001259.html

————, "Stuart Levy's War," via *nytimes.com*, November 2, 2008 www.nytimes.com/2008/11/02/magazine/02IRAN-t.html?pagewanted=5

Yoong, Sean, "Ahmadinejad: Destroy Israel, End Crisis," *The Washington Post*, August 3, 2006

Index